Faith and Understanding

Other titles in the Reason and Religion series:

Peter Byrne: *The Moral Interpretation of Religion*

Stephen T. Davis: *God, Reason and Theistic Proofs*

C. Stephen Evans: *Faith Beyond Reason*

Faith and Understanding

Paul Helm

WM. B. EERDMANS PUBLISHING COMPANY
GRAND RAPIDS, MICHIGAN

To Angela

© Paul Helm, 1997

Edinburgh University Press
22 George Square, Edinburgh

Typeset in 11 on 13 pt Sabon
by Hewer Text Composition Services, Edinburgh,
and printed and bound in Great Britain

ISBN 0-8028-4451-0

This edition published in the United States of America 1997
through special arrangement with Edinburgh University Press
by Wm. B. Eerdmans Publishing Co., 255 Jefferson Ave., S.E.,
Grand Rapids, Michigan 49503

Contents

Introduction

The aim of this book is to discuss and evaluate the relation between religious faith and philosophy as this finds expression in the 'faith seeks understanding' tradition. According to this tradition, philosophy is not an antagonist of faith but provides tools and doctrines which may be used to articulate the faith, and so understand it better.

Such an approach characterises much contemporary philosophy of religion, particularly in the analytic tradition, as it did the era of Christianity up to and somewhat beyond the Reformation. Indeed, the connections between the mediaeval and the Protestant scholastic traditions, and the techniques and concerns of contemporary analytic philosophy of religion are closer than the connection of such philosophy of religion with rationalism and empiricism, or the Kantian and post-Kantian tradition.

Faith seeking understanding is an attempt to articulate faith, to elucidate its metaphysical, epistemological and ethical implications. It has two main motives; to aid the believer's own understanding, of God and his ways, (an understanding that will find its consummation in the beatific vision), and to rebut objections and challenges to his faith, and particularly to individual doctrines of that faith, that arise from philosophical quarters.

The approach of faith seeking understanding is not, however, monolithic. Different thinkers in the tradition have different understandings of the powers of human reason, and of the exact role that reason plays in articulating faith, and different philosophical convictions. Certain issues remain matters of dispute, particularly the relation between faith seeking understanding and natural theology.

The book has two parts. Part One, the first three chapters, surveys and discusses various general features of faith and understanding. As befits a philosophical approach, the emphasis is on the exposition and, where appropriate, the critical appraisal of ideas and arguments rather than upon an examination of their historical provenance.

Part Two, the last five chapters, examines particular applications of faith and understanding. Of these the first three see themselves as self-consciously within that tradition, the fourth and fifth less so, but nevertheless, as I shall try to demonstrate, they exemplify it.

I have tried also to stress the diversity of the approach in another way. Some of the cases of faith seeking understanding that we shall discuss work out an understanding of their faith in terms of an examination of a particular doctrine; and this is the most natural way. But others consider a text of Scripture, others embark on general metaphysical reflection intended to support Christian faith, while others take as their starting point the seminal idea of a Christian thinker. Each of these approaches is represented in Part Two.

I am grateful to all, friends, colleagues and students, who have helped me to understand better the matters dealt with in this book, and especially to my wife Angela for her support and encouragement.

Part of Chapter 7 originally appeared in 'Jonathan Edwards and the Doctrine of Temporal Parts', *Archiv für Geschichte der Philosophie* (1979), pp.35–51.

Fifield
Oxfordshire

Part One
The Main Issues

1

The 'Faith Seeks Understanding' Programme

In this study we are aiming to investigate one important positive relation between faith and reason, one way in which philosophical concepts and arguments may be used to bring greater understanding and plausibility to the beliefs of a particular religious faith. On this view philosophical reason is an aid to faith, in clarifying and articulating what is believed, and setting out, as far as possible, its inner rationale.

In the eyes of many people faith and reason are always antagonistic, or potentially so. Matters of faith are thought to conflict inevitably with human reason. Faith is authoritarian, while reason is autonomous. Faith is biased, while reason is neutral, with no axe to grind.

The idea of an endemic, principled conflict between faith and reason is particularly strong in what we might term the 'Enlightenment tradition' of philosophy, the philosophy of what David Hume called 'the enlightened ages'. In this tradition 'reason' is thought of as a set of truths known by the unaided intellect of any person, or by any person whose mind is not predisposed by dogma. These truths are thus self-evident, or at least very highly likely, much more likely to be true than are any religious dogma, which are alleged to be the fruit of authoritarianism or escapism. On the Enlightenment view for any matter of faith to be rationally acceptable it must first pass the test of 'reason'. So, any matter of faith, if it is to be credible, must be self-evident, or must follow logically from truths that are self-evident. Or it must be more probable than not, and for any other religious belief to be reasonable it must be more probable than not given the belief that God exists.[1]

The Enlightenment approach to faith and reason has attracted most attention in connection with the question of whether belief in God's existence is reasonable, but in principle it can arise over any theological proposition. Thus Christian faith requires a belief in miracles which to many in the Enlightenment tradition is unreasonable; for such a belief requires a particular understanding of history, one in which God can and has intervened, whereas reason can keep an open mind.

Although the relation between faith and reason may be dominated by reason's suspicion of faith, if not their mutual suspicion, once the test of reasonableness is passed – if it is passed – then reason may befriend and support the propositions of faith. But in the eyes of many contemporary philosophers, though by no means most of those that form the mainstream of modern western philosophy from Descartes onwards, no propositions of religion pass, or could ever pass, the test of reason, and so all are 'irrational'. Because such propositions are unreasonable reason need not spend herself further on matters of faith. 'Faith' is another term for credulity.

The faith seeks understanding project, which we are to explore in this book, may be seen as part of the endeavour to respond to that conviction, and to display the reasonableness of faith. For in this project philosophical reasoning is harnessed to serve the interests of faith. How can this be? How can reason, which is seemingly antagonistic to faith, be harnessed to serve it? Part of the answer to this question is that the faith seeking under-standing project was underway long before the Enlightenment, and was based upon the conviction that the propositions of faith *ought* to pass the test of reason, or ought to be required to pass it.[2] Attempts to show the reasonableness of faith by providing general arguments in its defence are part of a tradition that existed long before the Enlightenment. Whether the appeal to reason intrinsic to the faith seeking understanding project is the same as the Enlightenment appeal to reason is something that we shall discuss later. However, it is hard to see how faith seeking understanding could exist as a viable project in a situation in which it is held that reason is needed to establish God's existence and fails to do so, or in which there is a principled distrust of reason on the part of religious believers.

The two ways in which faith and reason can be linked can be illustrated by reflecting on the Five Ways of Aquinas. In offering these proofs of God's existence, is Thomas proceeding, in typical rationalist fashion, to ground the propositions of faith in matters which are obvious or evident to everyone? And is he saying that the proposition that God exists is not credible if not provable? It would appear that he is, for Aquinas claims that 'from effects evident to us, therefore, we can demonstrate what in itself is not evident to us, namely, that God exists'.[3]

If so, he is making the convincingness of such arguments a necessary condition of reasonable belief. However, there must be some doubt that this is what Aquinas believes he is doing, for he goes on to state that 'there is nothing to stop a man accepting on faith some truth which he personally cannot demonstrate, even if that truth in itself is such that demonstration could make it evident'.[4]

He appears to allow that the propositions of faith may be taken for granted, and to employ the proofs both to seek greater understanding of the nature of God, and greater certitude in his existence.[5] We shall take up this question in more detail in Chapter 2.

REASON – SUBSTANTIVE AND PROCEDURAL

As we have just noticed 'reason' can be used as a name for a body of propositions, a set of truths which are held to be self-evidently true, or obviously true, or highly likely to be true, and on which all other truth-claims, including religious truth-claims, must be based. A prime example of a philosopher employing reason in this sense is Descartes, who appealed to the clear and distinct ideas of the mind as the sole sufficient criterion of knowledge. Descartes is a good case of a philosopher who held both that the proposition that God exists ought to be shown to be reasonable before one may believe it, and that it could be.

Reason may be used rather differently, however. It may be held to be sufficient for a religious belief to be reasonable that although it is not based upon such self-evident truths in the manner proposed by Descartes, the religious claims must be shown to be at least consistent with, or not inconsistent with, the self-evident or highly likely truths of 'reason'. Of course whether there are any such self-evident truths is itself a matter of controversy. It is certainly not self-evidently true that there are such self-evident truths. But for the remainder of the discussion of this chapter we shall assume that there are some self-evident propositions, or propositions that it is unreasonable for any person to deny, while not enquiring too closely what these might be.

Let us call the view that there are such self-evident or highly likely or obvious truths the *substantive* sense of reason; substantive because according to this view we all know, or are capable of knowing substantive, non-trivial truths about reality by using the senses, or by reason alone. Reason alone may deliver truths, knowledge of reality. For example according to Descartes, reason tells me that I exist, and that I can trust my senses, while my senses tell me that I am presently aware of a patch of green. According to others it is self-evident that all people are created equal. So reason alone, or reason and the senses, can tell us in authoritative fashion fundamental truths about what sort of world we live in.

What makes this use of reason _substantive_ is that it is held that by its use alone we may gain knowledge about the world, albeit of a fundamental or general kind. According to it, certain truths are obvious; any denial of them would be unjustifiable; or alternatively certain truths are reasonable, and any contradiction of these claims unreasonable.

But reason can also be understood in a narrower sense, a sense which is at once stronger and yet less ambitious than the sense just discussed. Let us call this second sense of reason the _procedural_ sense of 'reason'.

The prime function of procedural reason is to discriminate the fact of logical connectedness, either inductive or deductive. Using our reason in this sense it is reasonable to conclude that if the ball is orange then it is coloured, that if x is smaller than y then y is larger than x, and that if all men are mortal then some men are mortal.

Each of these pairs of propositions is such that the second of each pair is logically implied by the first. That is, one cannot consistently accept the first without accepting the second. If one accepts that the ball is orange then it follows that one ought – in consistency – to accept that the ball is coloured, because if the ball is orange then it follows in virtue of what 'being orange' means that it is coloured, since orange is a colour. And similarly with the other pairs. The logical connectedness in question is that of logical deducibility.

It is equally reasonable, as a principle of inductive logic, to conclude that if half the balls in the bag are white and half are black, and the distribution of balls in the bag is random, then the chance of the next ball out of the bag being white is 0.5. In the case of inductive reasoning, the conclusion, that the probability of the next ball out of the bag being white is .5 is true, but it is not inconsistent with that conclusion that the next few balls that are drawn out of the bag are all black. One might say that in these circumstances there is no more reasonable belief than the belief that the next ball to appear will be white, even though that belief may turn out to be false.

On this view of reason it is a tool, a procedure or set of procedures, which may operate upon propositions which may either be known or reasonably believed, or which may simply be assumed for the sake of argument or experimentation. So the procedural sense of reason is invariably conditional or hypothetical in character. It tells us that _if_ (for whatever reason) we take one or more propositions as given, _then_ some other proposition or propositions follow, or are likely to follow, from that initial proposition. In this it differs from reason used substantively, in the use of which nothing is taken for granted or assumed.

This second sense of 'reason', reason in the procedural sense, may be thought to be more basic than substantive reason, in that while the claims of substantive reason are challengeable and controversial, the claims of procedural reason are fundamental and unchallengeable, for they are the foundation of any reasoning about anything whatsoever. For it is necessary, in order to claim anything about anything, to make a distinction between what one is claiming and what one is not, and the only way of making that distinction is by the use of a little procedural reasoning. The claim that the car has four wheels, whether true or not, is distinct from the claim that it has only three wheels, and its distinctness is shown by the fact that if it has only three wheels it *cannot*, as a matter of logic, have four. Any reasoning about anything requires the acceptance, the use, of procedural reason. We are continually making judgements of what, given certain assumptions about how the world is, is likely to happen next, or what is likely to be true, and reason is necessary for making or assessing such claims.

But procedural reason, while being stronger and more fundamental than substantive reason, is also more modest, in that it is taken for granted that its tenets – the rules of deductive or inductive reasoning – cannot by themselves inform us about any of the truths of our world, nor do they claim to. They cannot, by themselves, claim to be informative about the nature of things. By contrast substantive reason makes the bolder claim that human reason can provide us with knowledge, even with indubitable knowledge about the world. For as we noted, Descartes thought that he could show by the use of substantive reason, by appeal to 'clear and distinct ideas', that he was indubitably an immaterial substance; others have claimed to show by reason in this sense that certain theological claims, perhaps all theological claims, cannot be true because they do not stand up to the light of reason.

Procedural reason may also perform another task besides that of showing what follows, as a matter of logic, from what. It may also show us that what seems to be illogical at first sight is not in fact so. Let us suppose two propositions, p and q, which seem to be self-contradictory, either because they are widely accepted as such, or because it seems obvious at first glance that they are. If it can be shown that there is a third proposition r, which (whether or not r is true) is consistent with each of p and q, then it follows that p and q are themselves consistent, and if they are consistent they cannot be logically contradictory.

So it has been argued, for example, that given the three propositions, *God is all-good*, *God is all-powerful*, and *There is moral evil*, which have been widely accepted as forming an inconsistent set, there is a fourth proposition *Moral agents have free will*, which is consistent with the three propositions and therefore the three are consistent with each other. One might say that used in such a way procedural reason may play a defensive role, showing that certain substantive claims of reason – the substantive claim, in this case, that because there is moral evil there cannot be an all-good, all-powerful God – are mistaken. Used in this way procedural reason defeats opposition rather than mounts an attack of its own.

A third way in which procedural reason may be employed is by showing that two seemingly unconnected propositions are in fact logically related.

The distinction between procedural and substantive reason is an important one. But as earlier remarks suggest, the wall between the two kinds of reasoning is not completely impermeable. This can be seen by briefly reconsidering the second and third ways in which procedural reason may be employed. What these two uses of procedural reason do is to defend the consistency of sets of propositions; the second way does this by showing that a supposed inconsistency is only *supposed* and has no basis in reason; the third way defends consistency by showing unanticipated logical connections between propositions. By doing these things, and other things being equal, procedural reason goes some way to supporting the truth of these propositions, and so performs a substantive role, albeit a modest one. For the consistency of a set of propositions is a necessary condition of its truth; if a set of propositions is inconsistent, there is good reason to suppose that at least one of the propositions in the set is false. But procedural reason only goes some way, and the substantive role that it performs is small. But it is nevertheless significant.

It may not be easy to discern which member of the set of self-contradictory propositions is false, but we can reasonably conclude that one of them is, since if the set is inconsistent, the members of the set cannot all be true. Now if we can show by procedural reason, in one or other of the ways indicated, either that a given set of propositions, previously believed to be inconsistent, is consistent, or that propositions which were previously thought to be unconnected in fact form a consistent set, then we have gone some way to establishing the truth of the set, by establishing one necessary condition of its truth. But a necessary condition is not a sufficient condition. The mere fact of consistency does not prove truth; if it did, then there would be no such thing as a consistent work of fiction. Nevertheless, though by the use of procedural reason we may not have gone very far down the road to establishing the truth of the set, we may have gone some way.

These uses of reason, the substantive and the procedural, are perfectly general in character; they may be applied to any claims of whatever kind, including the claims of a religious faith. We shall see each being employed in the 'faith seeks understanding' programme.

FAITH

'Faith' can also be used in at least two quite distinct senses, and each sense is important for this study. The word can be used as shorthand for *'the* faith', that is, for a body of beliefs of a theological or religious character which forms the cognitive content, or the core of the cognitive content, of some recognisable religion. Thus it is part of the faith of a Jehovah's Witness that they believe that Jesus Christ is a creature, whereas it is part of the faith of a Christian that they believe that Jesus Christ is God. When men and women confess their faith, whether they are Muslims, Hindus, or Christians, then what they are confessing is the set of propositions, together with the associated practices, which they regard as essential to their faith and which includes those beliefs which are distinctive of it. And the reason why this body of propositions is referred to as *the* faith is, quite simply, that it is that set of propositions which expresses what the holders regard as trustworthy truths about God, about themselves in their relation to God, and so on.

One could use 'faith' in this sense to refer to the convictions of an atheist, for the atheist also has a set of beliefs. Naturally, being an atheist, he does not include in this set any beliefs which he believes imply the existence of God. Nevertheless an atheist may, in this sense, be said to have a faith.

Sometimes there is misunderstanding at this point. When a person, in, say, reciting the Apostles' Creed, confesses as part of his faith that he believes in the resurrection of the body, though the faith is confessed in words, the person who confesses the faith does not place his trust in the words, but rather he trusts what the words denote or express. What the words 'I believe in the resurrection of the body' express, as they are usually understood, is some state of affairs, in this case some state of affairs about the future, which the one who confesses the proposition takes to be true, and also takes to be a fit object of religious confidence. In exercising such faith, the person may even be said to trust God insofar as he also believes that God has revealed certain propositions and so has warranted belief in those propositions.

Naturally enough a person's faith does not consist only in the faith that he confesses and in which he trusts. His faith involves emotions and actions and much else. Nevertheless, his faith – the faith that he confesses – has a core-content, a content of beliefs. Such faith involves understanding, for a person can hardly believe what he does not to some degree understand. But he may not understand it very much, and may seek to understand it more. Increased understanding of the propositions of the faith enhances the way of faith as a whole.[6]

It is sometimes suggested that there is a sense of faith which is 'personal' and which is to be contrasted with a 'propositional' sense of faith. But this distinction does not seem to be a watertight one. If my friend Jones says that he will lend me his ladders and I believe what he says, then my reliance upon him – my faith – must have both a propositional and a personal aspect to it. I believe Jones. I may or may not give him unconditional belief, believe him whatever he may say. But what is undeniable is that I believe him in respect of the ladders. The proposition expressed by the sentence 'Jones will lend Helm his ladders' is believed by Helm because it is taken to be a trustworthy assertion of Jones. In believing the proposition, I believe – trust – the person, and in believing the person on this occasion I believe what he says, his utterance about the ladders. So the two senses of faith, the personal and the propositional, are interconnected, and highlight two aspects of one situation. Though, understandably enough, the faith of an atheist cannot have this personal aspect, since he cannot regard the propositions of his faith as being the personal statements of anyone.

However, while there is no distinction in principle between faith as personal and faith as propositional, since faith necessarily has both aspects, the distinction is an important one in exploring the idea of faith seeking understanding. For in some accounts of faith seeking understanding the personal side of faith is stressed, faith as trust in a person, God. Moreover, on such an account faith is not only personal, it is based upon direct acquaintance with the person. It arises from such direct acquaintance but may, typically, be exercised and called forth in periods when there is no direct acquaintance.

The *Soliloquies* of Augustine (354–430) are written in this vein; the soul searches for God. It desires to know him, as a person knows his friend. The demonstration that God exists is contrasted with the knowledge of God.[7] The soul may know God as a friend in this life, but hope to enjoy the vision of God only in the life to come, a vision which is intellectual, but which is directed by love.

On this view what the gaining of understanding provides, insofar as it is achieved, is an increasingly informed acquaintance with the one who is, initially, trusted in faith, and so a richer experience. Here the dominant contrast is between faith and vision, or faith and sight; between the gradual replacement of what is indirect with what is direct as when, having had a letter from someone, I then meet them and make their acquaintance directly and more fully. One might even say that the personal trust of faith provides the one who trusts with a minimal direct acquaintance, as the one who receives a personal letter is minimally directly acquainted with the sender, and that the understanding which faith seeks enlarges this. Just as, in friendship, a person may come to know his friend better and better.[8]

Bonaventure (1221–74) is another example of someone who emphasised faith as direct acquaintance, as the beholding of God. According to him, contemplation of the world led to direct awareness of God:

> After our mind has beheld God outside itself through and in vestiges of Him, and within itself through and in an image of Him, and above itself through the similitude of the divine Light shining above us and in the divine Light itself in so far as it is possible in our state as wayfarer and by the effort of our mind, and when at last the mind has reached the sixth step, where it can behold in the first and highest Principle and in the Mediator of God and men, Jesus Christ, things the like of which cannot possibly be found among creatures, and which transcend all acuteness of the human intellect – when the mind has done all this, it must still, in beholding these things, transcend and pass over, not only this visible world, but even itself.[9]

What part does reason play in this process of faith turning into sight? Each person must pursue the life of faith for himself, because personal acquaintance with God is not something that can be passed on to others. Yet insofar as that personal acquaintance is informed, that aspect can be communicated to others. So reason performs a two-fold role. It is through reason that one understands the propositions on which faith initially relies. By reason faith is then transmuted into understanding, the understanding gained involves reason in a different sense, as rational insight into God himself. We shall look at this more closely in the next chapter

I have said that the faith in the sense in which we have been discussing it is a body of *beliefs*. It is important to stress that in saying this, no particular epistemological account is being offered of how these beliefs which form the core of the faith are rendered credible. 'Faith' in 'the faith' is being used in what is primarily a fiducial sense; the faith is that core set of propositions to which a person *entrusts* himself as embodying, in his judgement, the truth about God. What kind and degree of evidence the propositions to which he entrusts himself are supported by is another question, and one to which various answers can and have been given. But the following general points can be made.

The question of the evidential or epistemic backing which the propositions of the faith must have in order for them to be credible, at least in the eyes of the one who believes them, brings us to consider the other sense or aspect of 'faith'. Here the focus is not on what is believed – *the* faith – but rather on the act of believing upon or trusting. '*The* faith' is what is believed, *faith* is the personal attitude of commitment to what is believed.

The essential epistemological incompleteness of faith as belief, the fact that it falls short of knowledge, should be obvious; it is, to begin with, the epistemological incompleteness of belief itself. As ordinarily used, a person may believe that a proposition is true and be mistaken about the matter. This is perhaps most obvious in the case of beliefs about the future. I may believe that the rate of inflation will fall next year, and when next year arrives the rate of inflation may rise. My belief is mistaken; what I took to be true turns out not to be true. Faith, involving belief, partakes of this incompleteness, even though the belief may be reasonable, and it may be accompanied by a feeling of assurance or certitude. Even if there is an element of knowledge, *scientia*, in some of the propositions of the faith, as Aquinas, for example, argues that there may be, such knowledge does not extend to all the set.

Further, the incompleteness of faith is partly due to the particularity of what is believed, and the need to connect it up with other matters. What is believed needs to be worked out, its rational structure understood and displayed, and underlying this is the belief that it has such a structure, a belief based on a conviction about the rational and consistent character of God. Given the belief that God cannot be whimsical or capricious, even though his ways may not be fully comprehensible, it must be possible to gain some understanding of them by attempting to think them through in a consistent and coherent fashion.

'Faith' in this sense, the act or trust or reliance, is used in a wide variety of senses, and this variety can cause confusion. Thus, as we have already noted, faith may be contrasted with *reason*, but (as we have also seen) it may also be contrasted with *knowledge*, and with *sight*. To try to make clearer the differing ways in which what is believed may be grounded, I will distinguish between three senses of faith, which differ because of the different epistemological assumptions each has. These are not intended to be exhaustive, but it is fair to say that they are central to any reflections about the nature of faith.

One prominent view of faith is that it is an evidential gap-bridger or make-weight. On this account of faith, there is *some* evidence for the truth of what is believed; some evidence, say, that God exists, some evidence that he has promised certain things, and so on, sufficient evidence to warrant belief but not sufficient evidence to give knowledge. The fact that the evidence may be small, or ambiguous, does not rule out trust in what is believed, but it ought to qualify it. However, faith relies on the object of faith, what is denoted by the propositions which comprise 'the faith', with a strength greater than the evidence that the believer possesses strictly warrants, and so faith makes up for any evidential deficiency. From a strictly evidentialist point of view, belief of such strength is irrational, for the evidence does not warrant it. But on this understanding the assurance of faith makes up for the evidential 'gap' between faith and knowledge, making up for the lack of evidence by having a degree of certainty greater than the evidence warrants. One who has faith in this sense responds to the propositions of the faith as if he had more evidence for them than he in fact has.

According to Anthony Kenny, for Thomas Aquinas:

> Faith was certain: it involved a commitment without reserve to the articles of faith; a resolve to disregard evidence conflicting with them. In this, faith was a state of mind resembling knowledge.[10]

Such faith is not a case of knowledge but it resembles knowledge, or resembles the central cases of knowledge, in being certain. When measured by the standards of knowledge, *scientia*, faith falls short. Nevertheless, for Aquinas faith has that degree of certainty that it could or would have if it were knowledge, a certainty authorised by the Christian revelation, in rather the way in which the expertise of a scientist warrants a layman's trust in some theory beyond the degree to which the layman can understand it.

There are two different respects in which this idea of faith as knowledge might be taken. One stresses the certainty of faith, because it is reliance upon the authority of God, and there is no greater authority. Nevertheless, the believer may have a confidence in some proposition of faith p to the same degree that he had were he to have knowledge, *scientia*, of p.

A further way in which faith may be taken as knowledge is more Platonic. For Plato, knowledge, unlike belief, has to do with the direct apprehension by the knower, of that which is unchanging; belief has to do with shifting appearances. Hence knowledge excludes belief and *vice versa*. Platonically-influenced philosophers and theologians, such as Augustine and Bonaventure, have modelled faith in God, who is by definition eternal and immutable, not on belief but on knowledge, Platonic knowledge.

A *second* view of faith is that the certainty of faith is proportional to the evidence for the belief which is a component part of faith. If this proportion is not maintained then faith is weaker than it ought to be; if it is exceeded, then faith becomes hard to distinguish from credulity and foolhardiness. On this view what distinguishes trust from mere belief is not that trust makes up for evidential deficiency but that it is an act of reliance based upon, and proportioned to, the evidence in support of the beliefs. So there are cases of trust which depend upon belief and are correlated with the evidential strength or weakness of the belief. If we put to one side problems raised by weakness of will we may even say: weak belief, weak trust; strong belief, strong trust. Paraphrasing and parodying David Hume, on this view a wise man proportions his trust to his belief.[11]

Further, even where the evidence is not as good as may be, there is a significant difference between trust making up for evidential deficiency and trust being correlated with belief to the degree warranted by the available evidence. In both cases trust is the fiducial element of faith, but in the evidential deficiency view there is not sufficient evidence to warrant the trust having the strength that it has, whereas on the correlation view the good reason for faith having the strength it has is simply the degree of evidence that is available. Faith will have differing degrees of strength depending upon the evidential support for the particular propositions believed.

Because of the evidential gap that must necessarily exist between the evidence on which faith is based, and the incorrigible evidence of the Beatific Vision, all faith involves some risk, since incorrigible knowledge would exclude belief. And though knowledge that is less than incorrigible does not exclude belief, at least on most modern analyses of knowledge, all that this shows is that while faith and belief are distinct, they are not totally distinct.

The *third* conception of faith that we shall note is a view according to which evidence is irrelevant to the genuineness or the appropriateness of faith. As it is sometimes expressed, faith is inherently and necessarily risky. To seek evidence in order to minimise that risk would be to misunderstand what faith is. On such a view faith is often presented as 'offensive' to reason, an expression of confidence in God which runs counter to those who must regard matters of faith as reasonable before they are credible. Just as, on the Enlightenment view of reason, there is conflict between faith and reason from the side of reason, so on this view of faith there is a conflict initiated by faith; faith disregards the claims of reason.

> Without risk there is no faith. Faith is precisely the contradiction between the infinite passion of the individual's inwardness and the objective uncertainty. If I am capable of grasping God objectively, I do not believe, but precisely because I cannot do this I must believe. If I wish to preserve myself in faith I must constantly be intent upon holding fast the objective uncertainty, so as to remain out upon the deep, over seventy thousand fathoms of water, still preserving my faith.[12]

On this view faith is inherently risky, not because there is in fact little evidence for what is believed and more would be desirable, but because whatever evidence there is is in some way against the truth of the proposition believed, and thus faith 'contends' with evidence against. It is a mistake to think that such a view of faith cannot be defended; it does not follow that there are no reasons for holding the view that religious faith is not reasonable. Nevertheless, given the distrust in reason evident in such a view of faith it is hard to see how such a conception of faith could find a place for a faith seeking understanding project, since any attempt to show the coherence or rational defensibility of the propositions of the faith would tend to undermine that view of faith.[13]

What each of these three views of faith has in common, for all their differences, is that there is an essential incompleteness about faith; an evidential incompleteness which prevents faith from being knowledge, or a distance and opaqueness which prevents faith from being direct personal knowledge, or an inherent riskiness. Such incompleteness is usually regarded as unsatisfactory, but remediable to some degree, and hence not intellectually crippling. Only in the tradition represented by such figures as Tertullian and Kierkegaard, our third view of faith, is the incompleteness of faith regarded as essential to it, and the project of faith seeking understanding is correspondingly regarded as an unwarranted concession to the wisdom of this world, as an invasion of Jerusalem by Athens.

The chief feature of faith in 'faith seeks understanding' is that although it is essentially incomplete, incomplete either because it is evidentially deficient (as on either of the first two views of faith discussed) or because it falls short of full immediacy (as in Augustine[14] and Bonaventure, for example) the intellectual and evidential basis of faith is capable of being augmented by a process of reflection and investigation in which reason is necessarily employed, and that this process is inherently desirable and appropriate. The believer desires an intellectual deepening to the beliefs of his faith which he does not at present possess. In furtherance of faith seeking understanding the believer seeks to clarify and strengthen the grounds of the faith, grounds which edge it in the direction of *scientia*. So on this view faith seeking understanding is primarily an epistemological project.

How may faith as belief seek completeness? By as far as possible getting its beliefs turned into knowledge, and by gaining as much comprehension of its beliefs as possible. Either way, understanding is primarily epistemological in character; it seeks additional evidential support for what is believed in order to complete it, in order to transform faith into knowledge, or it seeks to link up the beliefs of faith with other beliefs of faith, or with other matters which lie outside the faith, and so increase the credibility of what is believed. There are certain matters which, unless I could link them up with other claims, I could hardly be said to possess understanding of them. Faith seek comprehension and comprehensiveness. It attempts to answer such questions as, Why am I required to believe this? Why am I justified in believing this? What inner principle or rationale does it express? How does this belief connect up with other things that I believe? On this view the understanding which faith seeks is the sort and degree of understanding which, when it is fully achieved, ensures that what is believed is no longer merely believed, but is *known*, because what is believed is true and the person who believes it now has adequate grounds for his belief; he has achieved understanding in the way in which someone who has an appreciation of the kinetic theory of heat has a greater understanding of why something is hot than if he lacks that knowledge. The understanding does not consist simply of gaining additional evidence for the belief in order to justify it, but in understanding the grounds of belief, or the meaning of what is believed, or both, better.

If I know anything at all I know that I have two hands and that they are presently tapping away at my word-processor. I could hardly have better grounds for the truth of any proposition than I have for the truth of this proposition. However, there is much about this state of affairs which I am convinced of the truth of which nevertheless I do not understand. For example, though I am familiar with my hands, and with my computer, there are many things about each that I do not understand, about the muscles and fibres of my hands, and the chips and electronic processes of my computer. To the extent that I gain more information about the physiology of my hands and the electronics of my computer, to that extent I am gaining understanding, in the relevant sense, of what I am already certain about. That is, I am increasing my comprehension, my grasp of what it is that I know, in that I am searching out and finding many of the implications and ramifications of what I know.

As briefly noted earlier this contrast between faith as belief and faith as knowledge is familiar in the writings of Thomas Aquinas. Thomas held that men and women may believe many propositions of faith which they do not know; most notably, the proposition that God exists. This is partly because all men and women exist in a state of epistemological pilgrimage. But it is not only for that reason. It also has to do with a person's intelligence and opportunities. For it is possible, Aquinas thought, for a person such as a theologian or a philosopher not only to believe that God exists, but also to demonstrate the fact of his existence from first principles, by one or other of the famous Five Ways. In succeeding in doing this, that philosopher or theologian converts his personal belief that God exists into knowledge, *scientia*; his belief ceases to be belief, with its essential incompleteness, and becomes knowledge, because the proposition in question has been demonstrated from reason. Faith, in these circumstances, is not more certain, but it is more comprehensive.

We shall have more to say about this project of Thomas', and how it fits into the 'faith seeking understanding' project, in the next chapter. But two things follow from it immediately. If this is what 'faith seeks understanding' means, or only what it means, then the project of faith seeking understanding is one that would seem to be somewhat elitist in character, for it is open only to men and women with certain aptitudes and education.

An understanding of matters of faith may be what all men and women of faith desire, but only those with certain gifts and opportunities will be able to satisfy this desire. Of course Thomas does not mean that those who have mere belief have no understanding of what it is that they believe. Understanding is not an all-or-nothing affair; it has degrees. Nor does Thomas mean to imply that those who achieve understanding gain a complete comprehension of what it is that they have come to understand. For Thomas that would be blasphemous. Even those who understand do so 'darkly', because of the gap that there is between the infinite and the finite, and the need to use language that is negative and analogical rather than literal and unqualified in character.

However, the elitist character of the relation between faith and knowledge is qualified when it is remembered that for Thomas the project itself is only of limited scope, for it is restricted to those propositions which are capable of rational demonstration, demonstration from first principles. And these, according to Thomas himself, are few in number.

So Thomas is not saying, in Enlightenment fashion, that in order for *any* religious belief to be reasonable it must first past the test of 'reason'; but he is saying, so it seems, that for any proposition to be demonstrated (to be a case of *scientia*) it must be derived from principles which are self-evident. Substantive reason does not here have the front-line importance that it had for the Enlightenment, but it does nonetheless have a subsidiary importance of a not too dissimilar character; it is that without which faith cannot become knowledge, not at least in this life. So on this understanding of the slogan 'faith seeks understanding' faith means, or implies, belief, and understanding means, or implies, knowledge. It is faith's desire, a desire intrinsic to it, to go beyond belief to knowledge, but this is a desire that can only be met in the case of certain matters, and in the case of those with the appropriate gifts to appreciate and be convinced by appropriate forms of reasoning.

Thomas does not mean that the understanding that faith may possess is limited to the proofs. But *scientia* is limited. But someone incapable of following the proofs may nevertheless gain some appreciation of them from analogies, and those matters which are not capable of demonstration are still capable of being understood better. Thomas' *Summae* may each to be said to be exercises *in extenso* in faith seeking understanding.

There is a further sense of understanding that is relevant here. Many in the faith seeking understanding tradition took themselves to be seeking understanding of the mind of God, at least as this had been revealed. God is by definition omniscient, and consistent in what he wills and does. What he wills may seem odd, or arbitrary, but this first impression cannot be the true one; it must rest on weak and imperfect understanding. To gain understanding of some divine action is to see how that action relates to the divine nature, and one chief way of doing this is by seeing how it relates with other divine actions and words; to ground the rationale of what is at first sight puzzling or unworthy of God in the character of God himself. And so, because God is necessarily what he is, to ground something in the character of God is to show that there is a certain necessity about it. This way of seeking understanding for the propositions of faith is prominent in Anselm (c. 1033–1109) as we shall see.

A desire for more information about objects of direct acquaintance such as hands and computers can be due to natural curiosity about oneself and the world around. In the case of religious faith, the desire has another source. So far we have stressed the intellectual, cognitive side of faith. It is trust, based either upon belief in or knowledge of certain religious or theological truths. But faith is more than that, for at least in Christianity faith is a fundamental component part of a person's relationship to God, including his love for God. As we have already stressed, *the* faith consists of propositions about God, information about him, and about what he has done. And in relying upon that information the person relies upon God himself who is the source of this information. But that act of reliance is not only an act of faith, it is an act of love as well. God is not only an object of faith but also of devotion. And as it is natural that when one person loves another, the lover should seek to know more about the one beloved, so in the case of faith seeking understanding the seeking is an expression not merely, or even, of natural curiosity, but of love and loyalty.

FAITH, UNDERSTANDING AND PHILOSOPHY

We have begun to isolate two or three different, though not necessarily incompatible ways, in which the slogan 'faith seeks understanding' may be understood, and more will be said in the following chapter. But for the remainder of this chapter I wish to consider an objection to what we have been saying; the objection that such an approach to the relationship of faith and reason is not genuinely or sufficiently philosophical. Is not the project of faith seeking understanding, however exactly it is to be understood, more an exercise in theology than in philosophy? For is not faith seeking understanding assuming the fact of revelation?

Is it true that whatever we know (or reasonably believe) we could in principle find out directly for ourselves, without relying upon anyone else? At first sight, it looks plausible to answer 'yes' to this question. As I glance out of the window at the garden I can see the colour of the trees and the movements of the birds and insects for myself. And it seems reasonable to suppose that I could discover more and more about such things, and about much else of a similar kind going on around me. And this supposition, that I am at the control-centre of my own epistemic world, is a basic tenet of both classical rationalism and classical empiricism. For all the fundamental differences between them, empiricism and rationalism have in common the view that whatever I know or reasonably believe about any aspect of the world around me I certify for myself, by my own reason or experience, without relying upon anyone else.

For a rationalist, such as Descartes, such personal certification comes from the clear and distinct ideas of reason; for an empiricist such as Locke, it comes from the self evident character of ideas, the immediate sensory states from which I build up a knowledge of the world around me by processes of inductive inference.

But besides the things which we get to know for ourselves, are there not many things for which we must rely on others? What about the testimony of others? Here, I think, we come to a fundamental philosophical divide, one which separates some of the formative figures in modern western philosophy, figures such as Descartes and Hume, from other philosophers such as Thomas Reid, and from the philosophical theologians whose views we shall be considering later. This division concerns the place and value of testimony in human knowledge.

No one can sensibly deny the important place that testimony plays in human affairs, in, for example, the authority of the expert scientist or the historian. The fundamental divide comes between those for whom the information conveyed by human testimony is a convenient shorthand for what each of us may find out for ourselves, and those who discern a more principled distinction between what we can know for ourselves and what we can know only on the say-so of others.

Hume, for example, recognises the importance of human testimony, but for him such testimony, at least insofar as it is judged to be reliable, must conform to his own present beliefs. In effect, credence is only to be placed upon the testimony of other people insofar as it is reasonable to believe that one could, with one's present stock of attitudes and beliefs, directly witness what is testified to. Thus in his famous discussion of miracles Hume bases his critique of reports of miracles on his (and our) present experience of natural and other uniformities.

> The reason why we place any credit in witnesses and historians, is not derived from any *connexion*, which we perceive *a priori*, between testimony and reality, but because we are accustomed to find a conformity between them. But when the fact attested is such a one as has seldom fallen under observation, here is a contest of two opposite experiences.[15]

In effect Hume says, had you or I been present when the alleged miracle took place, and believed that it was a miracle, we must have been deceived or self-deceived in doing so. On this view, the testimony of others is shorthand, and can and must be evaluated by present experience. Everything about the past must be evaluated by the present. The present can never be evaluated by the past. Let us call this the reductionist view of testimony.

But this is not the only view. Others argue that it is only so far as I have confidence in the testimony of others that I can gain knowledge, particularly knowledge of the past. Such credence is, so to speak, a primitive feature of the human cognitive situation, one that is not reducible to any other, and certainly not a shorthand or shortcut for one's own cognitive endeavours.[16] Of course I must evaluate the claims that various 'authorities' make, but it is a fallacy to suppose that I can do this in such a way as not to rely on any authority in doing so. Hume himself, despite what he says, has to rely upon the testimony of those who lived in other ages and who live in other places.

Thus Augustine, for example, says:

> I considered the innumerable things I believed which I had not seen, events which occurred when I was not present, such as many incidents in the history of the nations, many facts concerning places and cities which I had never seen, many things accepted on the word of friends, many from physicians, many from other people. Unless we believed what we were told, we would do nothing at all in this life. Finally, I realized how unmoveably sure I was about the identity of my parents from whom I came, which I could not know unless I believed what I had heard.[17]

Augustine says that such trust of another person is not something that one could gain from experience but is itself a pre-condition of understanding and accepting much that we presently experience. How could I gain from experience the knowledge that x and y are my parents? I need someone to tell me, since necessarily I could not, in infancy, have come to know such facts for myself, and I cannot now reach back in time. The idea that one might, even in principle, get down to a bed-rock of experience each item of which one had personally verified is an illusion.

Such an approach is sometimes characterised as one that rests upon the principle of testimony, the principle that one ought to believe the testimony of others unless there is good reason not to do so.[18] But the principle of testimony may be understood as simply a weaker version of the reductive account of testimony, depending upon whether or not among the good reasons for overturning the testimony of others are reasons which do not rest upon the principle. If they do rest upon it, then we are back to something like Hume's position. If they do not rest upon it, then the principle of credulity is an expression of the non-reductive understanding of human testimony.

As there have been those, such as Hume, who have argued a reductionist thesis about the evidential value of human testimony, so there have been those who have argued in favour of a reductionist thesis about divine testimony, i.e. divine revelation. They have seen a book such as the Bible as being essentially a 'republication' of truths that are otherwise available from the resources of human reason. In *The Reasonableness of Christianity* John Locke argues for the necessity of revelation on essentially pragmatic grounds:

> 'Tis too hard a task for unassisted reason, to establish morality, in all its parts, upon its true foundations, with a clear and convincing light. And 'tis at least a surer and shorter way, to the apprehensions of the vulgar, and mass of mankind, that one manifestly sent from God, and coming with visible authority from him, should, as King and law-maker, tell them their duties, and require their obedience, than leave it to the long, and sometime intricate deductions of reason, to be made out to them: such strains of reasonings the greatest part of mankind have neither leisure to weigh, nor, for want of education and use, skill to judge of.[19]

So the Bible is regarded, in this instance, as a specially vivid and pictorial way of presenting the truths of morality, a way that is necessary for those who do not have the benefit of a philosophical or theological education. The Bible or some other religious authority is on this view a divine public-relations or propaganda exercise, designed to portray, in story form, using myth and parable, eternal moral truths about human nature, or about human nature in relation to God, truths which can be discerned independently of the revelation by those who have sufficient wit and aptitude to do so.

Most if not all of those theologians and philosophers who have favoured the faith seeks understanding approach have taken a non-reductive view of the place of human testimony in acquiring knowledge. The faith seeks understanding project can partly be understood as an attempt to understand more fully for oneself what is accepted upon the authoritative testimony of another; in particular, upon the authority of God through his revelation. For faith to seek understanding is to go in a reductionist direction, while at the same time knowing that one can never succeed in such reductionism.

And they are not only non-reductionist in their view of human testimony but also non-reductionist in their view of divine testimony, or, more exactly, in their view of divinely-inspired human testimony to divine things. On their view, divine revelation discloses matters not otherwise known or knowable by unaided human powers. Of course such thinkers as Augustine, say, or Anselm or Aquinas (or Calvin or Luther, for that matter) who all took broadly this view, also believed that they have good reason for accepting the authority of the divine revelation. But those reasons did not include the belief that they already knew or could know, by reason alone, what the divine revelation already contained. On the contrary, they were at pains to emphasise that were it not for the divine revelation, there were truths (such as the truth that God exists in three persons) that were not otherwise discoverable. And also that there were widely-accepted beliefs, such as the belief that the world has always existed, which could only be known to be false because it is known, or reasonably believed, that God created the material universe, and this could only be known by faith alone. That the world had a beginning is credible (because it is revealed) but it is not demonstrable (because it cannot be proved by reason apart from revelation).[20]

What faith seeks to understand, therefore, in the eyes of such thinkers, is more of the implications of what God has revealed and which could not otherwise be known. And it endeavours to understand this by an exercise of the reason upon that revelation.

But, it may be said, how can such an approach be genuinely philosophical, building as it does on a theological foundation? Must it not be unphilosophical because it is insufficiently rigorous or critical of its starting point?

Why should this be so? Let us briefly consider some examples from other areas of philosophy. The philosophy of science investigates the logic and methodology of scientific operations and assertions, and in so doing takes the practice of science for granted. The political philosopher investigates such matters as equality, rights, and the nature of political obligation, taking for granted that there are political processes in which these issues arise. But just as the philosophy of science or political philosophy do not preclude an examination of the foundations of knowledge on which the practices of science or politics rest, so in theology it need not follow that faith seeking understanding necessarily excludes the practice of natural theology or a defence of the reasonableness of religious belief. One cannot do everything at once, and it is perfectly legitimate while doing one thing, to take certain other things for granted.

In his discussion of ancient scepticism Myles Burnyeat has drawn attention to what he calls the 'practice of insulation'. He puts the point in the following way:

> Nowadays, if a philosopher finds he cannot answer the philosophical question 'What is time?' or 'Is time real?', he applies for a research grant to work on the problem during next year's sabbatical. He does not suppose that the arrival of next year is actually in doubt. Alternatively, he may agree that any puzzlement about the nature of time, or any argument for doubting the reality of time, is in fact a puzzlement about, or an argument for doubting, the truth of the proposition that next year's sabbatical will come, but contend that this is of course a strictly theoretical or philosophical worry, not a worry that needs to be reckoned with in the ordinary business of life. Either way he *insulates* his ordinary first order judgements from the effects of his philosophizing.[21]

Are the faith seeks understanding thinkers guilty (if that is the word to use) of insulating their faith from philosophical scrutiny in the sort of way that Burnyeat identifies? To be guilty of insulation, they would have to claim that the starting-point propositions of faith are for ever beyond philosophical reach, so to speak. But as we have seen such thinkers are, typically, prepared to provide reasons of a general sort, sometimes positive, sometimes negative, for accepting divine testimony on matters not otherwise knowable. Furthermore, they are most certainly not prepared to allow that the understanding that faith seeks is a wholly theoretical matter. To achieve such understanding may require a measure of theoretical sophistication and detachment, the willingness to provide and consider definitions, to tease out the theoretical interconnectedness of one theological doctrine with another, and so on. But the attitude of such a thinker to the understanding he believes that he has gained is not typically one of theoretical detachment, or the satisfaction that is derived from a gain in knowledge for its own sake. Any such gain in understanding is meant to feed back into his faith and provide material for meditation, for worship and for ethics.

One prominent way of understanding philosophy is to see it as providing a rational reconstruction and justification of our ordinary beliefs. There is no conflict, on this view, between testing out arguments one may have against solipsism on someone else. In talking to others about one's arguments against solipsism one is not assuming that those arguments are sound. For such arguments are meant to strengthen the rational foundations for the belief in the existence of minds other than one's own mind, a belief which we employ when we talk to others. It is the *prima facie* reality of other minds that generates an interest in trying to put that belief on a rational footing. In a similar way there is no inconsistency in Anselm, for example, praying to God to provide him with arguments to put the question of the existence of God on a solid rational footing.[22]

Does the 'faith seeks understanding' approach 'leave everything as it is' in the sense made famous by Wittgenstein? In a way it does, and in a way it doesn't. It leaves everything as it is in the sense that the acceptance of the truth of certain propositions remains as the unquestioned starting point of enquiry. The understanding which faith seeks cannot be anything which could overturn the tenets of the faith, but necessarily builds on this starting point. But yet this starting point is not merely a set of first-order statements or expressions. For they may in their turn be open to philosophical scrutiny and argument.

The sort of insulation that one *does* find in faith seeks understanding thinkers is what one might call methodological insulation. In order to draw implications from a proposition or set of propositions one needs to take for granted, to accept or assume the truth of, the propositions which form the starting point of the exercise. In order to draw out the implications of the fact that God is the most perfect being, one needs to assume the truth of that proposition, or at least not actively to question its truth. This is simply because it is impossible to do more than one thing at once. If one is drawing out implications from a proposition one has – so to speak – to hold constant for the time being the proposition from which the implications are being drawn. But such insulation is philosophically innocuous, and even philosophically necessary, as we have seen.

Insofar as philosophical difficulties are met and elucidations offered, as part of the 'faith seeking understanding' project, these results help to meet any charges of irrationalism and special pleading. For as a by-product of such activities, the faith itself is seen as having the resources to cope with objections. While such arguments will not satisfy the sceptic – for what arguments will? – they nevertheless may go some way to meeting the concerns of the reasonable person.

But even if the 'faith seeking understanding' thinkers were guilty of insulating some theological judgements from the effects of their theorising, would this be such a bad thing? It is certainly a widespread practice in current philosophy, as Burnyeat indicates, and he may be correct in claiming that it is an approach that is characteristic of modern philosophical enquiries. If the way in which a contemporary philosopher approaches the problem of scepticism, or the nature of time, or the problem of other minds, is as a theoretical rather than as an 'existential' issue, and this is all right, then the 'faith seeking understanding' thinker could hardly be blamed if he took a similar approach.

NOTES

1. Swinburne, *The Existence of God*, presents a contemporary version of this approach.
2. For discussion of this issue, see Helm, *Belief Policies*.
3. Aquinas, *Summa Theologiae* 1ae 2,2.
4. Ibid.
5. For further discussion of Aquinas's views, see Wolterstorff, 'The Migration of the Theistic Arguments; From Natural Theology to Evidentialist Apologetics'; Stump, 'Aquinas on the Foundations of Knowledge'; and Vos, 'Aquinas, Calvin and Contemporary Protestant Thought'.
6. I am not denying that there are non-cognitivist or expressive understandings of the sentences of a faith such as the Christian faith. But such understandings are not central to the tradition and raise questions not germane to our present inquiry.
7. Augustine, *Soliloquies*, Ch.2.
8. For further discussion of this point, see Hoitenga, *Faith and Reason from Plato to Plantinga*, p.101.
9. Bonaventure, *The Journey of the Mind to God*, p.37.
10. Anthony Kenny, *What is Faith?* p.49.
11. In this account of faith I am intentionally ignoring the part that non-evidential factors may play in faith. A person may, on account of the strength of his purposes and desires, trust beyond what the evidence on which his belief is based warrants, but it is not of the *bene esse* of trust to do so. Though such trust may be overall rational because it may be rational to purpose what is important but for which there is little evidence, it is not epistemically rational.
12. Kierkegaard, *Concluding Unscientific Postscript*, p.182.
13. For further discussion of this view of faith, see Penelhum, *God and Skepticism*.
14. Augustine seems to present two views of faith, one more propositional, the other more personal, side by side, as we shall see later on.
15. Hume, *An Inquiry Concerning Human Understanding*, Section X, Part 1.
16. For discussion of this point, see Anscombe, 'What is it to Believe Someone?'
17. Augustine, *Confessions*, p.95.
18. For a defence of the principle of credulity by a contemporary philosopher of religion see Swinburne, *The Existence of God*, Ch.13.
19. Locke, *The Reasonableness of Christianity*, pp.60f.
20. Aquinas, *Summa Theologiae* 1a.46,2.
21. Burnyeat, 'The Sceptic in His Place and Time', p.225.
22. On this point see Adams, 'Praying the *Proslogion*'.

2

Faith Seeks Understanding

The slogan 'faith seeks understanding' gained currency from Augustine's preference for what was in fact a mistranslation of Isaiah 9:7, 'If you will not believe, surely you will not be established' (RSV). The Septuagint mistranslates it as 'If you will not believe you will not understand'. Augustine knew both the original Hebrew and the Septuagint versions, but in *On Christian Doctrine* he opts for the latter.[1] These facts matter less than does the fact that the phrase itself became a rallying cry for one way in which theologians and philosophers – not only Christian theologians, but Jewish and Islamic philosophers as well – from Augustine onwards have made a positive connection between faith and reason. Though, as was hinted in the previous chapter, and as we shall see more clearly in this, this one way of linking faith and reason is in fact several different ways. In this chapter we shall consider these different ways as clearly as possible, to try to indicate something of the richness and fertility of this tradition.

Augustine (and others) have different ways of expressing the basic point, and it is as well to consider these one by one. Among the ways Augustine himself has of putting the programme of faith seeking understanding are the following:

> Although understanding lies in the sight of the Eternal, faith nourishes as children are nourished with milk in the cradles of temporal things. Now 'we walk by faith and not by sight'. Unless we walk by faith, we shall not be able to come to that sight which does not fail but continues through a cleansed understanding uniting us with Truth. On account of this principle one said 'If you will not

believe, you shall not continue', and another said, 'If you will not believe, you shall not understand'.[2]

Therefore do not seek to understand in order that you may believe, but believe in order that you may understand[3]

If a person says to me, 'I want to understand in order that I may believe,' I reply, 'Believe in order that you may understand'.[4]

We want to know and understand what we believe.[5]

In these slogans sometimes the stress is placed not on the understanding as the outworking of faith, as what faith leads to, but on faith as the condition of understanding; if I want to understand, I must first believe. It is as if faith involves or possesses no understanding itself but is purely functional or instrumental. Though as we shall shortly see matters are not quite as straightforward as that. 'Now it is faith to believe that which you do not yet see; and the reward of this faith is to see that which you believe.'[6] Here faith is contrasted not with understanding but with sight, and 'the reward of faith' is equated with seeing, not vision in the strict sense, but with direct or immediate knowledge of the sort that vision conveys. As we noted in the first chapter, one thing that Augustine has in mind is the biblical contrast between faith and sight. Faith, unlike sight, is at best indirect; or perhaps it is more accurate to say that it is *less* direct than sight. Understanding makes faith more direct, more like sight, than it would otherwise be.

But sometimes the priority of faith over understanding appears to be reversed by Augustine, even in the same sermon:

> My opponent too . . . has something when he says: 'I would under-stand in order that I may believe.' Certainly what I am now saying, I say with the object that those may believe who do not yet believe. Nevertheless, unless they understand what I am saying, they cannot believe.[7]

Here understanding is a condition of having faith. These seemingly contradictory claims, that understanding follows faith and that understanding is needed for faith, can be reconciled if we bear in mind Augustine's view of faith. Faith has some cognitive content; and so a person needs to have some understanding of this content in order to have faith; otherwise how would his faith in God be distinguishable from faith in anyone else? It is this initial understanding which directs what ought to follow; the understanding that is to follow keeps to the parameters of the basic cognitive content of faith and attempts to fill out the detail and so deepen the understanding. For the primary cognitive content of faith is limited; and so understanding gains a fuller appreciation of this content without going outside its limits.

So in these words Augustine makes clear that faith involves some understanding, for understanding is a necessary condition of faith, and that the understanding which faith then seeks is further understanding, building upon the primary understanding involved in the first steps of faith.

Perhaps what Augustine takes to be the primary understanding of faith is not the direct comprehension of spiritual realities, but the understanding of words. What Augustine is saying is that it is necessary for anyone who believes anything first to have a form of words proposed for their belief, just as a novice joiner may believe that he needs a set-square without knowing what a set-square it. And then a fuller comprehension may follow this believing, a greater awareness of those realities which the language of their faith denotes and connotes. To understand is thus more than comprehending the meanings of words, it is an appreciation of those realities which the words represent.

Centuries later Anselm takes up the same slogan:

> I have written the following treatise in the person of one who strives to lift his mind to the contemplation of God, and seeks to understand what he believes.[8]

> Lord, I do not attempt to comprehend Your sublimity, because my intellect is not at all equal to such a task. But I yearn to understand some measure of Your truth, which my heart believes and loves. For I do not seek to understand in order to believe but I believe in order to understand. For I believe even this: that I shall not understand unless I believe.[9]

Here, as in Augustine, it is recognised that the understanding sought will be conveyed gradually and partially. Anselm never claims to comprehend the reality of God himself. Both belief and understanding are situated in a context in which there is a serious search for truth. Whether it is possible to convey any understanding to one who is not a serious seeker after truth is not a question that directly occupies Augustine and Anselm. For even if one could, there is an element of vanity or futility about the understanding conveyed, because such understanding will not be put to a good use.

Whether or not faith is necessary for understanding, Anselm is clear that the understanding he seeks is not necessary for faith:

> Just as right order requires that we believe the deep matters of the Christian faith before we presume to discuss them rationally, so it

seems to me to be an instance of carelessness if, having been confirmed in faith, we do not eagerly desire to understand what we believe. Indeed, assisted by the prevenient grace of God I am, it seems to me, holding so steadfastly to faith in our redemption that even if I were not in any respect able to understand what I believe, nothing could wrest me from firmness of faith.[10]

Clearly no Christian ought to debate whether something which the Catholic Church believes with its heart and confesses with its mouth is false. On the contrary, by clinging constantly and unhesitatingly to this same faith, by loving it and living humbly according to it, the Christian ought to search for the reason which shows why this faith is true.[11]

There are several characteristic Anselmian emphases here. Firstly 'understanding' is more consistently discursive in character than it is in Augustine. There is here little or no emphasis upon understanding as conveying a partial vision, though elsewhere, notably in the *Proslogion*, Anselm seems to catch more of this Augustinian emphasis, as we shall see later. Secondly, understanding involves possessing the reasons which shows why the faith is true. Faith initially accepts that it is true, while understanding comes to see (in a measure) how it is true, its basis in the principles of reason, in the nature of things, that is, ultimately in God himself. And so in seeing how it is true the mind comes to grasp something of the divine reality itself.

Anselm links the understanding that faith seeks with a particular normative view of what understanding is. For him, understanding is not simply the removal of anomalies and the gaining of information through the operation of reflective reason, but dispelling the appearance of irrationality or whimsy or arbitrariness in what God has willed. For doing what he did God must have had a good reason, even (in some sense) a necessary reason, and it is the place of understanding to unfold this. We shall explore this idea of a necessary reason more fully in the chapters on Anselm.

Like Augustine, Anselm lays emphasis on the cognitive content of the faith; his term 'faith' embraces not only the attitude of believing, but the propositions believed. The faith in question therefore has a propositional content. Those who have faith in these propositions do so on the authority of the Catholic Church. And it is one of the tasks of reason to look for reasons which show why this faith is true, which presumably provide grounds which do not in turn depend for their convincingness on the mere authority of the Church, but which have some independent validity. Not that Anselm wished to be free of submission to the authority of the Church, but he wished, in addition, to have some 'independent reason' for what he believed, a reason that would convey some of the inner rationale of his faith. Insofar as reason succeeds in this task, it gains understanding.

FAITH SEEKING UNDERSTANDING
AND NATURAL THEOLOGY

The slogan 'faith seeks understanding' appears to reverse the relationship between faith and reason of much natural theology. The prevailing understanding of natural theology since the Enlightenment is that it functions to make the propositions of faith reasonable. On this view, in order for any religious belief to be rational it must be supported on a foundation of natural theology, of propositions which any person can accept from reason and without any appeal to revelation. 'Faith seeking understanding' appears to turn this relationship round, or at least to ignore it, making faith a condition of a rational grasp of those propositions about God which faith relies upon.

In the presentation of his Five Ways in the *Summa Theologiae* Thomas might at first glance seem to argue that there are truths about God, principally the truth that God exists, which we can know by our natural powers of reasoning, and that these must be established before the articles of faith which presuppose them may be believed: 'For faith presupposes natural knowledge, just as grace does nature and all perfections that which they perfect'. Nevertheless, as we noted in Chapter 1, Aquinas goes on to assert that: 'there is nothing to stop a man accepting on faith some truth which he personally cannot demonstrate, even if that truth in itself is such that demonstration could make it evident'.[12]

We might hope to gain further light on the relation between natural theology and the faith seeking understanding project if we ask whether Thomas' approach to natural theology has the same character as the evidentialist natural theology of Locke and others. Nicholas Wolterstorff[13] thinks there is a sharp difference between the two, and that the natural theology of Aquinas is in the tradition of faith seeking understanding and not an early instance of the evidentialism characteristic of the Enlightenment:

> Aquinas was no different on these matters. He explicated the concept of knowledge somewhat more rigorously than did Anselm: a person knows only what is self-evident to him or evident to his senses, or what has been demonstrated from such. Likewise he conceives faith somewhat more rigorously, as accepting propositions on the authority of God the revealer. But the goal of natural theology for Aquinas

was exactly the same as for Anselm: to transmute what already one believed into something known. Demonstration was seen as indispensable to this transmutation project.[14]

Wolterstorff's chief reason for assimilating Aquinas to the faith seeks understanding project is that Aquinas begins from faith. This may be granted, provided that the qualifications noted above are made. But perhaps the sense of faith seeking understanding is somewhat different, it itself gets transmuted, from Augustine through Anselm to Aquinas. It is not that for Aquinas one believes *in order to* understand; that faith, and the propositions of the faith to which faith gives assent, is *and remains* a necessary condition for understanding, but that there is something inherent in faith which seeks to go beyond itself, that faith is inherently self-abnegating; faith is (from an intellectual point of view) second-rate, and ought wherever possible to be supplanted by knowledge, as one day all faith will be.

> The enterprise of natural theology is not only addressed to the unbeliever and is not only addressed to all who are interested in the pursuit of science. It is also addressed to the *believer*. It represents an *advance* for the believer, and that in the most fundamental way: an advance toward ultimate felicity. Our ultimate happiness lies in 'seeing' truths about God. And when we in this life manage to demonstrate some of the things that we unseeingly took on faith, so that now we 'see' them to be true, that is a step up the road toward felicity.[15]

From this it would appear that in Thomas' eyes the Five Ways are not exercises in natural theology in the Enlightenment sense, but are themselves an expression of faith seeking understanding. It is *desirable* that the existence of God is provable by natural reason, but perhaps not necessary. And certainly it is not necessary before that article of faith may be believed. There is, nevertheless, an appropriateness to natural theology, since 'faith presupposes natural knowledge'.[16]

Of course, if the existence of God is demonstrable, as part of faith seeking understanding, this fact is of some apologetic significance. For the demonstrability of the existence of God can then be detached from its original context and used to attempt to convince those who are sceptical of the existence of God. The proofs, having started life as part of a project of faith, come to have a life of their own. And it seems perfectly natural that this separation should occur. The proofs would then become *ad hominem* arguments addressed to the sceptic, still not cases of the evidentialism of the Enlightenment.

The 'proofs' of God's existence came to be considered as part of the 'prolegomena' of the faith, the *praeambula fidei*. While in classical Thomist apologetics the existence of God is established by a deductive or inductive argument via one of the Five Ways, the credibility of revelation is attested by reason in a weaker sense. Christian theology, on this view, is not a deductive system with the proposition that God exists as the axiom from which all else is derived. The matters which the divine revelation reveals, other than those matters which are separately demonstrable, are matters which it is overall reasonable for us to believe with confidence. We can be certain of what has been revealed, but we cannot know it, it cannot be demonstrated, in this life.[17]

It may seem to follow that the faith seeking understanding project is, in the hands of Aquinas, more restrictive than when in the hands of Augustine, and even more restrictive than for Anselm, being concerned solely with matters which are demonstrable from what is evident to all. But here we need to bear in mind that according to Aquinas the only theological proposition capable of *scientia* is the proposition that God exists. Demonstration, according to Aquinas, has only to do with universals.[18] So, though such demonstrability may be a sufficient condition of understanding, it cannot be necessary; not, at least, if Aquinas thought it was possible to gain understanding of matters that were nevertheless not demonstrable. And in fact there are places in which Aquinas distinguishes understanding from *scientia*.[19] If this is representative of what Aquinas thought then the proofs of God's existence were not cases of understanding, though they were cases of demonstration. So, far from being the paradigm cases of faith seeking understanding perhaps the proofs were not cases of it at all! And if it is possible to understand matters the truth of which is not rationally demonstrable, then the *Summae* may be thought of as exercises of faith seeking understanding *in extenso*.

Anselm himself anticipates a position very similar to that adopted by Thomas in introducing the Five Ways:

> If he [viz. the Christian] is able to understand, then let him give thanks to God. But if he cannot, then instead of tossing it about with his horns, let him bow his head in veneration before it. . . . For it is clear that they have no foundation of faith who, because they cannot understand what they believe, argue against the truth of the same faith as was confirmed by the holy Fathers. It is just as if bats and owls, who see the sky only at night, were to dispute about the midday rays of the sun with eagles, who with unblinded vision gaze directly at the sun.[20]

Anselm makes it clear that though having reasons for one's faith of the sort that he seeks would be sufficient for holding that faith acceptably, it is not necessary, for many who lack reasons nonetheless are justified in holding the faith that they do. Part of the reason for this is that 'the faith' is a complex of propositions. No one can hope in this life to possess a convincing set of reasons showing why every element of this complex is true. Even those who possess such reasons for some propositions will not possess them for all.

It should be clear, then, that the relationship between faith and understanding in the Augustinian tradition is not that faith is merely instrumental, or psychologically necessary, for understanding. There are undoubtedly certain conditions where believing p, even believing p against the evidence, are psychologically necessary for certain kinds of accomplishment, for gaining success in certain kinds of action, and even for gaining cognitive success. It may be necessary in order for a person to be cured of an illness that he believes that he will be cured even though, apart from such a belief, a cure is unlikely. Or, to use an example of William James, it may be necessary for a climber to believe that he will jump across a crevasse in order for him to succeed in doing so.

But faith does not function like this for Augustine or Aquinas. For as we have already seen, the faith in question is trust in *the* faith, in certain propositions. Augustine is not saying that faith is an irrational leap, but that there is an inherent and undesirable incompleteness in matters of faith which impels the believer on to gain understanding. Given that the propositions are about an object of love as well as of faith, who would not wish to understand more of the one beloved? And so the basic Augustinian contrast between faith and knowledge (where knowledge is understood as a condition of direct acquaintance to which understanding contributes) is well expressed as the contrast between faith and sight; partial but increasing sight in this life, full vision in the life to come.

This basic, positive connection between faith and understanding, a common thread running through the writers we have been discussing, involves a spiralling connection between faith and understanding, a spiral which in this life never reaches its zenith. Such a view is to be contrasted sharply with two other traditions of the relation between faith and reason, each of which may be more familiar to us than this.

For whatever may be the truth about Aquinas' and Anselm's view of natural theology, in the dominant and popular understanding of the place of natural theology, matters of faith come after, and are logically presupposed by, matters of reason. We do not believe in order to understand, but understand in order to believe. Such understanding involves coming to a positive view on the reasonableness of what we are called upon to believe. In order for faith to be reasonable, reason must precede faith, not even merely accompany it. This is the view of natural theology stemming from the Enlightenment, from philosophers such as John Locke. It is Locke's view that any of the propositions of the faith, in order to be acceptable, must be reasonable; that is, reasonableness is necessary for proper faithful believing:

> Whatever GOD hath revealed is certainly true: no doubt can be made of it. This is the proper object of *faith*; but whether it be a divine revelation or not, *reason* must judge; which can never permit the mind to reject a greater evidence to embrace what is less evident, nor allow it to entertain probability in opposition to knowledge and certainty.[21]

Here it is clear that in order for a proposition to count as a revelation from God it must first pass a test, the test of reason, substantive reason as we called it in the first chapter; and that the strength of one's belief must be proportional to the amount of the evidence that there is for it.

> Our assent can be rationally no higher than the evidence of its being a revelation, and that this is the meaning of the expressions it is delivered in. If the evidence of its being a revelation, or that this is its true sense be only on probable proofs, our assent can reach no higher than as assurance or diffidence, arising from the more or less apparent probability of the proofs.[22]

And in Locke's case, there is a more 'political' reason, namely that only by appeal to 'reason' in this substantive sense can arguments be found to repudiate the claims of religious enthusiasts of seventeenth-century England. More weakly, only where the propositions of the faith can be shown to be based on reason in this way can the faith be shown to be free from bias, to be 'objectively true' or 'reasonable'; only in this way can the faith be argued for with some hope of success in terms of showing that the propositions of the faith are soundly based. This Lockean approach is the characteristic Enlightenment position on faith and reason.

The *second* understanding of the relation between faith and reason which the faith seeks understanding tradition challenges is that which opposes matters of faith to matters of reason. Here one has in mind the anti-rationalism of writers in the tradition of Tertullian:

> The Son of God died. This is believable because it is ridiculous [*ineptum*]. And after having been buried he rose again. This is certain, because it is impossible.[23]

> Philosophy is the core of worldly wisdom, the rash interpreter of
> God's nature and plan. In fact, the heresies themselves are secretly
> nourished by philosophy. . . . After Christ Jesus, we have no need of
> curiosity; after the Gospel, no need of inquiry.[24]

According to this view there is a strict separation between the philosophical reason, which proceeds independently of revelation and so may be
thought of as 'worldly wisdom', and the word of God, which comes
through acts of special revelation and whose precise function is to
challenge the wisdom of the world by the foolishness of the Cross. On
such a view, as Terence Penelhum puts it:

> To seek to establish God's presence by reason is to attempt to bypass
> the spiritual regeneration which is the condition of recognising it, and
> which requires response to his special revelation. The Skeptic, by
> using reason to undermine our confidence in its power to establish
> such a conclusion, performs faith a service, whether or not he wishes
> to do so, in making us recognize that this attempt is doomed to
> frustration.[25]

There can be no co-operation or accommodation between such wisdom
and such foolishness, only mutual antagonism. Reason is not a neutral
tool; its very pretended neutrality is a challenge to the authenticity of the
word of God.

Whatever differences we may uncover between the various approaches
within the faith seeking understanding project, each has a similar negative
attitude to the anti-rationalism of Tertullian, though it is certainly possible
to combine a basic fideism with the use of the reason in elaborating the
meaning of the propositions believed by the leap of faith.

TWO CONTEMPORARY APPROACHES

We have seen that the faith seeks understanding motif appears to have been
taken up in rather different fashion by leading Christian thinkers. For
Augustine, the understanding which faith ultimately seeks is knowledge by
acquaintance or vision; for Anselm it is the provision of reasons grounded
in the nature of things, including of course the nature of God himself. For
Aquinas (if we make a distinction between rational demonstration and the
gaining of understanding) then understanding is gained through the
resolution of opposing opinions, as in the two *Summae*. These different
approaches are exemplified and sharpened in the different and conflicting
ways in which two contemporary philosophers of religion understand the
faith seeks understanding motif. Considering the issues that they raise will
lead us to a great clarification of the faith seeks understanding project.

Norman Kretzmann

According to Norman Kretzmann the main way in which the faith seeks understanding motif may be understood is as follows:

> A Christian philosopher, recognizing that many people, perhaps including herself, view the propositions of Christian doctrine as *prima facie* unlikely or even impossible, may be motivated to employ analysis and argument in the service of apologetics. In the second place, a Christian philosopher may engage in the intellectual exploration and development of fundamental doctrinal propositions in the conviction that the doctrine itself is eminently understandable and acceptable, but in need of clarification of a sort most likely to be accessible through analysis and argument.[26]

Here Kretzmann appears to be adopting an essentially modern view of religious faith as involving a propositional attitude which is necessarily deficient in the evidential support that it has, and because it is deficient there is an intellectual obligation on all who have faith to remove or to mitigate the deficiency. And so what primarily needs attention by believers are the grounds on which the propositions of faith are held, in an endeavour to show that they are more likely to be true than may at first appear. The gaining of understanding thus involves the removal of intellectual misapprehensions which block acceptance of such grounds. These may be misapprehensions about what the proposition in question means, or what grounds the truth of the proposition. Kretzmann does not say that such a stance is appropriate in the case of all Christian doctrine, but clearly he thinks that it is in the case of some fundamental doctrine. It is possible for that stance to differ from person to person, some regarding one doctrine as unlikely or impossible (depending on what in addition they believe or know), some another. So the faith seeking understanding project as Kretzmann understands it is primarily epistemological in character, though it involves matters which are ancillary to this epistemological thrust.

Further, Kretzmann distinguishes between what he calls *propositional faith* and *the way of faith*, 'professing Christian doctrine and trying to live in accordance with it, faith as a way of life, or what Augustine sometimes calls "the way of faith".'[27]

The way of faith involves the belief that certain propositions are true, but it involves more than this; for example it involves commitment and obedience. Propositional belief, arising from religious tradition or authority, is transmuted through reason into a religion, into the way of faith.

Insofar as propositional faith is based on reason then so is the way of faith which arises from it, which the propositional faith justifies. The goal of the Christian philosopher must be to replace as far as possible the acceptance of any proposition on authority with an acceptance based on reason, upon understanding. When faith gains understanding, understanding *supplants* faith based upon authority.

> For example, the authority-based faith that God exists, which is incorporated into the way of faith, would indeed be supplanted by the acquisition of understanding on the basis of a proof that God exists. What propositional understanding merely supplements or enhances is not propositional faith regarding some proposition in particular but the way of faith as a whole.[28]

According to Kretzmann, then, 'understanding' means the displaying of the credentials of religious belief by showing that such belief meets general standards of reasonableness, and it is a general obligation on all who aspire to the way of faith to seek to establish the reasonableness (in this sense) of what they believe.

The religious authority to which faith submits has itself to be submitted to reason before it is reckoned trustworthy. 'Faith is assent to a proposition in virtue of its having been put forward by an authority one has accepted on rational grounds',[29] so that the understanding which faith then seeks is of a piece with the primary understanding which is required to make the propositions of the initial act of faith credible. Understanding is assent to a proposition in virtue of its having been clarified or supported (or both) by one's reason on the basis of analysis and argument.[30] Such clarification would involve, for example, the removal of ambiguities which make for misunderstanding, the drawing out of the logical implications of the propositions of faith, and the rebutting of *prima facie* reasonable objections to the meaningfulness or the truth of such propositions. Whether by the acceptance of an authority on rational grounds Kretzmann means on grounds which should convince anyone, or whether he means 'reasonable' in some weaker sense, is not clear.

So, on this view, faith is to be contrasted with knowledge, and seeks, through the processes of reason, to gain knowledge, that full-fledged propositional understanding that typically involves both analysis and argument.[31] Such knowledge clearly bears a strong family resemblance to the sort of knowledge Plato and Aristotle ranked above 'mere opinion'.[32] Knowledge thus approximates to one feature of that condition to be enjoyed by believers in the Beatific Vision. It involves two elements, having a clear understanding or interpretation of some theological proposition, and assenting to that proposition as the conclusion of a convincing argument.[33] In fact this is putting the point unnecessarily abstractly. For it is not faith that seeks knowledge on this account, but the believer who seeks an elaboration of his faith. And this is how Kretzmann understands Augustine's account of understanding. It is primarily concerned with the meaning of the propositions of faith, and with arguing for their truth.

What, then, are we to make of Augustine's stress on immediacy, his use of visual terminology to characterise understanding? For example:

> when faith acted on what pertained to it, reason, following after, found something of what faith was seeking. . . . For faith has its own eyes with which it sees, so to speak, that what it does not yet see is true, and with which it most certainly sees that it does not yet see what it believes.[34]

Augustine's language of sight and vision is for Kretzmann a metaphorical expression designed simply to express in vivid terms the worked-out character of understanding, as when we 'see' the point of a joke or the validity of an argument. It is not meant to express the immediacy of direct acquaintance:

> Knowledge [*scientia*] is Augustine's other name for the full-fledged propositional understanding that typically involves both analysis and argument . . . [it] . . . might well be described in older terms as true belief accompanied by a rational account, or as involving a grasp of the causes of what the correctly interpreted proposition says.[35]

Natural theology and the intellectual processes which are indispensable for it are necessary for gaining such knowledge, which either is the condition of understanding, or a necessary condition of it. Knowledge is thus understood in exclusively propositional terms; a state of being convinced of the truth of some (set of) propositions by reason.[36]

According to Kretzmann, the propositional understanding which he explains and defends supplements the way of faith.[37] How? The way of faith has a propositional component, faith in which is a necessary condition of endeavouring to live a certain kind of life. The way of faith is for this life only, but the propositional understanding acquired in the way of faith 'carries over' (and is perfected) in the life to come, when faith becomes sight. Further, where propositional faith issues from (is a part of) active commitment to a way of life, then that propositional faith, in those circumstances, may be said to be seeking understanding.

For Kretzmann the progression from faith to understanding is essentially a two-stage affair; the stage of propositional belief augmented by rational reflection and argument. It is not fair to say that for him understanding is restricted to an elite, since he affirms that such understanding must be undertaken as opportunity and ability permit; all Christians will endeavour to gain it to a degree.[38]

What is also basic to this way of interpreting the faith seeks understanding motif is the idea of knowledge as justified true belief. Faith, though it involves belief, is necessarily unjustified true belief, for it falls short of knowledge Understanding aims at remedying this epistemic deficiency. There is a progression from belief, in which propositions are accepted upon authority, the authority of God in revelation, to knowledge. One way that such knowledge is achieved is when the internal connections between certain doctrines, each of which is taken to be embodied in the revelation, are demonstrated. Here there is the removal of arbitrariness. Another way is when the propositions of the revelation are shown to be demonstrably true in the manner of natural theology. Particularly in this last case, the true belief becomes knowledge by being justified, by the provision of adequate grounds.

Kretzmann identifies three difficulties with this view, difficulties which cast doubt on whether the faith-understanding distinction corresponds to the opinion-knowledge distinction. The first is over the idea that faith and understanding may co-exist and understanding be regarded as supplementing faith. But, 'a cognitive state in which authority-based opinion is merely supplemented rather than supplanted by reason-based knowledge seems incoherent'.[39] This is presumably because a reason-based account has a rational sufficiency which excludes the need to appeal to authority. The second difficulty is that faith must precede understanding; for this makes it seem as if understanding is additional to faith. And the third problem is that posed by Augustine's understanding of 'faith seeks, understanding finds', according to which faith is not only a precondition of understanding but also a means of attaining it.[40]

Kretzmann's key to the solution to all these difficulties is to pay attention to the 'religious side' of Augustine's account of faith and understanding. We need to remember what we have already noted, that for Augustine it is the life of faith which is essentially incomplete, necessarily falling short of the glories of the beatific vision. In such a life there are elements of both faith and understanding, but not of full understanding. Hence the need for faith. Faith, based upon what we can understand, and unreasonable without being so based, accepts what we cannot at present understand.

The problem of the combination of faith and understanding is solved by remembering, once again, that propositional faith involves belief in a complex of propositions; to gain understanding of some of the propositions in the complex is to supplement and so to strengthen the reasonableness of believing the complex as a whole. And furthermore, where there are difficulties in working out an understanding, a believer may use her faithful reliance on the proposition in question as a fall-back position.[41] Similarly, faith as a general disposition or habit seeks understanding, and remains in place even when some understanding of some propositions has been gained:

> Since the way of faith is a state of seeking theological understanding *generally*, there is no incoherence in the combination of that cognitive state with this or that particular instance of acquired propositional understanding, and so the subsidiary problem of simultaneously seeking and possessing what is sought does not arise for Augustinian Christian philosophy.[42]

Kretzmann comes down hard on the idea that faith, understood as propositional faith, must be a necessary condition of gaining philosophical understanding; it is, he says,

> an epistemological absurdity that is so blatant as to be harmless: it is just not true that one has to believe a proposition in order to acquire philosophical understanding of it. But if the essentially precedent faith under consideration is the way of faith, 'Believe in order that you may understand' looks like 'Become a Christian if you want to acquire any philosophical understanding of any proposition of Christian doctrine', which is wrong in a way that is more to be censured than pitied.[43]

While there is plausibility to Kretzmann's view that it is absurd to suppose that faith is a necessary condition for properly doing Christian philosophy, it is not clear that writers such as Anselm would agree with him. For one thing, Anselm seems to hold that having faith provides data which those who do not have faith do not have:

> He who does not believe will not understand. For he who does not believe will not experience, and he who has not had experience will not know. For the knowledge of the one who experiences is superior to the knowledge of one who hears, to the same degree that experience of a thing is superior to hearing about it.[44]

Here knowledge is a precondition of understanding, and the believer, through his experience of God, has knowledge that is not at present available to the unbeliever.

Where Augustine claims that faith is a precondition for understanding, Kretzmann interprets this as referring almost always to the *way of* faith:[45]

> For although no one can believe in God if he does not understand *anything*, nevertheless, by the very faith by which he believes he is restored in order that he may understand greater things. For there are some things we do not believe unless we understand them, and there are others we do not understand unless we believe them.[46]

Furthermore, while one does not have to believe a proposition to gain understanding of it, according to Augustine one normally does.[47] That is to say, while the writers we are considering, such as Augustine and Anselm, were believers, and sought to move from faith to understanding, it is not, according to Kretzmann, a necessary condition of understanding that one believes. There is nothing to stop anyone from treating the propositions of the faith for which understanding is sought as *assumptions*. This is unlikely to happen, since it is largely those who have faith who are interested in gaining understanding. But though it is not likely to happen, it may:

> The philosophically safest position is that doctrinal mysteries are introduced into philosophical theology as no more than assumptions, postulates whose coherence, credibility, and compatibility with other doctrinal propositions are to be determined by the analysis and argumentation to which they will be subjected. And although no Christian philosophical theologian would say *only* that much about them, he might well say that sort of thing and treat them in that way when he is attending not to the propositions themselves but to his job of clarifying them within philosophical theology. . . . Treating mysteries methodologically as mere assumptions is a sensible course of action available even to a Christian philosophical theologian whose religious commitment to those doctrines remains intact before, during, and after his work on them.[48]

So according to Kretzmann, understanding is concerned with displaying the coherence of propositions and with examining the rational grounds for them, tasks which can be carried out successfully independently of belief in any of them, by treating them as assumptions, assumptions which may well be held on faith, but which need not be held in this way in order to function as assumptions.

There may be a tension in what Kretzmann says at this point, and what he elsewhere claims about understanding supplanting faith. It is one thing to say that if one treats mysteries as assumptions then it is the task of philosophical understanding to show that they are not repugnant to reason, and so that they are 'reasonable'. But to demonstrate the reasonableness of a mystery in this sense, to defend it against objections which claim that it is repugnant to reason, is not to show that one has a reason for believing the mystery in the first place. One still is reliant upon authority for believing the mystery to be a truth, and such faith, while it can be supplemented by the operation of reason in mystery, cannot by supplanted by reason. Faith is not a temporary expedient until reason comes to the rescue.

So what about the initial credibility of the propositions of faith? Is it sufficient to echo the words of Augustine that Christ's existence and teaching is credible because reports about them have the 'strength of numbers, agreement and antiquity', and that heresies are few, confused and recent? Kretzmann claims that Bonaventure argues for the initial credibility of the Trinity, but in this he is surely untypical of the faith seeking understanding tradition.[49] What this shows is that among those who subscribe to the faith seeks understanding approach there were different estimates of the capabilities of the unaided human reason.

There is little suggestion in Augustine and Anselm that the authority of the Church needs rational support to make it credible; rather the reverse. Here, for example, is what Anselm says on the matter:

> No Christian ought to debate whether something which the Catholic Church believes with its heart and confesses with its mouth is false. On the contrary, by clinging constantly and unhesitatingly to this same faith, by loving it and living humbly according to it, the Christian ought to search for the reason which shows why this faith is true. If he is able to understand, then let him give thanks to God. But if he cannot, then instead of tossing it about with his horns, let him bow his head in veneration before it.[50]

Kretzmann's remarks make good sense when applied to attempts by reason alone to prove the existence of God, and as we know there is a long and formidable tradition of natural theology. But it is hard to see how the credibility of crucial Christian doctrines, such as the idea of *creatio ex nihilo*, the fall of the human race from innocence, and the trinitarian character of God, can be proved by reason, even if they are initially postulated as assumptions. For one thing, such doctrines are extremely hard to understand. How could conceptual analysis of the sort that Kretzmann proposes either demonstrate the inherent reasonableness of such matters, or their truth? Even those who, like Anselm in the *Cur Deus Homo*, used reason to support the doctrine of the Incarnation, and even to demonstrate its necessity, argued that the Incarnation was necessary given certain other beliefs, not that it was logically necessary, as we shall see in Chapter 6.

Dewey Hoitenga

As we have already noted, it is possible and quite natural to read the faith-understanding distinction in a different way, where the controlling idea is not (as with Kretzmann) the propositions believed, but the person believed, and where the knowledge sought in understanding is not demonstrable truth, or justified true belief, but what philosophers have sometimes referred to as knowledge by acquaintance, an immediate, direct awareness of an object, or a person, for oneself. In the first chapter we noted that faith, considered as trust, has both a personal and a propositional element to it. This second approach to the faith seeks understanding programme focuses more on the personal than on the propositional, without, of course, denying the centrality or importance of the propositional content of faith. But the point is, these are propositions the reference of which one knows for oneself, in direct fashion. Thus to understand the proposition 'God is love' one must have a direct acquaintance with the love of God; not merely a knowledge of the truth of proposition that God is love, or a belief in its reasonableness, but an awareness of the reality of that love directly, for oneself. One must recognise that one is loved by God, and be aware of that love.

This is the interpretation of the faith seeks understanding tradition, and particularly of Augustine, offered by Dewey Hoitenga in *Faith and Reason from Plato to Plantinga*. Hoitenga claims that Kretzmann has misinterpreted Augustine:

> Augustine teaches that the knowledge faith seeks is the direct knowledge of seeing God that is open to every Christian, unlike the inferential knowledge of natural theology available only to a qualified few. Such direct knowledge is a foretaste of the beatific vision because it is accompanied by the love of God, which is made possible by the 'way of faith' that constitutes any person who walks in it as a Christian. Insofar as Christians *see* God, it is correct to say that they *know* him; they do not just *believe* that he exists on some human authority, however well-attested that authority may be. Their knowledge, too, 'supplants' propositional belief, just as in Kretzmann's account, but it does not depend on the inferences of natural theology. The way of faith, likewise, is still a necessary condition for such knowledge; but such knowledge is the renewal by that faith of a direct knowledge of God already naturally possessed, not an indirect, inferential knowledge newly discovered by rational demonstration.[51]

Basic to this account is the idea of degrees of personal acquaintance. Faith, trusting in God, presupposes or includes some initial degree of direct acquaintance with God, that is, of personal dealing with God; for example, a trusting of his promises and a responding to them with obedience. This, however minimally, is a case of knowledge by acquaintance, as when one begins a friendship with another person by respecting what they say. The perfect vision of God is reserved for the next life, but increasing degrees of direct acquaintance are possible in this. Each of us, on this view, has an innate capacity for the knowledge of God because we are made in the image of God. But at the same time there is no assumption that only those seek understanding who are already Christian.

So faith is here understood to be an innate, though dormant or even repressed, natural knowledge of God, a state not exclusively propositional. It is qualitatively the same as, and continuous with, though it is vastly poorer than, the knowledge of the Beatific Vision, in that it is basically a case of knowledge as acquaintance. But it is also propositional in that the propositional content of the knowledge helps to identify and to structure the acquaintance in question, to distinguish it from false acquaintances and illusions.

So the basic contrast, on this reading of the faith-understanding distinction, is between some sight and more sight, not between faith and reason, or between faith and knowledge, where knowledge is understood propositionally. For faith is primarily trust in what is partly seen, and reason is needed to gain further sight. So at every stage in the transition from faith to sight knowledge and reason are employed, and the transition, a gradual one, involves increasing knowledge, as what is seen comes into clearer focus.

There are, according to Hoitenga, moral and psychological conditions for this knowledge and its growth as there are with human friendships. The friendship of another is not something that can be gained by effort alone, but by winning the confidence of the friend, showing oneself to be someone who is capable of friendship, and the like. So it is, on Hoitenga's understanding of faith and understanding, with a person's knowledge of God; one comes to know God by being appropriately 'open' to his approaches.

So faith is knowledge, though not full knowledge, and certainly not the fullest possible knowledge. And such faith is mixed with elements of doubt and intellectual confusion and unclarity. It is the role of 'understanding', which embraces further study of Scripture but especially (for us) philosophical reflection and clarification of what is already believed, to sharpen up and fill out that vision. (Others who do not share the vision may engage in the philosophy, but they will miss the main point, like someone who works for a charity but who does not share its objectives.)

Men on earth, whatever the perfection of understanding they may reach, understand far less than the angels. For we must remember that not even St Paul, for all his greatness, could say more than this: 'We know in part and we prophesy in part'.[52]

Knowledge, even the incomplete knowledge of this life, is not incompatible with faith, because faith for Augustine is not primarily belief, but it is primarily reliance upon what is known; it is the act of relying on what is known, as distinct from distrusting and departing from what is known. It is the role of faith to renew this natural or innate knowledge of God (the *sensus divinitatis*). What reason gives is a clarification and intensification of a person's own natural and direct (non-inferential) knowledge of God.[53]

Faith is thus at least partly a moral agency; through it the perversity of the will is progressively removed, a perversity which until it is fully removed blocks further knowledge. As it is removed, the knowledge progresses through love of the object of faith and increased acquaintance with it, in a sort of reciprocal, upward spiral.

But there is no need to think that the faith that seeks understanding, on this model, requires it to be based at all points upon the revealed (propositional) knowledge of God. If one thinks of the way in which Augustine traces his growing knowledge of God in the *Confessions*, for example, it is clear, according to Hoitenga, that he begins from a position of the innate knowledge of God. Faith seeks understanding, but already has some idea, before it seeks, of what it will find. As Augustine points out in the *Confessions* there is a paradox of searching; the one who searches needs to know what he is searching for before he looks for it.[54] And Hoitenga claims that this knowledge is provided, according to Augustine, in the natural, that is, the universal and innate, knowledge of God. Which is not to say that all who possess such knowledge search with the same intensity, or with the same wisdom, as others. God is the light of the mind, and to seek understanding is to seek for a better knowledge of what is already known.[55]

So what on this interpretation of the faith seeks understanding project is being inculcated by Augustine is more like an ethical practice or discipline than a set of intellectual procedures and techniques. It is necessary, for anyone who has faith leading to understanding, that he has faith and understanding *for himself*; he cannot have it for anyone else. What this means is that such knowledge is 'person-relative', both in the sense that it is related to a person's own dispositions and also in the sense that the knowledge gained in this way, being immediate, cannot be passed on, even though an account of such knowledge could be.

There are two difficulties with Hoitenga's approach. One is that he may be confusing immediate knowledge of truths with direct acquaintance with a person. This comes out particularly in his interpretation of John Calvin's *sensus divinitatis* along Augustinian lines, on which his account relies heavily. It is not obvious that for Calvin the *sensus divinitatis* is a case of knowledge by acquaintance; rather it is a basic conviction that God exists. But knowledge as immediate acquaintance with a reality or state of affairs, and knowledge as immediate awareness of a truth, are clearly different. Is Hoitenga correct in assimilating Alvin Plantinga and Calvin with that aspect of Augustine which is concerned with immediate awareness? We shall consider Calvin's *sensus divinitatis* and what it might imply in more detail in the last chapter.

The second difficulty arises from what might be called the nontransmissibility of understanding, on this view. In the case of the conceptual and rational analysis as proposed by Kretzmann as the model of Christian philosophy, the results of such analysis can be written down, and readily acquired by anyone with the necessary knowledge and intelligence and will to do so. As Kretzmann shows, while a Christian may use a proposition of his faith as a starting point in argument, the non-believer may simply assume the truth of that proposition, and in doing so contribute to developing an argument about it. By contrast, it is impossible for one person to transmit his knowledge by acquaintance to another person. The propositional content of such knowledge, insofar as it can be articulated, can be transmitted, but not the awareness itself.

On Hoitenga's view faith seeking understanding is gradualist, as is Kretzmann's, but in a different way; direct knowledge of God, however rudimentary, is a necessary feature of faith, and understanding seeks the filling out of this. For Hoitenga the basic epistemic category is what he calls direct knowledge. Understanding fills out the details of that knowledge, as one might fill out of the details of a panorama by closer and closer visual inspection of it. By contrast, for Kretzmann the basic category is belief, as a component of the way of faith, and of that general epistemic category which falls short of knowledge.

Is there a way of combining some of the emphases of Kretzmann and Hoitenga? Is it possible to argue that faith, as conveying rudimentary understanding (like the odour of the meal that the cook is shortly to place on the table) may be supplemented by further understanding? Such further understanding is incremental, and does not necessarily (*contra* Kretzmann) supplant propositional faith, though it may do so in some cases. (Perhaps one case is Anselm's ontological argument in the *Proslogion*.) At the same time (*contra* Hoitenga) the further understanding that is gained is certainly detachable from the life of faith.

It may certainly be possible for one person to combine both approaches, and perhaps this is what Augustine is doing, for example, in his discussion of time and creation in the *Confessions*. What Augustine wrote on these themes is certainly detachable from his own personal confession. Otherwise one would have to say that only those who share Augustine's faith can understand what he writes. For even if, in seeking understanding, Augustine follows the 'acquaintance', organic approach, it is undeniable that he combines this with conceptual analysis.

Perhaps the Kretzmann – Hoitenga debate is based upon a false polarisation of approaches in the faith seeking understanding tradition. There is undoubtedly an emphasis in that tradition on the direct knowledge of God as the aim of all Christian endeavour, including the intellectual endeavours of the Christian. This can hardly be interpreted, without serious distortion, as a series of metaphorical expressions. Similarly, the meditative framework in which much of the philosophising is carried out (by Augustine in the *Confessions*, and by Anselm in the *Proslogion*, for example) is the stance of direct acquaintance rather than abstract, propositional reasoning. Certainly for Anselm, the contrast is between seeing God and understanding him a little.[56] The writer addresses God as one with whom he has some acquaintance. And reason collaborates in this contemplative endeavour.

On the other hand there is also an emphasis upon argument, particularly (of the writers we shall consider) in Anselm. In the *Proslogion* he tells us that he is searching for 'one argument' to display the inner necessity of those matters he relies upon in faith. These arguments are not merely what Hoitenga calls 'negative apologetics', the answering of objections to the faith, but they contribute to filling out the intellectual character of the one of whom a visionary knowledge is sought.

Which of the two interpretations of the faith seeks understanding motif, Kretzmann's or Hoitenga's, gets nearer the truth, and whether elements of each could be satisfactorily combined to get even nearer the truth, the reader must judge, as he follows the discussion of the various cases we shall be examining from Chapter Four onwards.

OTHER POSSIBILITIES?

So far we have sought to clarify differing interpretations of the faith seeks understanding project as it is found in the seminal writings in that tradition, in Augustine and Anselm. But it is possible to think of the relation between faith and understanding in other ways.

A strong claim for the place of theistic belief in intellectual activity is made by Alvin Plantinga.[57] He characterises and advocates what he calls positive Christian philosophy. This involves theistic rather than distinctively Christian beliefs, and the relating of such beliefs to thinking about philosophical issues, not just issues in philosophical theology. Plantinga sees such beliefs not so much controlling as emancipating and fertilising philosophical thought (though in philosophy one person's control is another's release!). Perhaps viewing things from a theistic perspective we would have reason to think that, say, abstract objects are not causally inert but are themselves caused to exist (in the divine mind), and are themselves able to enter into causal relations, to be causes. Similarly with human action and intention; positive Christian philosophy will not look to non-human animals (an approach that is characteristic of naturalist theories of the mind) for models of philosophical theory but to the divine mind, to God himself, in whose image human beings are formed.

Although positive Christian philosophy has theological assumptions, it is not theology. Plantinga adopts the broadly Augustinian view, that there is no rigid separation between theology and philosophy. 'What we need is the best total understanding we can get, using all the resources at our command.'[58] As for the Thomist claim that only reason gives *scientia*, while faith depends upon testimony, Plantinga argues that most science does not in the event attain to the lofty heights of *scientia*; scientists of all kinds depend upon testimony; in this they resemble believers who depend upon the testimony of God for knowledge of what he has revealed. Since working out the implications of faith for philosophy and science is itself a work of the reason, Plantinga argues that the contrasting approaches of the Thomist and the Augustinian to the relation between philosophy and theology are largely nominal.

A more ambitious form of the same sort of claim is made by Nicholas Wolterstorff. In *Reason Within the Bounds of Religion* he argues that the religious beliefs of a Christian scholar ought to function as control beliefs. They are to further authentic Christian intellectual commitment in the devising and weighing of theories. That is, a Christian ought to weigh theories by his belief about 'what constitutes an acceptable sort of theory on the matter under consideration'.[59] These include beliefs about the requisite logical or aesthetic structure of a theory, as well as beliefs about the entities to whose existence a theory may commit us. By the use of such control beliefs a person is able to reject certain sorts of theories – because they are inconsistent with a person's control beliefs, for example – and he is able to devise theories consistent with them.

We might say that such a proposal is a case of faith seeking understanding which, though it includes theological understanding, extends beyond it; and it is more ambitious in scope than the Augustinian tradition that we have been examining, which focuses exclusively upon issues in philosophical theology. Whereas Augustine stated in the *Soliloquies* that he wished only to know God and the soul, Wolterstorff in effect extends the Augustinian approach to any aspect of God's creation and of human culture. He bids a believer not only understand the articles of his faith, but to see how that faith may bear upon theories in the humanities, and in the natural sciences. So that the scope of 'understanding' is without intellectual limit. For all we know to the contrary, faith may convey understanding in respect of anything for which understanding is sought.

But how would the beliefs of faith exercise their control and so give understanding? Wolterstorff makes the following proposals.

First, the authentic Christian commitment which is meant to exercise the control is relative to times and to persons, for the propositions which are common to the belief-content of the authentic commitment of all Christians are few and simple.[60] So it is a person's Christian belief which is relevant, not Christian beliefs in general or as a whole.

Second, utilising his beliefs as a control, the Christian ought to reject certain theories, and to devise theories of his own. So what theories ought he to accept? Or, better, what type of theory ought he to accept? Clearly, he ought to begin by rejecting those that conflict with or do not comport well with the belief content of his authentic commitment.[61] For example, behaviourism and Freudianism in psychology, because they deny human freedom and responsibility entirely, ought to be rejected, and theories which affirm such responsibility ought to be devised. In this way authentic Christian commitment enters into the devising and weighing of psychological theories. This seems an attractive proposal. But in evaluating it it is important to note the following qualifications which Wolterstorff himself introduces.

In the first place, the Christian commitment does not itself contain, or even imply acceptable theories, nor can the Bible be regarded as a black book of Christian theories.[62] So, presumably, whatever is devised as coming from the resources of faith will be contestable not only as an acceptable theory, but over whether or not it is properly grounded in an authentic faith commitment.

Secondly, often more than one theory about a matter will satisfy (i.e. be consistent with or comport well with) a scholar's authentic Christian commitment. There may be theoretical disputes about a matter among Christians. Again, even where faith directs understanding, it cannot do so unambiguously.

Thirdly, the Christian's authentic commitment is not by and large the source of the data for his weighing of theories, nor of the theories themselves. But if the role that the commitment plays is neither to be the source of theories, nor to furnish the data which support the theories and which they explain, then precisely what intellectual role is the commitment playing?[63]

Fourthly, a Christian's authentic commitment will only rarely contain all his control beliefs; and finally, a Christian and a non-Christian scholar may each justifiably accepted a particular theory, which may not be accepted by other Christians and non-Christians.

So it emerges that the control that a Christian's commitment exercises is never either necessary or sufficient for theory devising and testing, and it would appear that the role of Christian commitment being internal to and controlling the devising, accepting or rejecting of theories has, by these qualifications, all but vanished. Though whether this is a fair verdict is not something that presumably can be decided *a priori*, by reflection alone; if what Wolterstorff claims is correct, then theories controlled by Christian beliefs will be forthcoming.

An even more ambitious suggestion to which the faith seeks understanding motif might be applied is the claim that it is only on theistic or supernaturalistic assumptions that certain intellectual problems can be solved. For example, it has been argued that one can best account for the objectivity of moral values on theistic assumptions.[64] And in the final chapter we shall look at Plantinga's claim that it is only on such assumptions that a satisfactory account of epistemic warrant can be provided. At this point the faith seeking understanding project, and the project of natural theology, come together again. For anyone who, say, takes moral values to be objective, and who becomes convinced that such objectivity can only be accounted for on the assumption that God exists, has a proof of God's existence, though not a proof that uses premises granted by all rational people, but one that uses premises granted only by some.

NOTES

1. Augustine, *On Christian Doctrine*, p.45.
2. Ibid.
3. Quoted Kretzmann, 'Faith Seeks, Understanding Finds', p.11.
4. Quoted Kretzmann, 'Faith Seeks, Understanding Finds', p.12.
5. Evodius, quoted by Hoitenga, *Faith and Reason from Plato to Plantinga*, p.86.
6. Sermon 43, quoted by Hoitenga, *Faith and Reason from Plato to Plantinga*, p.59.
7. Sermon 43, quoted by Hoitenga, *Faith and Reason from Plato to Plantinga*, p.69.
8. Anselm, *Proslogion*, p.89.
9. Anselm, *Proslogion*, p.93.
10. Anselm, *Cur Deus Homo*, p.50.
11. Anselm, *On the Incarnation of the Word*, p.8.
12. Aquinas, *Summa Theologiae* 1ae 2.2. p.66.
13. Wolterstorff, 'The Migration of Theistic Arguments: From Natural Theology to Evidentialist Apologetics', and in 'Can Belief in God be Rational?'

14. Wolterstorff, 'Can Belief in God be Rational?', p.141.
15. Wolterstorff, 'The Migration of Theistic Arguments', p.71.
16. *Summa Theologiae* Iae 2,2. (p.66).
17. On this point, see McInerny, 'Analogy and Foundationalism in Thomas Aquinas': 'Thomas is not suggesting that by establishing those truths about God that he numbers among the praeambula fidei, any believer has or could deduce, come to know the truth of, or say he has evidence for truths of faith in the proper sense, namely, the Christian mysteries . . . The preambles of faith are not premises on the basis of which the truth of the mysteries can be established. The believer accepts all the truths God has revealed immediately – as a package, so to say – precisely because God reveals them, and his faith did not follow necessarily from any cognitive prelude and does not require that he engage in some research project of a philosophical or theological sort' (pp.285f).
18. See the quotations from Aquinas given in Stump, 'Aquinas on the Foundations of Knowledge', pp.133f.
19. Stump, 'Aquinas on the Foundations of Knowledge', p.135 for quotations from Aquinas.
20. Anselm, *On the Incarnation of the Word*, pp.8f.
21. Locke, *An Essay Concerning Human Understanding*, Vol. II p.287.
22. Locke, *An Essay Concerning Human Understanding*, Vol.II p.261.
23. Quoted in Kretzmann, 'Faith Seeks, Understanding Finds', p.5.
24. Quoted by Kretzmann, 'Reason in Mystery', p.20.
25. Penelhum, 'Skepticism and Fideism', p.308. For further discussion of this point see Penelhum's *God and Skepticism*.
26. Kretzmann, 'Faith Seeks, Understanding Finds', p.2.
27. Kretzmann, 'Faith Seeks, Understanding Finds', p.14.
28. Kretzmann, 'Faith Seeks, Understanding Finds', p.18.
29. Kretzmann, 'Faith Seeks, Understanding Finds', p.6.
30. Kretzmann, 'Faith Seeks, Understanding Finds', p.6.
31. Clearly 'knowledge' is not here used in the precise and rather specialised sense that Aquinas uses *scientia*.
32. Kretzmann, 'Faith Seeks, Understanding Finds', pp.7f.
33. Kretzmann, 'Faith Seeks, Understanding Finds', p.8.
34. Kretzmann, 'Faith Seeks, Understanding Finds', p.31 (quoted in footnote 21).
35. Kretzmann, 'Faith Seeks, Understanding Finds', pp.7f.
36. Kretzmann draws his data for this view mainly from Augustine's *de libero arbitrio*.
37. Kretzmann, 'Faith Seeks, Understanding Finds', pp.18f.
38. 'A person who has accepted but never sought understanding of "the Son of God died" cannot be plausibly described as a mature, reflective, actively committed Christian' (Kretzmann, 'Faith Seeks, Understanding Finds', p.21). See also Kretzmann's 'Evidence Against Anti-Evidentialism'.
39. Kretzmann, 'Faith Seeks, Understanding Finds', p.10.
40. Kretzmann, 'Faith Seeks, Understanding Finds', p.12.
41. Kretzmann, 'Faith Seeks, Understanding Finds', p.19.
42. Kretzmann, 'Faith Seeks, Understanding Finds', p.20.
43. Kretzmann, 'Faith Seeks, Understanding Finds', p.21.
44. Anselm, *On the Incarnation of the Word*, p.10.
45. Kretzmann, 'Faith Seeks, Understanding Finds', p.17.
46. Quoted by Kretzmann, 'Faith Seeks, Understanding Finds', p.17.
47. Kretzmann, 'Faith Seeks, Understanding Finds', p.23.
48. Kretzmann 'Reason in Mystery' pp.28f.
49. Kretzmann 'Reason in Mystery' pp.30ff.
50. Anselm, *On the Incarnation of the Word*, p.8.
51. Hoitenga, *Faith and Reason from Plato to Plantinga*, p.121.
52. Hoitenga, *Faith and Reason from Plato to Plantinga*, p.110.
53. Hoitenga, *Faith and Reason from Plato to Plantinga*, p.121.
54. Augustine, *Confessions*, p.195.
55. Augustine, *Confessions*, p.127 (Cf.Plato's *Meno* 81a).
56. Anselm, *Proslogion*, Ch.1.
57. Plantinga, 'Augustinian Christian Philosophy'.
58. Plantinga, 'Augustinian Christian Philosophy', p.314.
59. Wolterstorff, *Reason Within the Bounds of Religion*, p.67.
60. Wolterstorff, *Reason Within the Bounds of Religion*, p.75.

61. Wolterstorff, *Reason Within the Bounds of Religion*, p.76.
62. Wolterstorff, *Reason Within the Bounds of Religion*, p.78.
63. Wolterstorff, *Reason Within the Bounds of Religion*, p.80.
64. See, for example, Adams, 'Moral Arguments for Theistic Belief'. 'One of the most generally accepted reasons for believing in the existence of anything is that its existence is implied by the theory that seems to account most adequately for some subject matter. I take it, therefore, that my metaethical views provide me with a reason of some weight for believing in the existence of God' (p.145).

3

Understanding and Believing

In the last two chapters we have attempted to examine the faith seeking understanding programme in general terms. We have noted the ways in which the writers to whom we have already referred, thinkers such as Augustine and Anselm, were concerned to use their reason to draw out the implications of what they believed; to distinguish their beliefs from alternative views, to provide grounds for their belief, sometimes appealing to grounds from within the faith, sometimes to more general considerations. They believed that this increased understanding was part of a process which will culminate in the vision of God.

On their view, faith is reliance on what the believer takes to be true. For example, Augustine and Anselm each believed, as part of their faith, that God created the heavens and the earth. They sought answers to the question, What does this belief imply? They recognised that such a belief has wide metaphysical consequences, implications for our understanding of reality at the most fundamental level. What does it imply about the nature of creation, and about time and change, for example? They recognised that theirs was a distinctive position, distinct from views about the origin of the universe to be found in Plato and Aristotle, for example. Because they held that God necessarily exists, and that the creation is the result of his will, their view was fundamentally realist. God and the creation is in no sense a construction of the human mind; rather the reverse. The human mind is the construction, or rather the creation, of God. Had there been no creation, God would nevertheless exist. The faith seeks understanding tradition is an endeavour to conform the human mind to what God is and does, to understand it better.

Furthermore, in their view reality is one. This conviction also arose out of their belief that there is one God and one created order. This is why thinkers in this tradition had such difficulty over the existence of evil. How could evil be part of the creation of God? They found help in the idea that evil is not a part of the reality created by God, but a loss or lack, a privation of that reality. So in their view there is no separate religious or theological reality insulated from other 'realities' in such a way that it can make no contact with natural science, say, or with ethics. Natural science deals with the natures and powers of created things, and ethics with the prescriptive will of God, revealed in nature and Scripture. So that although, naturally enough, the propositions of the faith are only credible to those who have faith, these propositions have deep and wide implications for the reality of which we are all, believers and unbelievers alike, a part.

Reality is not a human construct, though it is no doubt unavoidable in practice that any understanding of reality is affected and even distorted by the particular circumstances and natures of the knowers, by error and ignorance. But if the universe is God's creation then it exists, as such, in an intelligible and orderly manner, a manner that holds true irrespective of what men or women may think or hope about it. We may make all sorts of mistakes in our belief, due to our incapacity, our ignorance, carelessness and a lack of imagination, but this does not alter the fact that there is one objective state of affairs to which, as far as possible, we ought to make our beliefs conform and which, because of its objective character, often corrects our beliefs in unexpected ways. The project of faith seeking understanding is part of this striving.

Let us call this view *unified realism*;[1] truths about the universe hold independently of the decisions or theorisings of human beings, and these truths form one consistent set.[2] There is no compartmentalisation. The writers in the faith seeking understanding tradition differed over the question of how we are able to know about the world, some attributing more power to unaided human reason than others in the process of discovery, but they were united in their unified realism. The only difference that is recognised is the broad and important distinction between necessary and contingent reality.

To understand is to grasp some of this manifold and mysterious reality; the greater the grasp, the greater the understanding. Because what we understand is part of God's creation, understanding and having a reasonable belief or having knowledge, are closely connected. One might understand something entirely fictitious, in which case understanding does not add to its credibility. But on Augustine's or Anselm's view to advance in understanding is to advance in knowledge of reality, of the one created order, to have a firmer hold on the states of affairs that God has willed, and so, even, to have a firmer grasp of the character and will of God himself.

A NEW PROPOSAL

Recently, however, the terms 'faith' and 'understanding' have been connected together in a very different way from the one that we have just outlined, a way which carries with it a sharply contrasting conception of the relation between religious belief and reality.[3] To appreciate how different this conception is, we need to begin by reflecting a little further on the idea of *understanding*, for quite different things can be meant by it.

There is, for instance, the sort of understanding that we possess when we know the meaning of a word or sentence. Part of what it means to have such understanding is that we appreciate proper occasions to use the expression, to know when and when not to utter it, and how the word or sentence may be appropriately combined with other words and sentences. We are able to paraphrase it into other words, perhaps to offer definitions. We can use the language to make statements, to ask questions, to make requests and the like. Understanding in this sense involves the possession of a range of skills in the use of language, the matching of our language to appropriate situations.

Understanding can also refer to the awareness of the logical presuppositions and implications of a particular belief or beliefs. As we have already noted this is one sense that is relevant to the faith seeing understanding project of Augustine and the others. We understand the proposition 'God created the heavens and the earth' better when we know more about the meaning of that proposition, about what 'God' means (and does not mean), the meaning of 'create' and so on. And to understand that proposition further is to see how it connects up with other beliefs, and to discern something of its inner rationale. As such understanding increases, so the ambiguities and obscurities, even the paradoxes, of the original assertion are resolved. We come to see what consequences, if any, it has for other sorts of propositions; propositions about time and cosmology, for example. And furthermore, coming to understand the proposition better also involves a better appreciation of the sort of truth the proposition has; whether it is a contingent or a necessary truth, for example. As we shall see later on, for Anselm (for example) the project of understanding a proposition of the faith involves coming to appreciate that there is a kind of necessity about the proposition in question, a necessity which is not at first apparent.

Understanding is also tied to the idea of explanation. When we explain something to someone, at least when we do so satisfactorily, we get them to understand something that they did not understand before. This is the sense of understanding that is relevant in the natural sciences and to some aspects of human actions. To understand an event or happening, in this sense, is to be able to subsume that event under some law of science or some other generalisation derived from human experience. Why did the car leave the road? Because it was travelling at speed when one of its tyres burst, as a consequence of which the car slewed round. And cars that slew round at speed usually – other things being equal – leave the road. Why is this liquid boiling? Because it has reached 100 degrees centigrade, and such liquid boils at that temperature. Why did Jones take the ladders? Because he had been promised the loan of them. Understanding in this sense usually leads to prediction and often, but not always, leads to an ability to control what we are able to predict.

This kind of understanding is vital for science and for some kinds of human activity, but is of less importance for our purposes. There is no suggestion in the faith seeks understanding tradition that to understand some propositions about God is to subsume that proposition under a general law in such a way that we can predict and control events better. This is because, in the view of that tradition, the propositions of faith are propositions which express the personal agency of God in a rather different way from those which the regularities of nature do, even though those regularities are evidence of the wisdom and faithfulness of God. The explanation, and thus the further understanding, of these propositions therefore often involves a proper description of the action of God in question, and an appreciation of its consistency or lack of consistency with the divine character.

There is a yet further sense of understanding, one which is more relevant here. To understand an activity is sometimes to gain an appreciation of the value and importance of that activity from the standpoint of the agent. It is a characteristic of human beings that not only do they interact with the world, but that they often do so consciously and intelligently, for reasons, and so are able to reflect upon the world. Such interaction with the world, if it is rational and intelligent, is bound up with how the world, or some aspect of it, is understood by the agent. We can take up an intentional stance to some aspect of our environment, even an aspect which is wholly imaginary or which is projected by us onto the future. Moreover, not only can we take up such a stance, we invariably do. We attribute significance and value to many of those features that we take the world to possess. So that in order to understand a human activity, particularly if it takes place in a remote or unfamiliar culture, one often has to gain some appreciation of the significance and value that agents in that culture attach to it and to its outcome; what they believe and hope about themselves and the world. This will involve coming to understand their beliefs from their point of view, a process which will involve some sympathetic identification with their stance to the world, including the network of their beliefs and values.

Understanding in this way does not involve accepting or identifying with the standpoint understood. One can understand why someone did something, their reasons and motives, without going along with them. It may be that the more one understands what lies behind an action, the less one is able to concur in it.

Two people may have conflicting understandings about some trivial or some deeper matter. We might say that at such points they understand the world differently; they have different sets of beliefs about what the world is like, and perhaps about what it ought to be like. So one might say that Colonel Gaddafi and Mother Teresa understand the world differently; they do not literally occupy different worlds, of course, but they have different beliefs about the world, and attach different importance and significance to their experienced world; they differ in how they conceptualise that world in terms of their respective beliefs – beliefs about international conflict and exploitation in the case of Gaddafi, about costly compassion in the face of suffering in the case of Mother Teresa. They understand the world differently, and because these differences are important for them, the personal significance that the world has for them differs also.

On this third account of understanding two things stand out; one is that 'understanding' is understanding the significance of an activity or belief for the one who has it or who engages in it; rather than understanding the meaning of a sentence, or the law-like character of some natural occurrence. The other is that beliefs and actions are often structured, so that to see the significance of one belief or activity is to see how it relates to other beliefs and activities.

It is something like this third sense of 'understanding' that D. Z. Phillips and others have recently drawn attention to in making their characteristic claim that 'One can only give a satisfactory account of religious beliefs if one pays attention to the roles they play in people's lives'.[4] To pay attention to the role of a belief in the life of a person who has it is to appreciate, for example, what relation such a belief has to evidence, or to the lack of such evidence, for that belief. And what sort of importance that belief has in that person's life.

Normally such understanding is *necessary* for assessing whether what a person believes is true or not. For naturally enough, one can only carry out such an assessment if one first has some grasp of what the proposition believed is. If this were all that Phillips was asserting, it would be uncontentious enough, but hardly novel. But he is not simply saying that in order to assess a belief one needs to know something about its content. What is interesting and controversial in Phillips' proposal is that such understanding is in his view not only necessary, but it is also *sufficient* for settling any philosophical or critical purpose one may have. If one appreciates the role that a belief or activity plays in the life of a person, then one understands that belief, and when one has understood that belief in this sense then philosophical reflection upon that belief is at an end. It is certainly not the job of philosophy to pass any critical judgement 'from outside' upon such a belief, or upon the 'form of life' of which it is a part. The role of philosophy is not to justify but to understand: 'Philosophy can claim justifiably to show what is meaningful in religion only if it is prepared to examine religious concepts in the contexts from which they derive their meaning'.[5]

There is, in this respect at least, a similarity between Phillips and the views we have been discussing in the earlier chapters. For both he and they fight shy of the idea of philosophy passing any overall critical assessment on religious belief. Neither are philosophical rationalists with respect to religious belief. But they reject such rationalism for different reasons. Those who follow the classical 'faith seeking understanding' programme do so because the belief for which a greater understanding is sought is accepted initially on the authority of testimony; Phillips does so because of his belief in the autonomy of religious belief *per se*. Religion has its own criteria of sense and nonsense, criteria which are internal to religion, and which it does not and cannot share with science, say. Religious belief is autonomous in the sense that it cannot, without gross misunderstanding and distortion, be subjected to any critical scrutiny except from within religion. The criteria of meaning and truth are to be found within religion; they cannot be imposed from outside. The same goes for science. It follows from this that the same utterance, with the same meaning, cannot be both an utterance in religion and (say) an utterance in science, for that would suppose a common standard of meaning and truth:

> I suggest that more can be gained if one compares the question, 'What kind of reality is divine reality?' not with the question, 'Is this physical object real or not?' but with the different question, 'What kind of reality is the reality of physical objects?' To ask whether physical objects are real is not like asking whether this appearance is real or not where often one can find out. I can find out whether unicorns are real or not, but how can I find out whether the physical world is real

or not? This latter question is not about the possibility of carrying out an investigation. It is a question of whether it is possible to speak of truth or falsity in the physical world; a question prior to that of determining the truth or falsity of any particular matter of fact. Similarly, the question of the reality of God is a question of the possibility of sense and nonsense, truth and falsity, in religion. When God's existence is construed as a matter of fact, it is taken for granted that the concept of God is at home within the conceptual framework of the reality of the physical world. . . . But to ask a question about the reality of God is to ask a question about *a kind of reality*, not about the reality of *this* or *that*, in much the same way as asking a question about the reality of physical objects is not to ask about the reality of this or that physical object.[6]

The term 'objective reality' is a hazy one. The objector may be suggesting that the believer creates his belief, or decides that it should be the kind of thing it is. This is obviously not the case. The believer is taught religious beliefs. He does not create a tradition, but is born into one. He cannot say whatever he likes about God, since there are criteria which determine what it makes sense to say. These criteria may develop or change partly as the result of personal decisions. But not anything can count as a religious decision or a religious development.[7]

So there is, for Phillips, not just one reality, but there are many realities. Science is one, religion another. These do not intersect, though of course what goes on in the world around him often has religious significance for the believer; it may tempt him, for example.[8] Is Phillips a realist about God? If he is, he is clearly not a unified realist in the tradition of Augustine or Anselm. In one sense, he is a realist, for he makes repeated reference to religious reality and to the reality of God. But in another sense he is not, since 'reality' is not used by him univocally. Religious reality is contrasted with the reality of science; each is a different *kind* of reality. There is also a further sense in which, even in his talk of religious reality, his realism is heavily qualified, as we shall see. So the issue of metaphysical realism, of what we have called unified realism, is one important difference between Phillips and the classical faith seeking understanding position. The latter seeks an integration of the one reality through the process of understanding. Phillips advocates the disintegration of reality into many realities by an appreciation of the many language-games, of which religion is one.

Two things are crucial, therefore, for understanding Phillips' position, for seeing how it differs from the classical faith seeking understanding model, and for critically assessing it. First, for Phillips understanding in the sense just given is necessary *and sufficient* for accepting a religious belief as genuinely so. To understand is to believe. Second, such understanding involves nothing more than an appreciation of the role that such beliefs and activities play in the life of the believer. One does not first understanding and then believe; or first believe, and then understand. Both faith and understand are capable of degrees, because understanding and believing are inseparable. Phillips' characteristic thesis can thus be spelt out in the following way:

Understanding and faith go hand in hand; there is not a temporal or even a logical priority of faith over understanding, as we have noted that there is in Augustine and Anselm. In these thinkers there is a two stage process; first faith, which though it involves some understanding does not involve much, and then understanding, filling out some of the incompleteness of faith by philosophical reflection and argumentation. Faith has some understanding, but the process of reflection and argumentation aims to provide more. If Norman Kretzmann is correct, it is possible to detach faith and understanding still further, to treat the propositions of faith as assumptions which anyone, believer or unbeliever, can examine. Faith is therefore not necessary for understanding; faith is a gift of God, while understanding may be a common human achievement.

Phillips does not deny the connectedness of faith and understanding, but he sees them as non-contingently connected or, if anything, he sees understanding as having the priority over believing, and understanding here is not exclusively intellectual in character, but participatory. It involves knowing how to behave; how to conduct oneself in the face of evil; how to pray. One cannot believe unless one understands; and to understand is to believe. It is only as one understands that one comes to have faith; in understanding, in gaining appreciation of the language-game of religion, with its characteristic values and significances, one gains faith. Not to understand is not to believe. One cannot understand and not believe.

In the last chapter we briefly noted Norman Kretzmann's point that it is just not true that one has to believe a proposition in order to acquire a philosophical understanding of it.[9] Phillips is not quite making the claim that Kretzmann emphatically rejects, but he is claiming that it is in believing a proposition that one acquires a religious understanding of it. But this looks to be either a trivial claim, or false. It is trivial insofar as Phillips may simply be interdefining 'belief' and 'understanding', and it is open to anyone to reject this definition. But if this is not merely a matter of definition, but the view as proposed by Phillips is a factual claim, then it becomes a matter of empirical enquiry. Initially at least, such a view would appear to be false, since many seem to have an understanding of religious utterances who nevertheless do not believe; indeed, it is precisely *because* they understand them that they are unbelievers. More on this later.

Phillips is not simply saying that in order to assess a belief one needs to know something about its content, its meaning, and particularly about how the holder of the belief takes it. To say this would be to make an obvious enough point. But he is saying that it is only by seeing how the belief operates as part of more general religious discourse and religious practices that one finds out what is meant by the reality of God. Finding out about God's reality is essentially the activity of a religious participant. Such discovery cannot be the result of empirical observation (by investigating the nature of religious experience, or reflecting on the nature of the world) or the result of metaphysical reflection (for example, by employing some version of the ontological argument) from the outside. Holding a religious belief reasonably cannot be the result of some impartial reflection and argument, for philosophy cannot adjudicate on whether religious belief is justified or on what counts as sense and nonsense in religion, though it is for some reason able to distinguish between a truly religious and a superstitious attitude. Rather, recognising the reality of God is appreciating how the concept of God functions in the lives of those who use it. There can be observation and appreciation of such functions from outside, but this will result in a theoretical approach which falls short of understanding. Understanding comes only from appreciation from the standpoint of a participant. Approaching the meaning and rationality of belief in God in any other way is bound to lead to misunderstanding. Understanding only arises out of, and is an expression of, commitment itself, or an appreciation of that commitment. Neutrality, non-committedness, will inevitably distort.

So, lying behind these claims about what makes a belief genuine is a thesis about meaning; that the meaning of the existence and reality of God can only be given or found *within* religion, where religion is understood as a characteristic way or form of life; as a practice or set of practices. The existence of God (or, as Phillips prefers to express it, the 'reality' of God), cannot be considered abstractly, via reflecting upon one of the proofs, say, for it is not externally or contingently related to the practice of religion, but internally or necessarily so. Where religion is practised, there the reality of God is known and felt, and nowhere else. Belief in God is thus unconditional, because religion is autonomous:

> There are some people the truth of whose religion depends on the way things go in their lives. Things may not go well here and now, but

unless the ultimate facts, the eschatological situation, are favourable in some sense or other, faith has been a hoax and a failure. For Hick, the kind of difference religion makes to life is the difference between a set of empirical facts being or not being the case. This belief is illustrated by a comment I heard a mother make about her mentally handicapped child: 'Only my religious faith keeps me going. Of one thing I am sure: my child's place in heaven is secure'. . . . Although I sympathise with the mother's hope, I do not find it impressive religiously. Indeed, I should want to go further and say that it has little to do with religion, being much closer to superstition.[10]

Were religion conditional it would then depend upon something outside itself, outside religion, and thus according to Phillips it would not be genuinely religious, but superstitious. So to be genuinely religious is to acknowledge the reality of God, a reality quite distinct from physical reality, a reality to which one relates in wholly distinct ways. For example, empirical evidence is obviously relevant to the way in which we react to what is physical, but not only is there no empirical evidence for the existence or non-existence of God, there could not be. The teleological argument for the existence of God is in principle mistaken; the idea that the existence of evil might count against the existence of God likewise so.

Not surprisingly, this thesis about the meaning of religious belief and what it means to have a religious understanding, carries with it a claim about the nature of religious truth. For Phillips 'truth' is not a term that is used univocally across all areas of human interest. There is not one unified reality, one network or edifice of true propositions which are related together at least by the relation of logical consistency. For the logical consistency of a set of propositions presupposes that the members of the set are commensurable in meaning. The question of overall consistency presupposes comparison in terms of meaning, and the idea of meaning being univocal across all 'forms of life' is precisely what Phillips denies. It is for this reason that he must eschew any kind of epistemological foundationalism, since foundationalism necessarily involves relating all propositions that it is reasonable to believe to one privileged set of propositions.[11]

We would normally say that whether the scientific propositions which express the hypothesis of the big bang, or the event of Jesus' changing of water into wine, or the possibility of life after death, could be part of one set of religious beliefs, is an issue which could be settled in principle, even if it is difficult to settle in practice. But Phillips demurs. To suppose that immortality has anything to do with a reality that is encountered after death is to make a mistake in principle.[12] For it is to suppose that religion is open to metaphysical or scientific test. Anything consistent or inconsistent with a religious utterance must itself be part of religion. Scientific utterances are not religious, and therefore they can be neither consistent with or inconsistent with religious utterances. They are part of a different language-game.

So for Phillips there is not one reality, but several realities, and the truths that express them are correspondingly plural. Epistemological pluralism is not for Phillips simply a contingent fact, one that might disappear had we all more information and greater impartiality and resourcefulness. Truth in religion differs *in kind* from truth in science. The pluralism is necessary. The two kinds of truth are incommensurable, and so to attempt to link them together by trying to 'reconcile' science and religion is a basic philosophical mistake, a sort of category mistake, like the mistake of supposing that thoughts have colours or numbers have shapes. Thoughts cannot have colours, because they are not the sort of thing that can be coloured, or colourless, and for Phillips religious language cannot have implications for scientific language. No scientific truth has any implication for any truth in religion, nor *vice versa*. Nothing that theologians or scientists say about the beginning of time, or the nature of the creation, or that philosophers have to say about the nature of the human person, could have any implication of a religious kind. (Phillips would add that theologians are misguided if they venture into making remarks about the beginning of time, since to do so is to stray into the area of cosmology and to leave the essential concerns of religion behind.) So truth is 'religionised' or 'scientised' for Phillips, since the criteria of what is true or false in religion or science is to be found within these 'forms of life', and thus the concept of truth differs in each case.

Despite the principled way in which the language-game of religion is to be distinguished from other language-games, Phillips is not simply saying that religious truth is only what forms part of the religious convictions of people at a given time. He is not denying that there can be discoveries in religion, or controversies within religion, or that mistakes can be made in religion which require correction. There can be unbelief as well as belief. There can be development in religion, and an increase in understanding. There can also be misunderstandings of religion, which it is the province of philosophers such as himself to remedy. There can be problems which arise within a religious tradition and which call for response. The point is however, that such mistakes, discoveries and developments are all within religion. By reflection and an increase in understanding a person can become more genuinely religious and less superstitious. He can discover mistakes about the nature of his own, and others', religious belief. But no facts of science or common sense or anything else outside religion have consequences such that a religious person will make a mistake or be in error, religiously speaking, if she does not pay attention to these facts.

These points can be amplified and illustrated with reference to Phillips' attitudes to the proofs of God's existence, and to the existence and problem of evil. For him, the proofs, including the very idea of proving God's existence from the world, or rendering belief in him rational, are metaphysically-inspired intrusions into religion which fail to understand what religion is. The ontological argument is not to be understood as a piece of metaphysics, but as a set of remarks about how the concept of God functions in religion.[13] Endeavours to prove God's existence amount to a series of religious mistakes. To treat religious issues in this way is to import alien standards of rationality into religion. Needing to prove God's existence supposes that there might be some doubt about God's existence, and that this might be settled by reference to some general features of the world. But this is to misunderstand the nature of religious doubt, and how it might be cured. For me to doubt God's existence is simply to say that religion means nothing to me.

To suppose that one needs to have a *theory* to account for the existence of evil in a universe created by a wholly good God, or a theory that proves the existence of God, is to make at least two fundamental mistakes. One mistake is to suppose that before the theory in question, a theory about why a good God permits evil, say, is invented or advanced there is some difficulty which the theory is intended to address. This supposes that there is no way of coping with evil in religion without theorising about it, and that coming to terms with the evil requires accepting a theory about it. But according to Phillips to suppose this is so is to neglect how religious people in fact relate to evil, how evil is handled in religion. Religious people do not cope with evil by invoking an explanatory theory; in fact they do so in a way which is necessarily not theoretical, by making a religious response to evil, a response which is religious precisely because it does not look for theories to account for evil. Thus they submit to the contingencies of life, to cancer or betrayal, recognising that they are the will of God. Or if evil is a temptation, they strive to overcome it; and these are not theoretical but religious responses.

As regards theories for the existence of God, the problem here, for Phillips, is that to entertain such theories seriously, to debate them and try to evaluate their strengths and weaknesses, and to suspend one's faith in God on the outcome of such enquiries, is to make the mistake of supposing that religious faith is hypothetical in character, to forget that it is uncompromisingly unconditional. For what makes something a case of religious faith, for Phillips, is precisely this unconditional character, and hence the irrelevance to it of proofs or evidence of any kind. Religion and theory are thus antithetical. Religion does not need support from science, or from observations about how things are going for a person in his life, nor could such support be offered. This underlines once more the participatory nature of 'understanding' for Phillips.

These claims, which are central to and characteristic of Phillips' account of religious understanding, raise serious questions. The plain fact is that many religious people, particularly those of a philosophical bent, have great interest in the proofs, and in the problem of evil, and in faith and reason, because of their concern for consistency in belief, and for the overall rationality of their beliefs. What mistake are they making? And there is the further fact that the history of Christianity, particularly since the seventeenth and eighteenth centuries, but also earlier, is littered with possible ways in which one might account for evil in God's universe. Again, why is this a mistaken strategy? It may be that these theodicies are not convincing, but why is the very endeavour to offer a theodicy misguided? Is it plausible to suppose that this entire tradition has made some fundamental philosophical error in even considering the question of whether God's existence can be proved, or whether there are general considerations which ameliorate the intellectual problem for theists posed by the existence of evil?

For Phillips religion is essentially a practice or set of practices, a way of life, and the beliefs that are religious are identified by such practices, and can only be understood in relation to, this form of life. And this is true, supremely, in the case of the existence or reality of God. Hence Phillips's dismissal of natural theology and of any other kind of metaphysical or general ethical enquiry about religious or theological matters. God's existence or reality is something that can only be understood from within, in relation to the religious language-game. If one attempts to take questions about the nature and existence of God outside religion, and then to ask general questions about the nature of God, one only distorts or falsifies or renders meaningless the expressions that one is considering.

Further, one cannot understand what the human activities of praising God, confessing to him and so forth are, apart from the belief in God that they presuppose. This may seem fair enough as it stands, but it must be remembered that for Phillips to understand in this sense is tantamount to being a participant. For to offer a philosophical criticism of a religious belief, or to assess it critically in some other sense, would be to adopt a standpoint outside religion, the very thing that Phillips eschews. So the only kind of criticism of religion permitted, because the only kind of criticism that is intelligible, is immanent criticism, criticism from within the standpoint of religion.

There is a further reason why, according to Phillips, God cannot be a metaphysical reality in anything like the usual sense, a reality who transcends the whole of the universe which he has created and which he sustains by his power. He cannot be this because to suppose this would be to give God a presiding role over all language-games or forms of life. But this, for Phillips, is a serious mistake, since the reality of God cannot be spoken of in an unqualified or context-less way, nor even in terms of some over-arching meta-context, but only in the context of religious belief. God is a religious reality.

From within religion it makes sense, according to Phillips, to affirm the creatorhood of God. In fact it is only from within religion that it is possible to talk of the creatorhood of God; for such talk has reference to the religious believer's recognition that the whole of his life is a gift from God. To talk of 'creation' as if it were a metaphysical idea is to miss the point that creation, at least as used in sentences such as 'God created the heavens and the earth', is a religious notion. So what such creatorhood means can only be understood in religious terms. To say that God is the creator, for example means that he is not an object to be investigated or manipulated. It is to recognise that life is contingent upon the will of God and that we owe everything to God; but it is emphatically not to recognise that God has created all that is, in the strong, metaphysical sense that this would be affirmed by Augustine or Anselm, say. The sense in which a religious person depends on God, and thus acknowledges the Creatorship of God, is different from the sense in which a classical theist would claim that all things depend upon God. It is religious dependence without metaphysical dependence, whereas for the classical Judeo-Christian tradition religious dependence arises out of and is only intelligible if one first presupposes metaphysical dependence.

So the reality of God, and hence the theistic realism that Phillips espouses, is of a highly qualified kind. God is real within religion; indeed the reality of God is constitutive of religion: 'To say that *the meaning* of God's reality is to be found *in* the world, is not to deny that God is *other than* the world in the sense important to religion'.[14] So in this sense Phillips is not a reductionist or subjectivist or relativist. He does not say that God is nothing but a projection of a person's needs, or nothing but a set of feelings, or that the language of religion is merely expressive and not cognitive in character. But on the other hand the reality of God is only a reality within religion; it is not something that overarches and presides over the whole of reality.

THE INFLUENCE OF IMMANUEL KANT

While Phillips appeals to Wittgenstein, and to what Wittgenstein says about language-games, as the inspiration of this view of religion, its roots may be found further back, in the attitude of Immanuel Kant to religion and especially to his attitude to the existence of God.

For Kant it is impossible to think of God as a metaphysical being existing beyond space and time, because attempts to do so generate antinomies. Rather, God's reality can only be invoked in moral contexts. Thus I cannot carry out the fundamental obligation to seek the *summum bonum* (that is, the highest good) unless I believe that it is possible to find it, since for Kant 'ought' implies 'can'. And since only God can be the provider of the *summum bonum*, according to Kant, it follows that God must exist. The *summum bonum* is necessary to ground the obligations of morality, and God is necessary for the provision of the *summum bonum*. The *summum bonum* is necessary for the rationality of morality. But the *summum bonum* is not possible unless the soul is immortal and God exists. Therefore, it is necessary to postulate it, along with its conditions: 'Therefore also the existence is postulated of a cause of the ground of the exact coincidence of happiness with morality.'[15] This requirement for the existence of the *summum bonum*, and of the existence of God as the provider of it, must be contrasted with, on the one hand, a mere wish for heaven as a place of pleasurable fulfilment, and a scientific hypothesis that it is likely that there is life after death, a hypothesis constructed after the manner of the argument from design.

> One must never consider morals itself as a doctrine of happiness. For morals has to do only with the rational condition (*conditio sine qua non*) of happiness and not with the means of achieving it. But when morals . . . is completely expounded, and a moral wish has been awakened to promote the highest good (to bring the Kingdom of God to us), which is a wish based on law and one to which no selfish mind could have aspired, and when for the sake of this wish the step to religion has been taken – then only can ethics be called a doctrine of happiness, because the hope for it first arises with religion.[16]

Instead of the idea of the *summum bonum* as a reward, Kant comes to rely on the fact that the commands of the moral law, the obligation to seek the *summum bonum*, cannot command what is impossible, and the *summum bonum* would be impossible if God does not exist. The practice of morality is valid only if the truth of a theoretical proposition, that God exists, is assumed, it being neither demonstrable nor refutable. The moral law does not require the existence of God, it requires that I postulate God's existence. So practical reason, the fulfilments of the requirements of *reason*, still apply: that God's existence is required. God cannot be known, not even somewhat.

So according to Kant it is reasonable to postulate the existence of God, but we can know nothing about the character of the God who is postulated, certainly nothing about his metaphysical character as a putative object of knowledge. All we know is that he is the provider of the *summum bonum*, the rewarder of virtue and the punisher of vice, and hence the vindicator of morality.

On Kant's view of the reality of God it becomes impossible to prise apart any features of God's existence from his purely moral character, as one who makes provision for men and women in the life to come, as the rewarder of virtue and the punisher of vice. For Kant the one and only thing that one can reckon to be true about God is that he is the provider of the *summum bonum*. His existence can be postulated, and must be postulated, but the God thus postulated is a wholly moral being, a being whose knowable functions and powers as God are wholly exhausted as the provider of the *summum bonum*. So for Kant God cannot not be trustworthy in this moral role that we must postulate for him. His existence is essentially connected – as a postulate – with his character as a rewarder and provider. The truly moral person is religious, for he see all duties to be divine commands.

Kant's view of the nature of religion and the stance taken by Phillips differ, naturally enough, in important ways. Nevertheless, there is an interesting degree of convergence. For Kant is saying about God essentially what Phillips says about God, that God's reality does not connect with the reality of anything else, certainly it does not bear any presiding role over reality as a whole, but that it holds only in certain specific human contexts; in the context of morality for Kant, in religion, for Phillips.

As Kant is at pains to stress, what God provides concerns only what relates to the provision of the *summum bonum* in the life to come. He does not and cannot make himself known in this life, and so he cannot connect up with any other features of our lives. It is to Kant, not to the later Wittgenstein, that we owe the insight that belief in the reality of God is part of a game or conceptual scheme; in Kant's case, the conceptual scheme of morality. One might say that for Kant, belief in God is internally related to the practice of certain moral duties, or at least the intelligibility of intending to practice them. God has reality only as a moral provider; he has no reality in the worlds of science or religion. These are the very points that Phillips is insisting on.

OBJECTIONS

The chief reason for drawing attention to Phillips' proposal in this treatment of faith seeking understanding is to identify the sharp contrast between it and the faith seeking understanding tradition of Augustine and Anselm. But Phillips' position is not without difficulties, and it would help to draw this contrast more sharply if we consider some of them.

As we have seen, central to Phillips' view of the relation between faith and understanding is a particular view of religion. Among the multitude of religions and religious views, how is such religion to be identified? Phillips would answer, By its own distinctive internal logic, that which characterises it as a 'form of life'. But (as with Kant) it is hard to avoid the conclusion that Phillips is not so much describing a religion, some existing religion, or the essential core of religion, as prescribing, as laying down, by means of examples, what is to count as authentically religious, what is to be regarded as superstitious, what is unintelligible and so forth. Far from leaving everything as it is, such a philosophical approach to religion results in a distinction being drawn between certain practices which are said to be truly religious, and others which, although they go under the guise of religion, are not truly religious but superstitious.

To illustrate this point further, let us take prayer, a religious activity of central interest to Phillips.[17] One may agree that there is a distinction between religion and superstition, and between prayers that are truly religious and those which are an expression of a superstitious attitude, without allowing that this is the entire story. Phillips thinks that religion is exhausted by certain practices and the attitudes to God which such practices sustain; he is not reductionist in his account of religion, for he is not proposing a reduction of religion to something else, but he might fairly be called an attitudinalist in his view of religion. Because of this, because for him prayer is to be understood as an attitude of a certain sort, and as nothing more, his idea of prayer must be very different from that of mainstream Christianity, for example.

In Christianity a distinction is commonly drawn between different types of prayer; between prayers as acts of praise and thanksgiving, and petitionary or intercessory prayers. In petitionary prayers the one who prays asks for something, perhaps believing that God has promised to provide it. But for Phillips such petitionary prayer, prayer which hopes for or expects an answer, is essentially irreligious. Although such prayer takes place in an act of worship, say, it exhibits an attitude to God which makes religion, or an aspect of religion, depend upon how things go. But is it not a part of religion to expect God to answer prayer? The question of whether a prayer is answered or not would, in this sense, be an empirical question. If a person prays to God for healing, and is healed, or is healed in unusual circumstances, then that person would be entitled to say that God had answered his prayer; otherwise, not. Certainly in such a case religion is in some sense involved in the way things go; but it is hardly accurate to say that the offering of petitionary prayers makes religion *depend* upon how things go. This would only be so if a prayer was like a scientific hypothesis, and if a failure to have a prayer answered was like the falsification of the hypothesis. But religions often have ways of coping with any failure to obtain an answer to petitionary prayer; mostly commonly and obviously by saying that the failure is God's refusal of what has been asked.

For Phillips any petitionary prayer is, to say the least, religiously 'sub-standard'. It is sub-standard because it connects the activity and value of religion with how things go. In this instance, the religious person has a need for something to happen and, hoping that God will meet it, he prays to God for it. But such a hope is an essentially irreligious or superstitious attitude, for it attempts to harness the supernatural to the fulfilling of our mundane needs; it is essentially selfish, self-seeking. Rather, according to Phillips, a truly religious prayer cannot be petitionary. Prayer which, on the surface, appears to be a petition, in fact expresses the believer's attitude to the contingencies of his life. It is not a way of making requests to God, based upon what God has promised, but a way of acknowledging that many things in life are beyond our control, and that in this sense our lives are not in our own hands, but in the hands of God.

Phillips may or may not be entitled to the view that prayer is attitudinal in this way. But what is undoubtedly true is that in saying that this is the only kind of prayer, or the only kind of prayer that is adequate from a religious point of view, Phillips is stipulating the meaning of 'prayer'. He is telling us how the term is to be used. And he is doing so at the behest, if not of a theory of religion (because the idea of a *theory* of religion would be unacceptable to Phillips), then of an *a priori* view of what any religion must be like. This is not a case of humility before the facts, of looking to see how the religious form of life operates, of the philosopher leaving everything as it is, but a piece of dogmatising.

One way of vividly distinguishing Phillips' proposal about how we are to understand the significance of prayer, and the established faith seeking understanding tradition, is to note that it is precisely through petitionary prayer that the search for understanding begins. For Augustine and Anselm, as we shall in more detail in later chapters, understanding came only in answer to prayer; and in this sense it was a gift of divine grace. Neither Augustine nor Anselm suggest that such prayers are religiously improper; they are central to their philosophical quest.

A second illustration of the problems that beset Phillips' view of religious understanding can be taken from his conception of truth. We have already noted the ambivalent attitude that Phillips must take up over the question of realism. The reality of God appears relative for Phillips, relative to religion considered as a practice or set of practices. Within these practices God really exists, but it makes nonsense, in Phillips' view, to suppose that God might exist above all human practices, so to speak. It is not that God does not exist outside religion, but that the very question of his existence outside religion cannot sensibly be raised. But a view of truth which relativises that notion to various forms of life, no matter that Phillips continues to speak of religious reality, is fundamentally anti-realistic. Phillips faces the objection that for all his professions to the contrary he *epistemises* truth (as William Alston puts it).[18] That is, Phillips defines truth in terms of certain human states, particularly (in the case of religious truth) in terms of those states which are in his view characteristically religious. He fails to grant that truth has to do with what is the case, not with what some person or group of people believes is the case. But as we noted, it is such a realist, non-epistemological conception of truth which lies behind the entire faith seeking understanding enterprise as initiated by Augustine and Anselm. For understanding is gaining a wider or deeper grasp of the truth, of some state of affairs or other, some aspect of the unified reality that God has created. There is the same conception of truth in all these endeavours after understanding even though – it may be granted – there may be different ways of gaining it.

Phillips takes religion to be natural in the sense that it is given in human life; it is certainly not contrived, nor in any way a conventional matter. It is 'given', a brute fact about human communities. But let us suppose that due to some cataclysm, or to some systematic malfunction, the prayers or at least the hopes of humanists were realised, and everyone came to adopt a completely secularised attitude, the religious concerns of mankind vanishing to zero. Perhaps in this situation an interest in the history of religion would remain, but there would be no religionists, just like, at present, there are people who are interested in the history of the idea of phlogiston, but none who actually believe in phlogiston.

Phillips would be bound to say of this situation that God no longer had any reality, and this is surely equivalent to the claim that he does not exist, or perhaps that he no longer exists. The question of his existence could not arise. He ceases to exist as the last religionist becomes extinct, just as a language may die when the last user of the language dies. Those who, by contrast, assert that God exists as a metaphysical reality, would take the view that in such a benighted situation God would still exist, for his existence does not depend on any human states such that if those states disappear he also vanishes. In such a situation, where no one believes in God, it is perfectly true that no-one recognises or believes that God exists, and that the belief that God exists would make no positive difference to any human life. But there is a clear distinction to be drawn between the propositions 'No one believes in God' and 'There is no God'. They are logically independent of each other. The first may be true while the second is false, and the second may be true while the first is false. Even when no one believes in God the question of the reality of God is unaffected; the reality of God cannot be altered by whether or not people acknowledge his existence.

As we have seen, one of the things which Phillips persistently stresses is that religion is autonomous; that is to say, it cannot properly be criticised from outside itself, even though certain religious practices, e.g. the practice of petitionary prayer, may be criticised from within, for being superstitious. Religion can only be criticised from the standpoint of religion; anything else is imperialism. It is not easy to see what arguments Phillips has or could have for this position. All that seems open to him at this point is to renew his attempt to display the internal logic of religion as he sees it. But, as Alston says, it is hard to see how one can stop the language-game of religion being criticised from outside that language-game, from the standpoint of some other language-game. Perhaps there are

> language-games specially designed for examining, describing and evaluating other language games. There is also the (putative) possibility to be considered that there is free-floating, unregimented intellectual activity that does not proceed on the basis of any fixed set of standards and procedures such as defined language-games, and that we could be engaging in that when we subject language-games to critical scrutiny.[19]

Even if one grants that religion is not primarily a theoretical matter, some religions nevertheless have some commitment to what the world/universe is like; theories about creation and providence, the nature of morality, the possibility of surviving death, and so on. The practical is important, but it is not all-important. Phillips has made the elementary mistake of taking one necessary condition of religion – its practical aspect – to be a sufficient condition:

> Religion is not primarily a theoretical matter; it is, when deeply entered into, primarily a 'form of life', essentially involving emotional and practical involvement, shaping one's life in certain ways, 'seeing'

things in certain ways. But all this is quite compatible with what also seems obvious – that religion typically involves commitments to certain states of affairs obtaining in the world.[20]

And, it can be added, these states of affairs, at least in Christianity, involve not only metaphysical matters of the sort we have been discussing and will discuss further, but also historical and geographical matters. This is one of the consequences of saying that Christianity is a historical religion, crucial elements having been enacted in the objective world of space and time which we all occupy.

In the Augustinian tradition, as we shall see in more detail in the following chapters, one may believe but fail to understand; not fail totally to understand, but fail to understand as much as one might. So that faith can hold steady while understanding increases (or, presumably, decreases). Similarly one can understand and not believe. Since understanding is a matter of the theological and philosophical elaboration of the propositions of the faith, such an understanding may even be conveyed to those who do not have faith. On this position there is a logical primacy attaching to understanding, since any degree of faith entails some degree of understanding, and it is possible to understand to some degree and not to believe.

Interestingly, Anselm's argument in the *Proslogion*, and particularly his *Reply to Gaunilo*, depends upon the very point that Phillips is here denying, that understanding is separable from believing. For the fool allegedly understands what 'God' means, but does not realise that, given this meaning, God must exist.

Where one *identifies* understanding and believing, as Phillips does, philosophical problems arise. In particular, the problem of how one may then give an intelligible and persuasive account of rejection or rebellion in religion. For surely the point about the rejection of some position is that a person rejects the very same matter that others accept, and that he might in other circumstances have accepted. Otherwise rejection would be impossible. For if believing and understanding go hand in hand, then rejection, which involves unbelief, or at least non-belief, must always, as a matter of definition, be based upon misunderstanding. So that no-one ever could rejects Christianity, or Islam, or any other religion, one could only reject misunderstandings of these religions. Because if Christianity, or Islam, were truly understood then their claims would be believed, since understanding is believing.

Phillips recognises the difficulty, though he does not think that it poses any threat to the identification of belief and understanding in religion,[21] and offers two answers to it. The first is that there is a place for rejection in religion provided one understands this as the rejection of an entire 'form of life'. The one who rejects or rebels in effect says 'religion means nothing to me'; he opts out of religion.

But what about rejection as rebellion against God? Is there a place for this? In answer to this Phillips says that 'belief in God' has a wider application than 'belief in John', in that a person may believe in God whose basic relation to God was one of fear. He cites Norman Malcolm:

> Belief in God encompasses not only trust but also awe, dread, dismay, resentment, and perhaps even hatred. Belief in God will involve some affective state or attitude, having God as its object, and those attitudes could vary from reverential love to rebellious rejection.[22]

And Phillips himself says:

> I should still want to argue, however, that the love of God is the primary form of belief in God if only because the intelligibility of all the other attitudes Malcolm mentions is logically dependent on it. The rebel must see the kind of relationship God asks of the believer before he can reject and defy it. He sees the story from the inside, but it is not a story that captivates him. The love of God is active in his life, but in him it evokes hatred. To say that he does not believe in God is absurd, for whom does he hate if not God?[23]

So there is *some* modification of Phillips's thesis. Phillips here claims that since belief in God involves hatred, even the hater of God is a believer. One can grant this point; it is intelligible to suppose that someone might believe in God and yet hate him. But even if we grant Phillips the point about hatred, what he proposes has a distinctly stipulative ring to it. Phillips simply defines belief in God in a way that suits exactly what he wishes to say about religion as a language-game. He offers no grounds for this re-definition. Understanding and believing go hand in hand, but believing in God is now said to include not only trust but fear.

Such an attitude might involve the belief that there is a God, but why should such an attitude be called belief in God, for belief in God usually connotes not only belief in the existence of God, but trust in God. Someone who is said to believe in God but who fears God in the sense meant by Phillips can hardly be said to trust him, but rather to believe that it is true that God exists, and to fear or hate the fact of God's existence rather than trust him.

On Phillips's own admission there is one proposition, 'God exists', which may arouse both trust in A and fear in B. But why should responses be restricted to trust and fear? Why may not one response be indifference,

indifference to the question of whether God exists? What reason is there for supposing that all the philosophically acceptable attitudes must be *strong* attitudes. (Here, surely, is another case where description and prescription are blurred together.) Why may not someone believe that God exists and be indifferent to the fact that he does? Are not many like this?

In any event, these remarks about believing and hating do not quite meet the objection. What about the one who rejects God in a different manner, the person who says that he has no good reason to believe that there is a God? Does he, for all his protestations to the contrary, nevertheless believe in God?

Someone might see how much Phillips' position differs from that of the classical faith seeking understanding tradition, and yet argue in the following way. At the outset of this chapter we distinguished between various kinds of understanding, including the understanding of language. Taking a cue from this, it might be argued that the understanding that Augustine, Anselm and the others seek is not, let us grant, the understanding of a different kind of reality, an autonomous religious reality, but it is more like the understanding of language. For Augustine, say, to gain understanding is like learning a new word, or learning another meaning of an existing word. It is to come to learn a new language, the language of the Christian Church, perhaps; and that it is only in the context of the Church, the believing community, that true understanding can be gained, as one comes to learn the language of faith. This would be another way of connecting together understanding and believing.

There is no reason to suppose that gaining understanding may not involve understanding words in new ways. However, there are several reasons for thinking that this is not the whole of the faith seeking understanding endeavour. For one thing, Augustine and Anselm were already in the Church, the Christian community, and yet they sought understanding. But more importantly, the understanding that they sought was such that, when it was granted, it was generally available, public property so to speak, and not only church property; there is no guarantee that those who are outside the Church would understand, but no principled objection to the suggestion that they may.

The chief purpose of this chapter has not been to provide criticism of Phillips' views, but to show that despite superficial similarities his account of faith and understanding is radically different from that of the tradition we outlined in the first two chapters and that we shall discuss in more detail in the chapters to follow. Phillips' proposal is not one that falls within that tradition, but it is a radically different conception of religious understanding.

It is possible to summarise our discussion by drawing attention to three main differences. First, the Augustine–Anselm tradition is metaphysically realist. For this tradition metaphysics is a handmaid of theology; indeed theology is a branch of metaphysics. And the metaphysical account Augustine and the others give of the relation between God and the world is a unified realist conception. Such an account of God and the world, if it is true, would be true even if religious belief ceased. By contrast, for Phillips religion (and with it the recognition of the reality of God) is a matter of engaging in a set of important practices, and nothing more. Should those practices cease, God's reality would vanish, he would cease to exist. (And, since presumably the fact that these practices exist is a contingent fact, God's existence is likewise contingent.) Secondly, Augustine and Anselm and others in the main tradition distinguish between faith and understanding, whereas, as we have seen, Phillips identifies the two. Finally, Phillips regards religion as an autonomous form of life, while they see it as in principle (and in fact) open to the influences of human culture, of science and philosophy, and *vice versa*, since all cognitive enquiries address aspects of the one real world which is God's creation.

NOTES

1. We can remain agnostic on whether Augustine and Anselm, say, were realists in the much-discussed further sense of holding that there are truths which are unknowable in principle.
2. Some philosophers, for example the Muslim Averroes (1126–98), advocated a system of two-fold truth; that a proposition could be true in philosophy and false in theology and *vice versa*. For example that it could be a philosophical truth that creation is impossible, but a theological truth that God is the Creator. Such a view seems incompatible with unified realism. For an interesting discussion, see Brown 'Christian Averroism, Fideism and the "Two-Fold Truth"'.
3. Phillips, *Faith and Philosophical Enquiry*, and many other writings.
4. Phillips, *Faith and Philosophical Enquiry*, p.67.
5. Phillips, *Faith and Philosophical Enquiry*, p.17.
6. Phillips, *Faith and Philosophical Enquiry*, p.3.
7. Phillips, *Faith and Philosophical Enquiry*, p.59.
8. Phillips, *Faith and Philosophical Enquiry*, p.100.
9. Kretzmann, 'Faith Seeks, Understanding Finds', p.21.
10. Phillips, *Faith and Philosophical Enquiry*, p.127f.
11. Phillips, *Faith After Foundationalism*.
12. Phillips, *Death and Immortality*.
13. Phillips, *Faith and Philosophical Enquiry*, p.35.
14. Phillips, *Faith and Philosophical Enquiry*, p.59.
15. Kant, *Critique of Practical Reason*, p. 129.
16. Kant, *Critique of Practical Reason*, p.135.
17. Phillips, *The Concept of Prayer*.
18. Alston, 'Taking the Curse Off Language-Games: A Realistic Account of Doxastic Practices', p.21.
19. Alston, 'Taking the Curse Off Language-Games: A Realistic Account of Doxastic Practices', pp. 33f.
20. Alston, 'Taking the Curse Off Language-Games: A Realistic Account of Doxastic Practices', p.26.
21. Phillips, *Faith and Philosophical Enquiry*, p.31.
22. Cited by Phillips, *Faith and Philosophical Enquiry*, p.31.
23. Phillips, *Faith and Philosophical Enquiry*, pp.31f.

Part Two
Five Case-studies

4

Time and Creation in Augustine's Confessions

As we have already noted, Augustine of Hippo may be regarded as the fountainhead of the faith seeks understanding tradition. In this chapter we shall consider Augustine's reflections on the idea of divine creation chiefly as they centre on the opening words of the book of Genesis, 'In the beginning God created the heavens and the earth . . .'. As we have stressed in Chapter 2, the faith seeks understanding programme starts from the propositions of faith, and these are rooted in divine revelation. So it is natural that that programme should be closely connected with biblical interpretation, and the example of faith seeking understanding we consider in this chapter is such a case. Augustine accepted the opening words of the book of Genesis as an important part of his faith; but he attempted in the *Confessions* (and elsewhere in his writings, though here we shall concentrate chiefly on the *Confessions*), to gain further understanding of the words by reflecting on them in relation to God's relation to time and change. As we shall see, Augustine believed that every detail of this passage was of significance, and had a rich and compressed meaning which he sought to unpack. Though these reflections about the creation story in Genesis are to be found chiefly in Book XII of the *Confessions*, we shall take up the account in Book XI, Augustine's discussion of the nature of time, and the relation of time to eternity, a series of reflections on the words 'In the beginning God created the heavens and the earth'.

Although Augustine does not explicitly appeal to the faith seeking understanding motif here, his procedure obviously falls within this framework. In the opening of Book XII, to be considered later, Augustine takes

himself to be seeking and knocking, words indicating a search for understanding. And later he believes he has received understanding in answer to
his search; the Lord stirred him to knock, and opened to his knocking.[1]

TIME AND ETERNITY

Augustine considers the nature of time in the course of an extended
meditation on God and his relation to all that he has created. In addressing
God, and reflecting in his presence, Augustine implies that he is personally
related to God, and wishes to learn more about God from God himself. He
wishes to 'hear and understand how in the beginning you made heaven and
earth. . . . You have granted to your servant to utter these things; grant
also to me the power to understand them'.[2] Augustine's meditation is in the
form of a dialogue in which he believes God gives him illumination about
the nature of things. He believes the words; he wishes now to understand
the reality that the words express. This intellectual insight is expected in
answer to prayer.

Augustine affirmed, as part of his faith, that God created everything out
of nothing. Such a view sharply contrasts with the idea of creation in
classical Greek philosophy (for example in Plato's *Timaeus*), where
creation is the fashioning of eternally existing stuff. One of the errors of
the Manichees, the sect that had so greatly influenced Augustine as a young
man, and from whom he became emancipated by reading Platonist
philosophy, was the belief that evil was a material substance. In asserting
the doctrine of *creatio ex nihilo* Augustine was asserting not only the basic
metaphysical contrast between Creator and the creation, but also that
matter was not *per se* evil, since God had created it and God is good.

So, in creating, God could not use anything that was already created.
This does not register a lack of power, it is simply an implication of what
creation out of nothing means. If creation were not from nothing, then the
material from which he created would not itself be created, and God would
not be the creator of everything. In speaking his creative word God does
not literally speak, for speech takes time and before the creation there was
no time, since according to Augustine (as we shall shortly see) time is the
measure of change. (He does not appear to consider the possibility that the
speech of God might itself be the beginning of time.) Time, for Augustine,
is merely a logical consequence of the creation of things which change; it is
not itself a stuff or substance, like gold or orange juice, which was created,
but it is a relation between created things or, more precisely, between
changes in the states of those created things:

> If therefore it was with words which sound and pass away that you
> said that heaven and earth should be made, and if this was how you

made heaven and earth, then a created entity belonging to the physical realm existed prior to heaven and earth; and that utterance took time to deliver, and involved temporal changes.[3]

Understanding is partly a matter of logic. But often logical implications are not clear. Hence Augustine's prayer to God that he would make them clear. Augustine comes to see that God's relation to the creation cannot be like that of one created thing to another. This is one reason for Augustine's belief that God, because he is uncreated, is timelessly eternal. Similarly, creation cannot be through the power of words, which come and go, because the words would then be created intermediaries. Creation is through the eternal Word. And so time itself is created; not as a substance or entity, but as the measure of change. As, in creating a cup, say, God does not create two things, the cup and the edge of the cup, so God does not create things which change, and time. The edge of the cup is created in creating the cup. So time is not created separately, but as a consequence of the creation of things which are liable to change.

So if one distinguishes broadly between those thinkers that have held that time is absolute, who have held what is sometimes called the container view of time, with the universe placed at some temporal point 'within' it, and those who think of time as relative,[4] simply as the measure of change, then Augustine sides with the latter. He does not, as far as one can see, consider the idea that before the creation there was a period of empty time, a period of time without change,[5] since there could be no events before the creation, not even events in the mind of God, since God is timelessly eternal. This is because, with one significant exception to be discussed later, for Augustine the categories of 'Creator' and 'created' correspond to those of 'timeless' and 'temporal', on the principle that only what is created changes or could change.

In thinking about God's relation to time, there have been two contrasting traditions. Some argue that God is in time; that he has a past and a future, but that his past is immeasurably backward, literally immeasurable since until the creation of an orderly universe by God there was no temporal metric. God is eternal in the sense that he exists necessarily, backwardly and forwardly without limit. According to the contrasting view, the view that Augustine's discussion of eternity and time in Book XI of the *Confessions* did much to establish as Christian orthodoxy, as the dominant view, God has created the world, but this act of creation was not at a time, since God is not in time; rather, the universe was created (or perhaps timelessly 'is' created) through an eternal though not a necessary act of God's will.

So when Augustine says God exists 'before' the universe exists, 'before' is understood in a hierarchical sense, in the sense in which age is said to come before beauty, or duty before pleasure. God does not exist before the universe in the sense in which breakfast comes before lunch. Rather he is before the universe because he has his being necessarily, while the universe exists contingently, in virtue of his will. He is before the universe in the sense that the universe exists because of him, and not *vice versa*.[6] So God's temporal relation to one period of time, say the period when the Battle of Hastings took place, is exactly the same as his relation to some earlier or later period; he neither exists before or after such events but 'before' them in the sense described.[7]

Later on, in Book IX, Augustine makes this point explicitly:

> For it is rare to see and very hard to sustain the insight, Lord, of your eternity immutably making a mutable world, and in this sense being anterior. And then who has a sufficiently acute mental discernment to be able to recognise, without intense toil, how sound is prior to song? The difficulty lies in the point that song is formed sound, and something not endowed with form can of course exist, but can what does not exist receive form? In this sense matter is prior to that which is made out of it. It is not prior in the sense that it actively makes; it is rather that it is made. Nor is priority one of temporal interval here. For it is not that first we emit unformed sound without it being song, and later adapt or shape it into the form of a song, in the way we make a box out of wood or a vase out of silver.[8]

While the creation is not an event in time, not even an event at 'the beginning of time', but is an expression of the timelessly eternal will of God, nevertheless God and the universe do not exist as two co-eternally necessary things, since the created universe is contingent. So the creation has an absolute beginning *ex nihilo*; there could be no physical cause of the universe, since either such a cause would be before the beginning of the universe (which it could not be, since the beginning of the universe is by definition the first physical cause) or simultaneous with it, which would mean that a physical part of the universe could be the cause of itself. Augustine held these positions *de fide*. This book of the *Confessions* is an attempt to elucidate this aspect of his faith. There is no attempt here to provide a rational proof of these positions, by a version of the cosmological argument, for example, though in claiming that the heaven and earth 'cry out' that they are made, Augustine indicates that he would be sympathetic to such an argument.[9]

The words of Genesis are part of Augustine's faith, and so he accepts them as true. The question is, what truth – exactly – do they express? Augustine's outline answer to this question is that the words express truths which are not at first apparent, but which only become apparent when one receives a (God-given) understanding, part of which involves avoiding the pitfalls which the surface grammar of Genesis 1 suggests. Augustine himself draws a contrast between the surface and the depths of the passage:

> What wonderful profundity there is in your utterances! The surface meaning lies open before us and charms beginners. Yet the depth is amazing, my God, the depth is amazing.[10]

Part of Augustine's appreciation of the words lies in the fact that they combine together both a surface and a deep meaning. Reflection on the words raises a number of problems which must then be answered, and in answering them one gains understanding, an understanding which is not private but which one is able to publish for the benefit of others, as Augustine does in his *Confessions*. What is gained is a greater understanding of the actions of God, and so of God himself.

AUGUSTINE'S THREE PROBLEMS ABOUT TIME

Having established the categorical distinction between the Creator and his creation, Augustine then presents himself with a number of problems about time which he addresses in Book XI. Let us briefly look at these in turn.

Augustine's first problem about time concerns the way we have of talking about time as past, present and future. We, as creatures of God, are in time, subject to change. Because of this, we refer to various times in a way which presupposes that we ourselves have a position in time. We who are alive in 1997 say, for example, that Napoleon lived in the past, our past, and that our progeny will live in the future. The past is (roughly) what is over and done with, what we cannot now in principle causally affect, the future is what we can now causally affect. The past is what has been brought about, or has occurred, the future what will be brought about or occur. Granted this distinction between past, present and future – a grasp of which is essential to our ability to live as temporal beings – Augustine asks how can the past and the future exist when the past is no longer and the future is not yet?[11] If the past and future exist, where are they? More worryingly, Augustine goes on to question the status of the present, since it is, in his view, simply the conceptual boundary between the past and the future:

> One hour is itself constituted of fugitive moments. Whatever part of it has flown away is past. What remains to it is future. If we can think of

some bit of time which cannot be divided into even the smallest instantaneous moments, that alone is what we can call 'present'. And this time flies so quickly from future into past that it is an interval with no duration. If it has duration, it is divisible into past and future. But the present occupies no space.[12]

Richard Swinburne expresses this point in the following way:

> A 'period' which did not contain smaller periods would be really not a period, but an instant. It is a mistake to think of a period of time as (in any natural sense) composed of instants – for example, the hour between 2 p.m. and 3 p.m. as the collection of instants between 2 p.m. and 3 p.m. Instants are boundaries of periods and have no duration.[13]

Augustine's understanding of the present is like this; the present has no duration, but it is an instant, a mathematical point separating past and future, and so itself has no temporal length. This raises an acute problem for the coherence of Augustine's overall view of time; for if the present has no duration, and if the past and future are simply presents that have been and presents that will be, it looks as if the entire temporal series must collapse into zero.[14]

Perhaps Augustine would have been wiser to emphasise here the vagueness and indefiniteness of what we refer to as 'the present', something which he draws attention to elsewhere.[15]

Augustine's second problem about time concerns another aspect of the status of past and future. Times are spoken of as being long or short, but neither the past nor the future can be long or short, since neither now exists:

> Where then is the time which we call long? Is it future? We do not really mean 'It is long', since it does not yet exist to be long, but we mean it will be long. When will it be long? If it will then still lie in the future, it will not be long, since it will not yet exist to be long. But if it will be long at the time when, out of the future which does not yet exist, it begins to have being and will become present fact, so that it has the potentiality to be long, the present cries out in words already used that it cannot be long.[16]

The past is what has been, and the future is what has yet to be. Augustine appears to get himself into even greater difficulties at this point. As we have seen, he is already committed to the view that the present is infinitesimally small, a mathematical point. He now claims that the past no longer exists, since only the present exists, and likewise the future does not yet exist.

Thus since neither the past nor the future now exist, they are not, and so can be neither long nor short.

Augustine's view of time seems to contain the following paradoxes: that when times are (i.e. are present) they have no length, and when they are said to have length (or shortness) then they are not. Once again, it looks as if everything that is real about time collapses into the present, but that the present itself has no duration.

The third problem concerns time and its measurement. We measure time easily and without any problem and yet we know that time is such that it cannot be measured:

> Nevertheless, Lord, we are conscious of intervals of time, and compare them with each other, and call some longer, others shorter. We also measure how much longer or shorter one period is than another, and answer that the one is twice or three times as much as the other, or that the two periods are equal. Moreover, we are measuring times which are past when our perception is the basis of measurement. But who can measure the past which does not now exist or the future which does not yet exist, unless perhaps someone dares to assert that he can measure what has no existence?[17]

It is impossible to measure time, since time is not there all at once (unlike a length of cloth) to be measured. Nor can we measure the present since the present has no length. Nor can the future or the past now be measured, since what does not exist cannot now be measured. In using time as a measure we seem to do something that it is impossible to do.

AUGUSTINE'S RESPONSES

Augustine's basic response to these three problems or paradoxes, problems generated by human creatureliness, by the fact that we are individuals existing in time, is a constructivist or reconstructivist one. Since for Augustine all that exists for creatures in time is the present (though even the present exists rather precariously, as we have seen), our accurate descriptions of what is past or present, and our assertions about the past and future, cannot be based upon a power of retrovision or prevision. To have such a power, to be able to see into the past or the future, would imply that past and future had, at present, a real existence, that they were visible or at least sensible, and this would be to treat past and future as if they were places which we could see by looking backwards or forwards, just as we can see the sofa in front of us, and the wall behind us.

Rather the justification of our talk about past is based upon presently existing traces, features of the present which we judge to be about the past and on the basis of which we construct the past and impute features to it. When what is now past was present it 'left an impression on our minds'. This memory, for example Augustine's memory of his childhood, is a present phenomenon.[18] Remembering is something we do now, and we build up and retain our understanding of the past on the basis of memory. Similarly our ability to describe features of the future is based on the present, on anticipations, though our powers with regard to the future are less sure and secure because the traces are fewer and less secure in the case of the future. Those, like the prophets, who claim to foretell the future do so not because they can see into the future, as one can see a far horizon (for there is no future to see), but on the basis of what they presently know.[19]

Although it is clear that we do succeed in measuring time, and that we measure time as it passes, it is not at all clear what it is we are measuring. Nor is it clear what the standard of measurement is. (And, as we have already stressed, all that exists to be measured is the present, which has no duration.) Augustine rejects the view that time is the movement of the stars and that we therefore measure time by celestial movement.[20] The stars exist contingently; had they not been, nevertheless time would still have existed, had other things which change existed. Furthermore, it is possible to conceive of the heavenly bodies rotating at different speeds from those at which they presently rotate.[21] What applies to the stars applies equally to anything else that is created. We may use the heavenly bodies to measure time, but such movements do not define what time is.

Augustine asks, How can we measure sounds which have no exact length until they are completed, and when they are completed are past, and so no longer exist? What is measured when we measure time must be something in the present, and the only thing that is present is something which remains fixed in the memory.[22] Memory is not an impression that is now caused by a past event, it is a present impression that something has occurred and no longer occurs. According to Augustine, therefore, and consistently with the constructivism that we noted earlier, time is measured by the mind, by the impression which the passage of time leaves behind. The future diminishes and the past increases because we expect less and remember more.[23] In making these claims Augustine is not saying that human memory is infallible, but that it has a primitive (non-analysable) power of awareness, necessary for the measurement of time, perhaps occasionally necessary and sufficient for the measurement of time, but usually other data are also necessary for accurate measurement.

It is Augustine's view that this account based on human memory solves the problems that time poses, at least for those whose standpoint is creaturely, within time. The length or shortness of times is an impression. We measure time not on the basis of a direct acquaintance with the future or the past *per se*, but by what is conveyed by our present impression of the future and of the past.

Perhaps it is not altogether accurate to call Augustine's view of time and its measurement constructivist. It is more accurate to say that it is retentionist; the mind is able to think about the past because of what it retains of past presents in the present. But only the present is now real.

Can Augustine's retentionism really provide a solution to the problems of the measurement of time? Each memory impression to which we appeal in giving an account of the past is itself an event or state, only momentarily present. How can appealing to such momentary *impressions* do what appealing to momentary *events* cannot do? These impressions are beliefs. What is the difference between a long expectation of the future and a short expectation? Is what Augustine is drawing our attention to the intentionality (directedness) of the impressions? It is not so much that impressions (considered as events in the consciousness) have a unique role, since such impressions are no different in their logical character from events of other kinds. It is certainly mistaken to suppose that what Augustine is saying is that 'time is the extendedness of impressions, memories and expectations'. Rather time is extendedness *as measured by* memories and expectations, the beliefs which are intrinsic to these events in our consciousness.

Are there, on Augustine's understanding, truths about the past and the future? And is he saying that our knowledge of these truths is based upon the present awarenesses? Or is he saying that the only truths that there are, are truths about the present? How would he distinguish between the past, say, and a piece of fiction? We said, a moment ago, that for Augustine only the present exists, or is real. If so, then Augustine must be a realist about the past. For the past is what really occurred; it is unlike a fictional narrative, for example. In which case his retentionism is purely epistemic in character, since he holds *a priori* that as creatures we must have a past and a future.

Whatever the difficulties with Augustine's account of time and eternity, it provides him with the background for his discussion of the nature of the creation of the universe, and also for considering time from the standpoint of the timelessly eternal Creator.

TIME AND CREATION

As we noted earlier, there have been two broad traditions of thought about God's relation to time; some have argued that God exists at all times and, since he exists necessarily, he is backwardly and forwardly everlasting. In the mediaeval period it would appear that William of Ockham took such a view;[24] many at present, such as Richard Swinburne,[25] also take this view.

Others, such as Boethius,[26] and of course Augustine, and a number of contemporary philosophers,[27] argue that God exists in a timeless eternity. He cannot have a past or future, for such change is incompatible with the divine fullness of being.

So according to Augustine God creates the universe not in time, but with time. He timelessly eternally wills the changes that inhabitants of a temporal changing universe such as ourselves, undergo and witness. Addressing God, Augustine says:

> It is not in time that you precede times. Otherwise you would not precede all times. In the sublimity of an eternity which is always in the present, you are before all things past and transcend all things future, because they are still to come, and when they have come they are past. 'But you are the same and your years do not fail' (Ps. 101:28). Your 'years' neither go nor come. Ours come and go so that all may come in succession. All your 'years' subsist in simultaneity, because they do not change; those going away are not thrust out by those coming in. But the years which are ours will not all be until all years have ceased to be. . . . You created all times and you exist before all times. Nor was there any time when time did not exist.[28]

These words underline the fact that basic to Augustine's view of reality is a contrast between what is eternal, immutable and uncreated, and what is in time, created and mutable. (Though we shall have some reason to discuss a possible modification to this view in the following discussion.) Augustine claims that anything that is subject to or undergoes change and variation 'proclaims' that it was created. For Augustine, change implies contingency, both in the sense that what is changed might not have been, and also because what is changed depends upon whatever changes it. But as we shall see, while change implies contingency, contingency does not imply change. According to Augustine, there is one exception to the equation of contingency and temporality, one case of timeless and therefore of changeless contingency.

Augustine claims further, that *everything that is subject to change has a beginning*. He takes this to be a significant claim, since if something has a beginning then something else must have begun it. As he puts it, 'The manner of our existence shows that we were made. For before we came to be, we did not exist to be able to make ourselves'.[29] But there are at least two problems with this claim. First, why should whatever changes have a beginning? And secondly, why should whatever has a beginning have a *beginner*, a purposive intelligent agent, one agent? Why may the universe not just *be*? Or why may not the universe have come into being causelessly?

In his study on Augustine, Christopher Kirwan suggests that since Augustine excludes God from the 'everything' that is required to have a cause, why should Augustine not exclude other beings who might then share in God's creative activity?[30] The problem with this suggestion is that in Augustine's eyes it would appear to be arbitrary; any such individuals would themselves, for Augustine, be creatures, and hence would ultimately depend upon the Creator. It would flout Augustine's principle that anything that is not God is a creation of God. To be uncreated beings they would fall foul of another of Augustine's principles, that whatever changes must have a beginning. However, there is no reason why there should not be a backwardly infinite overlapping series of such individuals.

As we have seen, Augustine conceives of divine creation as a timeless act in which the creation of all things and events is brought about as a whole. And even if he did not, even if (like a modern philosopher such as Richard Swinburne) Augustine gave up his principle that all that exists in time is created, and thought of God as existing everlastingly backward in time, still there would be a distinction between creation and adaptation. On this metaphysical conception of creation it makes sense to ask, Is the whole of the physical order (however physically explained) due to a creator? This question cannot be satisfactorily answered by postulating some physical theory, since such a theory must itself posit initial conditions and laws which are part of physical reality and which (it is plausible to suppose) might have been other than they are in fact. Even if we suppose that the laws of physics could not be other than they are, nevertheless the initial conditions, the primeval slime or whatever, could have been different. And even if this is not so, even if the primeval conditions could not have been other than they were, this does not remove their contingency, for they might not have been.

The idea of *creatio ex nihilo* is the idea of the willing that x exist being necessary and sufficient for the real existence of x, x not being fashioned out of something already existing. We need, as Augustine does, to observe the distinction between grammatical and logical form here: 'He made the table from a plank'; 'He made the universe from nothing' (where the matter of no existing thing forms part of the substance of what is willed into existence). There is something from which the table was made but nothing from which the universe was made. What is the difference between such creation, and something's coming into existence by chance? One crucial difference, presumably, is that in the case of *creatio ex nihilo* it would be possible to be able to specify independently of the existence of x what x was to be. The ability to do this would imply both power and control over x. There seems to be no incoherence in such an idea. Perhaps *creatio ex nihilo* is a basic action or capacity of a *sui generis* kind.

To support his belief in divine *creatio ex nihilo* Kirwan says that Augustine appeals not to reason but to the Bible alone to justify it. But this is not strictly correct. Augustine appeals to the divine self-sufficiency:

> For if he was helped in making the things he willed to make by some other things that he had not made, he was not Almighty, and to believe that is blasphemy.[31]

Despite these qualificatory comments, however, the two problems identified above remain embarrassingly unanswered.

The idea of *creatio ex nihilo* is one area where Augustine clearly departs from the Neoplatonism which so influenced him in his articulation of Christian doctrine, repudiating it on what he believes to be Christian grounds. Despite this, he does provide what is obviously a Platonically-influenced account of what follows the act of creation, in Book XII, to which we shall shortly turn. Before doing this, it is necessary to understand and underline the fact that for Augustine creation is a metaphysical and not a scientific idea. Such a distinction is often missed, and it is claimed that some scientific event could be the first moment of creation. Thus in *A Brief History of Time* Stephen Hawking writes in a number of places as if creation is a scientific concept, or as if, due to increased scientific understanding, it is possible for science to take possession of the concept of creation from theology and metaphysics. Augustine, for one, would find such a supposition impossible to take seriously.

Hawking makes two points which are relevant to our discussion of Augustine and time. The first concerns the status of the big bang, in which he appears to argue that the big bang is the moment of creation.

For example, one argument that Hawking employs is as follows:

> Hubble's observations suggested that there was a time, called the big bang, when the universe was infinitesimally small and infinitely dense. Under such conditions all the laws of science, and therefore all ability to predict the future, would break down. If there were events earlier than this time, then they could not affect what happens at the present time. Their existence can be ignored because it would have no observational consequences. One may say that time had a beginning at the big bang, in the sense that earlier times simply would not be defined. It should be emphasized that this beginning in time is very different from those that had been considered previously. In an unchanging universe a beginning in time is something that has to be

imposed by some being outside the universe; there is no physical necessity for a beginning. One can imagine that God created the universe at literally any time in the past. On the other hand, if the universe is expanding, there may be physical reasons why there had to be a beginning. One could still imagine that God created the universe at the instant of the big bang, or even afterwards in just such a way as to make it look as though there had been a big bang, but it would be meaningless to suppose that it was created *before* the big bang. An expanding universe does not preclude a creator, but it does place limits on when he might have carried out his job![32]

Again,

In fact, all our theories of science are formulated on the assumption that space-time is smooth and nearly flat, so they break down at the big bang singularity, where the curvature of space-time is infinite. This means that even if there were events before the big bang, one could not use them to determine what would happen afterwards, because predictability would break down at the big bang. Correspondingly, if, as is the case, we know only what has happened since the big bang, we could not determine what happened beforehand. As far as we are concerned, events before the big bang can have no consequences, so they should not form part of a scientific model of the universe. We should therefore cut them out of the model and say that time had a beginning at the big bang.[33]

We might express this argument as follows:

1. It is possible that there are events before the big bang
2. But predictability breaks down at the big bang
3. Therefore, events before the big bang can have no (predictable) consequences
4. Therefore, we should say that time had a beginning at the big bang.[34]

Bringing these two passages together we obtain the following conclusion. Hawking appears to be saying both that it is possible that there are events before the big bang but that we should say that time had a beginning at the big bang. The fact that we may not be able to know anything about the happenings before the big bang is irrelevant to the question of whether there could be events before the big bang. Is the big bang the beginning of time or not? If it is, then it cannot have been preceded by any event, either knowable by us or not. If it is not the beginning of time then it cannot be equivalent to a divine act of creation, supposing (with Augustine) that creation is the act of beginning time.

Hawking's second point concerns the freedom of God to choose some particular universe,[35] or not. He believes that, assuming the occurrence of the big bang, 'God would still have had complete freedom to choose what happened and how the universe began'.[36] However if, as his later speculations suggest, it is possible to combine quantum mechanics with general relativity, and the universe is completely self-contained, with no singularities (such as the big bang) and no boundaries, and completely described by a unified theory, Hawking thinks that this has profound implications for the role of God as Creator:

> Einstein once asked the question: 'How much choice did God have in constructing the universe?' If the no boundary proposal is correct, he had no freedom at all to choose initial conditions. He would, of course, still have had the freedom to choose the laws that the universe obeyed. This, however, may not really have been all that much of a choice; there may well be only one, or a small number, of complete unified theories, such as the heterotic string theory, that are self-consistent and allow the existence of structures as complicated as human beings who can investigate the laws of the universe and ask about the nature of God.[37]

Hawking's speculations, if true, would have profound implications. For if God is to create a universe, then any universe that he creates must have the physical character of this universe. This consequence may be a reason for doubting the truth of Hawking's speculations, but in any case it is a far cry from saying that the unified theory is so compelling that it brings about its own existence, and so eliminates the very possibility of the universe being the creation of God.[38] This supposition is surely nonsense. There is no difference in logic whether we opt for the cosmology of a big bang, or favour Hawking's later speculations; even if God's choice was narrowed down to a universe of one physical type, he still has the option whether or not to create this universe, and, if he does opt to create, which token of that type to create. So it does not follow from this that the universe must necessarily exist; what does follow is that were God to choose to create a universe he must create this universe, or a universe governed by these laws, having this physical character. It is one thing to understand the underlying order of the universe, it is another thing to propose that this understanding is logically sufficient for the real existence of what this is an understanding of. If any cube must, of necessity, have six sides, it does not follow that there must be cubes; only that if there are cubes, each must be six-sided.

As Richard Swinburne has said:

> There can be no scientific explanation of the existence of a universe; for all that science can do is to explain how a present state of the universe was brought about by a past state. It cannot explain why there is a universe at all.[39]

As we have seen, Augustine had a quite different conception of creation from that presupposed by Hawking. Time is a relation between created things; these created things are necessarily liable to change. But there could be no events before the beginning of the universe, not even events in the mind of God, who is timelessly eternal, and therefore without change. So if the big bang is the first moment there could be no events before it, not even unknowable events. And so God exists 'before' the universe in a sense different from the temporal 'before'.

Just as there is no necessity about the big bang, so scientific laws cannot ensure that, tomorrow, say, there is not a big silence. Scientific laws, however basic, cannot ensure that the universe continues in being, any more than they can ensure that the universe comes into being. What does ensure this, Augustine would say, is the will of God that there be, and that there continue to be, a created universe.

But does not such a creation imply change in God, and so flout Augustine's basic thought about God, that he is timelessly eternal? Here we are faced with a trilemma; either God was at rest prior to the creation, in which case there was no reason not to continue to do nothing, or God was in motion (in which case God is not truly eternal), or God began to be in motion (in which case, also, he is not truly eternal). But Augustine rejects each horn of this trilemma, for he holds that God can eternally will a change. What God eternally wills is not itself eternal in the sense in which God himself is eternal; for though there was no time when what he eternally wills was not, what he eternally wills is nevertheless contingent upon his will. This response is sufficient for Augustine to rebut the claim of those who may argue that since any act of creation implies a change in God the universe must have been created an infinitely long time ago. Augustine's answer is that God can immutably will to create, or immutably will to change what he has created. Willing a change does not imply changing a will.

Although there was no time when God could have decided to create a universe different from the one that he did in fact create, nevertheless, his eternally free decision to create was not necessary. It was an act of God's will. The world may be created timelessly and nevertheless be contingent. As Anthony Kenny has expressed it, in commenting on Wyclif's views:

God cannot change from knowing that p to knowing that not-p, or from willing p to be the case to not willing that p be the case; but when he knows that p is the case, sometimes (where p is a contingent truth) it would have been possible from all eternity that he knew that not-p was the case. If this seems difficult to grasp, Wyclif reminds us that even in human affairs it is often possible that p's being the case is something that depends on a free action of mine, and yet there has never been a time when I can alter the truth-value of p.[40]

GOD AND THE CREATION OF THE WORLD

Now to Book XII of the *Confessions*. Having looked at Augustine's treatment of 'In the beginning God created the heavens and the earth' we shall examine his reflections on the remainder of the words of Genesis 1:1–3, according to which the heavens and the earth were created without form and void and in darkness.

As with his meditations upon time, Augustine begins with a prayer to God for understanding. 'Speak to me, instruct me.'[41] He believes that he has already received understanding from God. He has come to recognise that God alone is eternal and immortal; that he has created everything that exists that is distinct from himself, and that time does not exist apart from the creation but is the measure of the changes that the created realm undergoes.

Augustine's view of the creation must be understood against the background of Neoplatonist thought which greatly influenced him. This influence was not unconscious. Part of the understanding that Augustine is seeking comes from his desire to integrate the Christian revelation with non-Christian forms of thought, and particularly in discerning where that integration should stop. He was prepared to use resources beside the Bible and his own unaided reflection on it in order to gain understanding. This is not surprising when one considers the influences that reading Neoplatonist writers had on the formation of his mind during his conversion recorded earlier in the *Confessions*. He recounts what he regards as the favourable influence of the Platonists, for he learned 'from them to seek for immaterial truth'.[42] It is not so much that he uses such sources eclectically as that he greatly valued the Platonists, and what he derived from reading them became part of his permanent intellectual equipment. However, he did not hesitate to differ from them where he believed that Christian teaching required it.

To see this we need particularly to have in mind Plato's account of the creation in the *Timaeus*, which portrays the Demiurge as someone who brings intelligibility to eternal matter as a craftsman works on wood or stone.

God therefore, wishing that all things should be good, and so far as possible nothing be imperfect, and finding the visible universe in a state not of rest but of inharmonious and disorderly motion, reduced it to order from disorder, as he judged that order was in every way better.[43]

Although there are very similar structural elements between this account and the account of creation that Augustine favours, he is emphatic on the point, against the Platonists, that creation is *ex nihilo*.

Augustine begins his extended meditation on Genesis 1:1 by making a sharp distinction between the heavens and the earth on the one hand and what he calls the 'heaven of heavens'.[44] The heaven of heavens is not a physical realm, the set of remote galaxies, say, but a metaphysical realm the nature of which we shall need to try to get clearer about as we proceed with our understanding of Augustine. He sees himself as drawing out the implications of this verse in a way – one way, but perhaps not the only way – that is consistent with the account he has already given of God's relation to time and his creation and the rest of his beliefs. His treatment of the verse indicates that he regards is as a kind of cryptic and abbreviated metaphysical statement, and his exegesis of the text is designed to unpack its meaning, or one of its meanings, in a way which is consistent with his general metaphysical reflections on time.

So, when God is said to create the heavens and the earth, we are to understand two things. 'The earth' is the totality of the physical creation; and 'the heavens' are not the starry heavens (because the starry heavens are part of the physical creation and, at this point in the Genesis story, not yet formed) but a

> kind of creation in the realm of the intellect. Without being coeternal with you, O Trinity, it nevertheless participates in your eternity. From the sweet happiness of contemplating you, it finds power to check its mutability. Without any lapse to which its createdness makes it liable, by cleaving to you it escapes all the revolving vicissitudes of the temporal process.[45]

These obscure words not only express Neoplatonic ideas, but the New Testament conception (as conveyed, for example, in the Epistle to the Hebrews) that what is on earth is a pattern or replica of what exists in a perfect form in heaven, and that this heaven, the destiny of the Christian, is where the vision of God is to be enjoyed. The heaven in question appears to be a sort of ideal, divinely-willed archetype which exists in complete form in the mind of God. By contrast, when God made the heaven and earth out of the formless void, the void which he himself created, the heaven referred to here is the visible heaven. At first glance it may seem from this that the earth and heaven received shape or form in accordance with the forms of the divine intelligence, forms expressed in or conveyed by the heaven of heavens.

Augustine personifies the heaven of heavens. It contemplates God; it is created, yet does not change, and so is a counter-example to what we earlier took to be Augustine's principle that whatever is created changes. What does Augustine mean by these rather opaque expressions? Bearing in mind Augustine's Platonist leanings, an initial suggestion might be that the creation of the visible heavens and the earth is in accordance with the divine will or pattern which though it exists in contemplation of God's eternity is not necessary, as God himself is necessary, since God might in principle have created a universe in accordance with a different pattern. With our discussion of Hawking in mind, we might even think that the heaven of heavens contained sets of equations which any heaven and earth to be created must be created in accordance with.

How more exactly the heaven of heavens is to be thought of partly depends upon settling the question of what precise function the 'heaven of heavens' plays, according to Augustine. And it is not easy to answer this question. As hinted already, it is natural to think of the heaven of heavens functioning as Platonic ideas, as the eternal, immaculate prototypes or paradigms of those general features of the world which are liable to change and to be corrupted. While there is, most certainly, this contrast between the eternal and the mutable throughout Augustine's discussion, there is little *direct* suggestion that the forms of the created universe of change are patterned after the changeless forms of the heaven of heavens. But there is some:

> For this physical totality, which is not in its entirety present in every part of it, has received a beautiful form in its very lowest things, and at the bottom is our earth. But in comparison with 'the heaven of heaven', even the heaven of our earth is earth. And it is not absurd to affirm that both of these vast physical systems (viz. the heavens and the earth) are earth in relation to that heaven whose nature lies beyond knowledge, which belongs to the Lord, not to the sons of men.[46]

As we have seen, 'heaven and earth' is Augustine's way of referring to the whole of created reality. So there was first the creation of the formless void (Genesis 1:2) and then the shaping of that void. The shaping, the receiving of a beautiful form, is in some obscure way derived from the pattern of the 'heaven of heavens'. But there is no direct suggestion of a conceptual relation between the heaven of heavens and the heaven and the earth, such that the heaven and the earth were given form *in accordance with* the forms of the heaven of heavens.

Augustine makes the contrast between the creation of two things created without changing; one is the heaven of heavens, 'so given form that, although mutable, yet without any cessation of its contemplation, without any interruption caused by change, it experiences unswerving enjoyment of your eternity and immutability'.[47] It is by contemplating the divine nature that the heaven of heavens is saved from change; though liable to change, it does not change. By contrast, at the other end of the scale is formless matter which, because it is formless cannot change, because in order to change what changes must have form, since change is the movement from one form to another:

> Only a person whose empty heart makes his mind roll and reel with private fantasies would try to tell me that temporal successiveness can still be manifested after all form has been subtracted and annihilated, so that the only remaining element is formlessness, through the medium of which a thing is changed and transformed from one species to another. It is absolutely impossible for time to exist without changes and movements. And where there is no form there can be no changes.[48]

However, not everything that Augustine says about the heaven of heavens favours this interpretation. For Augustine also states that this template, if that is what it is, is not co-eternal with God.[49] 'Without being coeternal with you, O Trinity, it nevertheless participates in your eternity'.[50] So the heaven of heavens is not part of the character of God. For unlike God, it is not necessary. At places Augustine personifies this 'heaven of heavens'; it has 'affection';[51] it is a creature experiencing happiness. It is 'the House of God', it has 'citizens'.[52] These words suggest that the heaven of heavens is a realm of being, not a set of abstract ideas, and thus casts doubt on the idea that the 'heaven of heavens' is a sort of blueprint in terms of which the heaven and the earth were created.

A further reason for doubting that the heaven of heavens is the pattern for the creation of the heavens and the earth is that Augustine says that the heaven and the earth were made out of the original created formlessness. When Augustine says that by comparison with the heaven of heavens even the heaven of our earth is earth, this may suggest a relation similar to that between the incorruptible Platonic forms and the changing qualities of perceptible things. Yet there is no direct textual evidence to support the view that the heaven and the earth participate in and gain their beauty from the forms of the 'heaven of heavens'.[53]

A final reason for doubting this interpretation is that some of Augustine's language about the heaven of heavens suggests not so much a template as an end, the *telos* of the creation of the heaven and the earth. It is heaven, the prospective abode of the people of God, the place or state in which they too will enjoy the presence of God directly and so be kept in purity. Augustine thus says that the 'heaven of heaven' is

> the intellectual, non-physical heaven where the intelligence's knowing is a matter of simultaneity – not in part, not in an enigma, not through a mirror, in total openness, 'face to face' (1 Cor.13:12)[54]

So when it is written that God created the heavens and the earth, and the earth was without form and void, Augustine interprets the words with great precision, with greater precision that he did in his earlier writings on this theme. Thus in his work *On Genesis Against the Manichees*, written around AD 388 (*The Confessions* was written about ten years later) Augustine states that:

> All these expressions, whether heaven and earth, or the earth invisible and without order, and the abyss with darkness, or the water over which was borne the Spirit of God, are names for unformed matter . . . beneath all these names there was the invisible and formless matter, out of which God created the world.[55]

But in *The Confessions* Augustine takes 'heaven' to be the 'heaven of heavens' and the 'earth' to be formless matter, 'invisible and unorganised'.[56] The creative word of God gives form to the matter, while the heaven of heavens continues changeless, supported in this by its enjoyment of the divine eternity.

Despite the way in which Augustine lays out his account in terms of the eternal God, the heaven of heavens, the creator of a void, and then the forming of that void into an intelligible creation, it would be a mistake to think that Augustine held that God first, temporally speaking, created a formless void, and then, after creating it, imposed form upon it. Rather there is a temporal simultaneity here; the creation of the void and its being given form are two temporally indistinguishable actions; the priority of the formless void is simply a conceptual priority. Augustine's argument for this priority is that being formless the void would be incapable of change and so would not be in time. 'For the changes of things make time as their forms undergo variation and change'.[57] If the void were thought of as a temporally separate creation, such a supposition would contradict his account. The creation of a formed physical totality logically requires that there be something which is formed, but what it is formed out of does not have a temporally distinguishable identity.

Matter is conceptually prior to that which is made out of it. Furthermore, it is passively prior. The matter does not itself contribute to its own form, but it 'waits' for the Creator's imprint in accordance with the pattern of the heaven of heavens. So it is not prior in the sense that it actively contributes to what is made; it is rather that it is made. Augustine draws an analogy between a singer and a song:

> Nor is priority one of temporal interval here. For it is not that first we emit unformed sound without it being song, and later adapt or shape it into the form of a song, in the way we make a box out of wood or a vase out of silver. . . . When a song is sung, the sound is heard simultaneously. It is not that unformed sound comes first and is then shaped into song. . . . That is why a song has its being in the sound it embodies, and its sound is its matter. The matter is given form to be the song.[58]

He stresses that the earth which was at first (conceptually speaking) created 'was not such as we now see and touch'.[59] It was 'almost nothing because it was still totally formless'.[60]

Both the 'heaven of heavens' (the 'House' of God, as Augustine expresses it) and the formless void are outside time, though of course it would be nonsense to suppose that they existed like this *for a time*. Rather Augustine's point is that both form and matter are created, and it is only upon matter being shaped by form that change occurs and there is time:

> Out of this were made a second heaven and a visible ordered earth and beautiful waters and everything else mentioned in the creation narrative after days had come into existence. These things are such that they are subject to ordered changes of movement and form, and so are subject to the successiveness of time.[61]

UNDERSTANDING AND BIBLICAL INTERPRETATION

What we have sketched so far is Augustine's endeavour to gain understanding of one of the central and formative propositions of his faith. The rather anthropomorphic language of Genesis 1 is given a theoretical interpretation, one which, Augustine believes, is its deep meaning. What is noteworthy is that Augustine takes the text of Genesis with great seriousness, and gives the words a metaphysical import of the sort which, at first sight, they do not have. So in this case at least, to gain understanding is to gain insight into a truer, deeper meaning of a text of the Bible. As we have seen, Augustine distinguishes between the surface meaning, and the depth of God's utterance.[62] He sees philosophical reflection and biblical interpretation as a joint enterprise. He does not see what he is doing as the imposition on the biblical text of philosophical ideas, nor is he interested only in a jejune, literalistic interpretation of the text. He sees his own philosophical ideas derived from the Platonists and the biblical text as each providing mutual support and confirmation. So philosophical or conceptual understanding is tied very closely to the gaining of understanding of the meaning of a text.

In a kind of refrain Augustine refers to the inner ear,[63] a sort of direct intuition, through which God teaches Augustine, and gives him 'understanding'. He uses the metaphor of an 'ear' to emphasise the receptive character of the understanding that he has achieved. What he has gained is not primarily the result of human effort but is a gift of God's grace in answer to his prayer. This inner ear is clearly being distinguished from an ordinary ear, through which we receive sounds in some natural language or other. The products of the inner ear are what we understand from what comes to our minds through our outer ear.[64] It is the 'inner ear' which, by processes of inference,[65] gives a matching of text and philosophical reflection.

Further, what Augustine offers the reader in Book XII is his 'provisional understanding', his 'interim judgement'.[66] This is perhaps not so surprising given the fact that Augustine had only come to this view comparatively recently. His hesitancy here is in rather stark contrast to the definiteness of his views on Genesis 1:1, God's relation to time, and what follows from these views. He sees a limit to what understanding is possible, within which various interpretations are allowable.[67]

Augustine recognises that it is possible to love the words of Genesis as he does and yet to give them a different meaning, though one that does not contradict what he is saying, but which is complementary to it. He shows this by considering seriously an objection to his own account. The objection he considers is that since Moses, (whom he takes to be the author of the book of Genesis) cannot have had in mind what Augustine says the words of Genesis 1:1 mean, those words cannot bear that meaning. On the view that lies behind the objection, meaning is tied to intention in that the meaning cannot be inconsistent with, or even other than, what the author intends. 'They say "What that man had in mind was what we say he meant, and this is what he expressed in those words".'[68] And Moses intended to speak in a 'rough and carnal' way to people who could not understand in any other way, and so to refer only to the visible works of

God. So that on this interpretation the text of Genesis 1:1 is restricted in its scope to cover only that which is physical and has no further reference because there is no authorial intention to refer to the intelligible ground of what is physical.

Augustine reviews several other possible interpretations of the words.[69] For example that 'heaven and earth' is a compound phrase equivalent to unformed matter.[70] Augustine is appealingly charitable with these other interpretations. There is nothing wrong *a priori* with a variety of interpretations, providing that each one is true:

> In Bible study all of us are trying to find and grasp the meaning of the author we are reading, and when we believe him to be revealing truth, we do not dare to think he said anything which we either know or think to be incorrect. As long as each interpreter is endeavouring to find in the holy scriptures the meaning of the author who wrote it, what evil is it if an exegesis he gives is one shown to be true by you, light of all sincere souls, even if the author whom he is reading did not have that idea and, though he had grasped a truth, had not discerned that seen by the interpreter?[71]

So in certain cases there can be a range of understandings, the criterion for which is whether they are true, that is, whether they accord with other elements of the faith.[72] So the original text, the text accepted by faith, is ambiguous; while certain interpretations of the text may be ruled out, there remains a range of meanings that are possible. By this Augustine clearly does not mean that in the interpretation of the Bible anything goes, but rather that there are levels of understanding. And provided that the interpreter of the text of Genesis 1:1 agrees with him on the basics of *creatio ex nihilo* as Augustine understands them, then a variety of understandings of how the creation was effected are permissible. He lists a further five permissible interpretations of Genesis. 1:1.[73]

What point about understanding (in our sense) is Augustine making here? Simply that there are limits to the extent to which understanding can be refined, and beyond those limits is a permissible divergence, permissible when measured against the text that is being interpreted. He makes the further point that if two people hold true but different beliefs, these beliefs are true because they correspond to the will of the immutably true God; hence they are not the private property of the one who has formulated them and who holds them, and we should therefore be tolerant of the truth wherever it is to be found.[74] If we prefer our own true belief to those of others we reveal that our love is not so much for the truth as for our own opinion because it is our own.

NOTES

1. Augustine, *Confessions*, p.252.
2. Augustine, *Confessions*, pp.223f.
3. Augustine, *Confessions*, p.225.
4. To say that time is relative in this sense is not to be confused with the theory of physical relativity. Neither depends upon the other.
5. See Shoemaker, 'Time Without Change', and particularly Swinburne, *The Christian God*, Ch.4.
6. See Augustine's later discussion of the different senses of 'priority' in *Confessions*, p.269.
7. For this reason Augustine would be able to rebut the argument that since God's timeless existence is simultaneous with, say, the Battle of Hastings and the Battle of Arnhem, these two events are themselves simultaneous. His existence is not simultaneous with any event in time. (For an example of this argument see Swinburne, *The Coherence of Theism*, pp.220f.)
8. Augustine, *Confessions*, p.269.
9. Augustine, *Confessions*, p.224.
10. Augustine, *Confessions*, p.254.
11. Augustine, *Confessions*, p.231.
12. Augustine, *Confessions*, p.232.
13. Swinburne, *The Christian God*, p.74.
14. Cf. Gale's critique in *The Nature and Existence of God*, pp.231f.
15. Augustine, *Confessions*, p.232.
16. Augustine, *Confessions*, pp.232f.
17. Augustine, *Confessions*, p.233.
18. Augustine, *Confessions*, p.234.
19. Augustine, *Confessions*, p.234.
20. Augustine, *Confessions*, pp.235f.
21. Augustine, *Confessions*, pp.238f.
22. Augustine, *Confessions*, pp.240f.
23. Augustine, *Confessions*, p.243.
24. For a discussion of Ockham's views see Gerard Hughes, *The Nature of God*.
25. Swinburne, *The Christian God*, Ch.4.
26. Boethius, *The Consolation of Philosophy*, v.6.
27. See, for example, Kretzmann and Stump, 'Eternity'; Helm, *Eternal God*; and Leftow, *Time and Eternity*.
28. Augustine, *Confessions*, p.230.
29. Augustine, *Confessions*, p.224.
30. Kirwan, *Augustine*, pp.154f.
31. Quoted by Kirwan, *Augustine*, p.153.
32. Hawking, *A Brief History of Time*, p.10.
33. Hawking, *A Brief History of Time*, p.52.
34. Hawking, *A Brief History of Time*, p.46.
35. Hawking, *A Brief History of Time*, p.192.
36. Hawking, *A Brief History of Time*, p.192.
37. Hawking, *A Brief History of Time*, p.192.
38. Hawking, *A Brief History of Time*, pp.192f.
39. Swinburne, *The Existence of God*, p.286.
40. Kenny, *Wyclif*, p.34. The issue is discussed further in Helm, *Eternal God*, Ch.10.
41. Augustine, *Confessions*, p.251.
42. Augustine, *Confessions*, p.129.
43. Plato, *Timaeus*, p.42.
44. Augustine, *Confessions*, p.246.
45. Augustine, *Confessions*, p.250.
46. Augustine, *Confessions*, p.246.
47. Augustine, *Confessions*, p.253.
48. Augustine, *Confessions*, p.252.
49. Augustine, *Confessions*, pp.250f.
50. Augustine, *Confessions*, p.250.
51. Augustine, *Confessions*, p.251.

52. Augustine, *Confessions*, p.252.
53. Further support for this view can be gained from the description that Augustine earlier gives of his vision, *Confessions*, p.171.
54. Augustine, *Confessions*, p.253.
55. Augustine, *Two Books On Genesis Against The Manichees*, p.60. See also pp.151f.
56. Augustine, *Confessions*, p.253.
57. Augustine, *Confessions*, p.250.
58. Augustine, *Confessions*, p.269.
59. Augustine, *Confessions*, p.249.
60. Augustine, *Confessions*, pp.249f.
61. Augustine, *Confessions*, p.253.
62. Augustine, *Confessions*, p.254. This, the idea of layers of meaning in a scriptural text, is one aspect of what Stump calls the 'dynamic view of revelation'. Every text has at least one good and true interpretation, and probably more than one. 'Revelation and Biblical Exegesis: Augustine, Aquinas and Swinburne', p.184.
63. Augustine, *Confessions*, p.251.
64. Augustine, *Confessions*, p.254, 260.
65. Augustine, *Confessions*, p.255.
66. Augustine, *Confessions*, p.253.
67. Augustine, *Confessions*, pp.258f, 260f, 270f, 267f.
68. Augustine, *Confessions*, p.258.
69. Stump, 'Revelation and Biblical Exegesis: Augustine, Aquinas and Swinburne'.
70. Augustine, *Confessions*, p.259.
71. Augustine, *Confessions*, pp.259f.
72. Stump, 'Revelation and Biblical Exegesis: Augustine, Aquinas and Swinburne', p.191.
73. Augustine, *Confessions*, pp.260f. Augustine's views on biblical interpretation are given at greater length in *On Christian Doctrine*.
74. Augustine, *Confessions*, p.265.

5

Anselm's Proslogion

The importance which Anselm, Prior of Bec and later Archbishop of Canterbury, attached to the idea of faith seeking understanding may be gauged from the fact that 'Faith Seeking Understanding' is the sub-title which Anselm gave to the *Proslogion*. The work is chiefly known today for its presentation of the ontological argument, but Anselm intended its scope to include not only the question of the existence of God, but also the co-possibility of his attributes, particularly a reconciliation of the idea of God as the supreme good with what was necessary for human redemption. He contrasts what he is attempting in the *Proslogion* with what he achieved in his earlier work, the *Monologion*:

> I began to ask myself whether perhaps a single argument could be found which would constitute an independent proof and would suffice by itself to demonstrate that (1) God truly (really) exists, that (2) He is the Supreme Good, needing no one else yet needed by all else in order to exist and to fare well, and that (3) He is whatever else we believe about the Divine Substance. . . . I wrote the following short work on this subject (and on various others) in the role of someone endeavouring to elevate his mind toward contemplating God and seeking to understand what he believes.[1]

Despite the modesty of Anselm's expression the ambition is clear; one independent argument to demonstrate some of the central tenets of the faith. The entire work is intended as an expression of this Augustinian idea, though the economy of Anselm's style compared with the rather florid, rhetorical style of Augustine could hardly be greater. In these chapters Anselm reflects on the reality and the character of God as (he believes) this is revealed in Scripture as 'that than which no greater can be conceived'. By faith he accepts the existence of this God on the authority of the Christian revelation, and he is a participant in the Christian way of life. But, as he tells us, he wishes to gain understanding of the nature of God, in whom he trusts, and this involves him in attempting to discern the inner necessity of God's existence. Identifying and establishing this necessity and drawing out some of its implications is a good part of what Anselm means when he refers to the rational basis of faith. He is not striving to show that the faith is 'reasonable' in some vague sense, but that it has an inner necessity; God necessarily exists, and what God does is congruent with what he is.

What then is this single argument? It would be a mistake to identify this solely with the argument for which the *Proslogion* is most famous, the ontological argument, because Anselm sees the scope of the *Proslogion* to be wider than this. But Anselm cannot mean that the *Proslogion* is in the form of one continuous argument, because it obviously is not. Perhaps the most plausible suggestion is that the one argument is encapsulated in Anselm's formula 'a Being than which no greater can be conceived'. This is the one pivotal concept, the one overriding consideration of the *Proslogion.*[2] According to Anselm such a concept, when properly understood, implies the real existence of that to which the concept refers. And though this concept presents certain *prima facie* difficulties for other areas of Christian belief, it is in fact the means of resolving these difficulties.

For Anselm, to gain understanding is to gain an appreciation of the inner nature of things by being able to remove or explain elements of the faith which seem accidental or *ad hoc* or even incoherent, or in some other way unworthy of God. These difficulties are only apparent, and disappear once we take into account the true nature of God. Having discerned, as he believes, the inner necessity of God's existence, Anselm then extends his treatment to the character of God as the supreme good. But there is a difference in Anselm's procedure as the work unfolds. He believes that God has shown him that there is an inner necessity to God's existence, and the demonstration of this rests on the idea of God as the most perfect being. The remainder of the work is then occupied with showing that the nature of God as the most perfect being is consistent with his being the Redeemer. Chapter 5 is crucial, for Anselm establishes there that God is whatever is better to be than not to be, reiterating the point in his reply to Gaunilo, who had written a response to Anselm's ontological argument. Anselm then proceeds to show that with respect to whatever it is that God is, in virtue of being that than which a greater cannot be conceived, is consistent with other things that need to be said about God. That, for example, his justice, which is part of his perfection, is consistent with his mercy, another part.

Anselm endeavours to establish the inner necessity of God's existence in the first four chapters of the work, while in the remainder he reflects more fully on the being and character of God, the being than which no greater can be thought. These later chapters are characterised by the same meditative and reflective spirit. Anselm expresses incomprehension and bafflement at some aspect or other of the character of God, and prays to God for enlightenment; this is followed by the achieving of insight and illumination through intellectual reflection, the gaining of understanding, the removal of paradox and apparent self-contradiction.[3] But this is not regarded by Anselm as an easy or automatic process, nor is it one without limit. He does not believe that the inner necessity of all the ways of God can be discerned. He recognises that God dwells in inaccessible light which his understanding is not able to comprehend. God is not only greater than which can be thought, but he is something greater than that which *could* be thought, 'than which nothing better can be thought'.[4] One example of Anselm hitting the intellectual limits concerns God's choice of some and not others for salvation:

> But if we can somehow grasp why You can will to save the wicked, surely we cannot at all understand why from among those who are equally wicked You save some and not others because of Your supreme goodness, and condemn some and not others because of Your supreme justice.[5]

Earlier, in Chapter 1, we contrasted two accounts of the faith seeking understanding project, one more propositionalist, the other more personalist in character. In the *Proslogion*, at least, these two aspects are found intertwined together; the work is an address to God, and hence has a deeply personal cast, but it is also intensely intellectual. Thus in his Chapter 1 Anselm expresses the believer's intense longing for direct acquaintance with God:

> He pants to see You, but Your face is too far removed from him. He desires to approach You, but Your dwelling place is inaccessible. He desires to find You but does not know Your abode. He longs to seek for You but does not know Your countenance. O Lord, You are my God and my Lord; yet never have I seen You. . . . I was made for seeing You; but not yet have I done that for which I was made.[6]

And again in *Proslogion* Chapter 14:

> My soul, have you found that for which you were looking? You were
> seeking God, and you have found that He is something highest of all –
> than which nothing better can be thought. [And you have seen that]
> this being is life itself, light, wisdom, goodness, eternal blessedness,
> and blessed eternity, and that this being exists everywhere and always
> . . . Lord my God, my Creator and Renewer, tell my yearning soul
> what else You are other than what it has seen, so that it may see
> clearly what it longs [to see].[7]

And in the final paragraphs of the work:

> O Lord, I ask for what You counsel through our marvellous
> Counsellor; may I receive what You promise through Your Truth,
> so that my joy may be full. God of truth, I ask to receive it, so that my
> joy may be full. Until then, let my mind meditate upon (what You
> have promised), let my tongue speak of it. Let my heart love it; let my
> mouth proclaim it. Let my soul hunger for it; let my flesh thirst for it;
> let my whole being desire it until such time as I enter into the joy of
> my Lord, the triune God, blessed forever. Amen.[8]

The understanding that Anselm seeks consists in the clarification of
statements about God. Anselm sees the faith seeking understanding
project, which results, he believes, in 'understanding God a little' as
helping him towards the direct acquaintance with God, but as always
falling short of that goal in this life. So for Anselm there is no incompatibility between the two approaches to the knowledge of God, provided that
one is seen as anticipatory and preparatory for the other. Such an approach
as this would hardly seem to justify Richard Campbell's verdict that
'Anselm's contemplation seem to be essentially intellectual in character,
concerned with rational apprehension rather than affective experience',[9]
for clearly enough the two were inseparable in Anselm's life. But at the
same time, one can hardly classify Anselm as a mystical theologian!

Anselm's procedure here may be contrasted with that of rationalist
theology. Rationalism requires the elimination of mystery and paradox
from theology as a condition of believing; or at least as a condition of
continuing to believe. The propositions of the faith have to meet some *a
priori* criteria of intelligibility, either rational or empirical, before they are
worthy of belief, though even in the case of text-book rationalists such as
Descartes there is a recognition of divine mystery and inscrutability; in the
case of Descartes, such mystery was the result of divine omnipotence.

By contrast, Anselm is first a believer and a follower of Christ, and then seeks the resolution of the problems that arise once faith becomes reflective, once the believer begins to reflect rationally on the propositions he believes. But the resolution of the problems that arise can only ever be partial. For God remains incomprehensible. By this Anselm does not mean that all human language about God is mumbo-jumbo, but that the nature of God is not fully comprehensible by the finite mind, though it is partly comprehended:

> Truly, O Lord, this is the inaccessible light in which You dwell. For truly nothing else can penetrate this light so that it sees You dwelling there. Truly, then, I cannot stand to look at this light because it is too resplendent for me. Nevertheless, whatever I see by means of this light – even as a frail eye sees what it does by means of sunlight, which it could not stand to look at in the sun itself. My understanding is not able to comprehend this light, which shines forth so brilliantly.[10]

Comprehension is a matter of degree. Anselm hopes and believes he will achieve at least some comprehension as the result of his search, comprehension sufficient to discern the inner rationale of his faith. Even in the life to come, when faith turns to sight, the finite creature will be unable to comprehend the infinite Creator. So Anselm would see nothing strange or embarrassing in having a measure of understanding accompanied by remaining bafflement. For him this is the normal intellectual condition of any reflective Christian. And this is not unreasonable; why should the creature expect to penetrate the mind of the Creator?

This attitude of Anselm's to what he believes is characteristic of many other philosophical attitudes. For example, we take for granted the reality and objectivity of the furniture in the room. This taking for granted may be said to correspond to Anselmian 'faith'. But if we have any amount of philosophical curiosity, we shall wish to enquire more closely into precisely what it is that we accept. Is the furniture objectively there? What does this mean? What is the best account that may be given of the relation of what is objective to what is undoubtedly subjective, my sensory states and my thoughts as I look at the furniture? Satisfactory answers to these questions, if they are forthcoming, correspond to Anselmian 'understanding', and like that understanding such answers do not solve every philosophical question that may be asked about the furniture.

In the remainder of this chapter we shall concentrate on Anselm's exposition of the ontological argument (or arguments) in Chapters 1–4 of the *Proslogion*, with a sidelong glance at Gaunilo's objection to it, and at Anselm's reply. We shall not primarily be concerned with the validity and soundness of the arguments, but with what by his deployment of them

Anselm believed that he was achieving; we shall explore the character of the arguments in the hope of getting clearer the sort of achievement that counted for him as a gain in understanding.

As we have already noted, the context is one of prayer and meditation on God, not the development of a natural theology to be deployed in the furtherance of apologetics. In the Introduction Anselm indicates that in offering his 'independent proof' of God's existence he is adopting the style of a meditation. This meditation is not a relaxed procedure, but one of great intellectual intensity. In it Anselm devotes himself to God, and one might say that the ontological argument is the way that Anselm has of intellectualising that devotion; or rather, of intellectualising the idea of that being who alone is worthy of such devotion.[11]

> Supposing, then, that to record what I had joyously discovered would please its readers, I wrote the following short work on this subject (and on various others) in the role of someone endeavouring to elevate his mind toward contemplating God and seeking to understand what he believes.[12]

This is a conscious decision about the literary character of the work he is writing. Nevertheless Anselm clearly thinks that this is a natural stance to adopt, one entirely consistent with his starting point, that of someone who already believes. The existence of God, and faith in him, are thus presupposed. One can take it that even if his endeavour to gain understanding were to have failed (and Anselm recognises that there is no guarantee of success), he would not reject his faith but return to the stance of someone who believes upon authority, and who continues to live the life of faith.

The meditative form of the work has led some to suppose that the famous ontological argument, which forms the intellectual heart of these passages, is not an argument after all, but a prayer, and that we deform or distort what Anselm is saying if we consider it 'abstractly'. But if this were true then the generations of philosophical discussion of the ontological argument must be based upon a distortion of Anselm's original intention, and of his procedure.

But such a polarising between meditating and arguing must be a mistake. Why? We have already seen that while the work has a meditative stance it is not wholly meditative in character, for Anselm intersperses his addresses to God with reflections of a more abstract kind on the being and character of God. Another reason for thinking that this is not wholly meditation, is that it is Anselm's central concern to offer what he calls an 'independent argument' for God's existence, a point to which we shall return later. In any case it has not proved difficult to show that an argument (or arguments) can be extracted from these meditative passages. But while this is true, it might not quite meet the point, since perhaps an argument is being extracted from the text in violence to Anselm's original intentions. The fact that we can extract an argument from his words does not mean that Anselm intended to offer an argument. But there is no reason to think that Anselm was not intending to offer an argument; for as we have seen, he explicitly tells us that he is.

AN INDEPENDENT ARGUMENT

But do we need the eye of faith in order to discern the validity of the argument, or to be persuaded of its soundness? By calling this an *independent* argument Anselm seems to have thought of it as one which has a validity independent of the presuppositions of faith; it is not an appeal to authority. On Anselm's view one who assumes a certain definition of God (for whatever reason) ought, if he has the necessary intellectual ability, to conclude that such a God cannot fail to exist.

It has been debated whether 'God' functions as a proper name, a word that is primarily denotative in character, like 'John Smith', or as a description, like 'the man in the iron mask'. There is little doubt that Anselm is using the word as an abbreviation of a description, the description of 'a being than which no greater can be conceived'. And what he is endeavouring to show is that this description, one which all Christians (he believes) and others will accept, implies the necessary existence of God, and so to show that God's existence is capable of an 'independent' proof, independent of special revelation, one that does not rely upon the sole authority of that revelation. So Anselm can be seen as wishing to remove the seeming arbitrariness of belief, that it depends solely on the say-so of the Church, and so to show that it has an inner necessity to it which gives it an independence from the Church's proclamation, but at the same time vindicates that proclamation. God's nature is such that he cannot not exist. But this, though true, does not answer the question of whether the meaning that is given to 'God ' is derived from Christian special revelation alone, or is one that is more widely available.

A good reason for thinking that this is what Anselm means by an independent argument, and that he wishes it to be considered as such, is Anselm's behaviour when faced with the objections made by Gaunilo. It is striking that Anselm does not say 'Gaunilo, your objection to what I say about God's existence is beside the point; it is only of value if I am arguing for the existence of God. But I'm not doing that at all; I'm meditating on his existence.' Rather, Anselm does his best to answer the objections put by

Gaunilo, and in so doing develops his ontological argument further. So Anselm, here at least, would recognise no sharp contrast between meditating and arguing.

It is more pertinent to ask whether his argument is intended to be a piece of natural theology. Natural theology may be thought of as the project of deriving significant theological conclusions from premises which are non-theological and which any or most rational people would accept. Here the crucial thing for our purposes is whether Anselm starts from a position which might be generally acceptable to theist and non-theist alike. Is this not at least part of what Anselm means by presenting what he terms an 'independent argument'?

The ontological argument for God's existence is manifestly *a priori* in character. Unlike the cosmological and teleological arguments (for example) it does not depend upon premises which in turn depend on observation for their credibility. Rather, Anselm's argument depends solely on his belief that God is 'something than which nothing greater can be thought', a form of words which even the fool who says there is no God can understand. Or, at least, which even the fool thinks he can understand. For perhaps this is the thrust of his reply to Gaunilo, that while Gaunilo thinks that he understands he fails to.

But if this is so, then how can the fool say in his heart that there is no God? Perhaps he can if we bear in mind the distinction between thinking of the word, and thinking of that to which the word refers:

> For in one sense an object is thought when the word signifying it is thought, and in another when what the object is (i.e. its essence) is understood. Thus, in the first sense but not at all in the second, God can be thought not to exist.[13]

He can be thought not to exist only if the words for God are not fully understood. And the trouble with the fool who does not believe in God, according to Anselm, is that he rests content with the words, and does not go on to meditate on the character of that reality to which the words point. Here, perhaps, Anselm comes close to asserting that understanding ought to lead to believing; the fool does not believe because he does not understand.

In developing his argument Anselm draws a contrast between something which is merely understood and what really exists. Here one may note once again the ontological realism that is a presupposition of the entire faith seeking understanding tradition. For God to really exist is for him to have an existence that is independent of any human belief or speculation. Anselm says that the fool must have in his understanding the words 'something than which nothing greater can be thought'. Yet one may have these words in the understanding and yet not understand them; this was the fool's predicament. But the question is, can these words *only* exist in the understanding? If they are in the understanding, must there not also be in reality what these words describe? For is not what really exists greater than what exists in the understanding alone?

The question of whether the ontological argument is a piece of natural theology, or more precisely whether it is intended by Anselm to be a piece of natural theology, depends solely on the question of whether or not this account of God depends upon sources that would be accepted by any or most rational people; in short, does Anselm's account of God as a being than which no greater can be conceived depend upon special revelation, the Bible or church tradition, in a way that only those who accept these authorities will accept his definition? If it does, then though the ontological argument for God's existence is an argument, it ought not, strictly speaking, to be regarded as a piece of natural theology. If, by contrast, though Anselm derives his definition of God from special revelation, but it is in any case a definition that would be generally acceptable, then whether or not the argument convinces, it is a piece of natural theology, and those who, in the long tradition of discussion of the argument have treated it as such, have been correct to do so.

There is certainly room for investigating where Anselm's account of God came from. Did it come from the Bible? Did it come exclusively from the Bible? It has been argued by Karl Barth and others that both the argument of Chapters 1 and 2, and that of Chapters 3 and 4, depend upon the revealed Name of God. Barth claims that the phrase 'that than which no greater can be conceived' is not an abbreviated statement of the nature of God, but is simply a prohibition:

> *Aliquid quo nihil maius cogitari possit* is therefore on no account the condensed formula of a doctrine of God that is capable of later expansion but it is a genuine description (*significatio*), one Name of God, selected from among the various revealed Names of God for this occasion and for this particular purpose, in such a way that to reach a knowledge of God the revelation of this same God from some other source is clearly assumed.[14]

> Anselm did not regard this designation for God as a non-essential theologoumenon and certainly not as a constituent part of a universal human awareness of God, but as an article of faith. . . . Thus in no sense is he of the opinion that he produced this formula out of his own head but he declares quite explicitly the source from which he

considers it to have to come to him: when he gives God a Name, it is not like one person forming a concept of another person; rather it is as a creature standing before his Creator. In this relationship which is actualised by virtue of God's revelation, as he thinks of God he knows that he is under this prohibition; he can conceive of nothing greater, to be precise, better, beyond God without lapsing into the absurdity, excluded for faith, of placing himself above God in attempting to conceive of this greater.[15]

Barth recognises that the identification of the one and only being who is such that none greater can be thought with God has yet to be made. So it is not strictly true that Anselm simply assumes that his account of God as a being than which no greater can be conceived is straightforwardly derived from special revelation:

But this equation which is vital for the Proof in its general and special form, is it valid? Does God really bear this Name? Must everyone who conceives of God really conceive of the prohibition expressed in this Name. . . . How do we know that God is really named 'that than which a greater cannot be conceived'? We know it because that is how God has revealed himself and because we believe him as he has revealed himself. But this knowing can be explained: We know it because on the basis of revelation and faith, we know that when we stand before God, we do not stand as any one being before any other being, but as a creature before his Creator.[16]

If Barth is correct then what Anselm is doing cannot be regarded as natural theology, but must be an exercise in revealed theology. For on Barth's view Anselm's argument that the God revealed in the Bible necessarily exists will only be acceptable to someone who first accepts this definition of God, and in accepting this definition one accepts the authoritative teaching of the Bible.[17] Is what Barth says about Anselm's procedure correct?

It does not follow that because a concept has a particular authoritative source, that there are no independent grounds for accepting it. I might accept my bird guide's description of a kite and then see one for myself. Anselm may as a matter of fact have derived the concept from the Bible but it may nonetheless have an independent plausibility.

Further, there is some circumstantial evidence which does not support the Barthian approach. In his work *On the Incarnation of the Word*, Anselm says:

If anyone will deign to read my two short works, viz., the *Mono-logion* and the *Proslogion* (which I wrote especially in order [to show] that what we hold by faith regarding the divine nature and its persons – excluding the topic of incarnation – can be proven by compelling reasons apart from [appeal to] the authority of Scripture). . . . I advanced these points (1) in order to defend our faith against those who, while unwilling to believe what they do not understand, deride those who do believe, and (2) in order to assist the devout striving of those who humbly seek to understand what they most steadfastly believe.[18]

This seems clear enough. In seeking to defend the faith it seems reasonable to suppose that Anselm thought that he was appealing to considerations that would convince those who did not believe because they could not understand.

It is true that in *Proslogion* Chapter 3 Anselm does identify the one than whom no greater can be conceived with the 'Lord our God', and this confirms the faith seeking understanding motif. But one must distinguish the fact that Anselm already has faith from the question of whether the concept of God which he employs is solely an article of faith. The one who is the being than which no greater can be conceived is the God in whom he has faith, but it does not follow from this that the concept depends upon special revelation alone for its validity. As Richard Campbell expresses it:

> The God who is believed by the Church to be something-than-which-nothing-greater-can-be-thought is the God whom *Anselm* now understands to be the one who exists so truly that he cannot be thought not to be. Anselm is confessing that the God who is Lord of the *Church* is also his God, the God of the inquiring *theologian*.[19]

Since God, the God of revelation, is supremely great, it is possible to develop rules for thinking about him. For example:

> For we believe about the Divine Substance whatever, absolutely speaking, can be thought to be better than its contradictory. For example, it is better to be eternal than not to be eternal, better to be good than not to be good, – or rather, to be goodness itself than not to be goodness itself.[20]

These rules are not themselves derived from special revelation, and are justified by the supremacy of God, by his worshipfulness; Anselm is developing the idea of a perfect being, of worshipfulness, *a priori*. And the particular great-making properties which he imputes to God are partly, at least, the result of rational reflection and of Anselm's own ideas about what constitutes perfection.

From such a passage it is clear that for Anselm 'perfection' has a purely formal character; for although he tells us that certain properties are perfections of God, greatness-making properties, nevertheless if he could be shown that these properties are not appropriately applied to God other properties would be and these, the replacement properties, would be the divine perfections. Whatever essential characteristics God has are perfections. So whatever turns out to be a perfection, God is by definition that than which a more perfect cannot be conceived. And for Anselm existence is unquestionably a perfection.

It does not matter for Anselm's purpose here that, say, being in time is not a perfection whereas being eternal is. Whatever is taken to be perfect would do, because it is the move from all perfection in the mind to all perfection in reality that Anselm needs for the development of his argument. Nevertheless, the list of divine perfections that Anselm favours sets the agenda for what is to follow, so in this sense it does matter.

Anselm stresses that the ontological argument was *conveyed* to him; he did not invent it as an apologetic strategy. It was not devised for that specific purpose. It 'began more and more to force itself insistently upon me, unwilling and resisting as I was'.[21] By meditation upon God it was borne in upon him that God is the most perfect being, whose existence is necessary. Yet while Anselm may be said to be doing natural theology, his procedure is quite different from that of another philosopher who employs a version of the ontological argument, Descartes.

In the *Meditations* Descartes was concerned not to meditate on the existence of God as an exercise in faith seeking understanding, but rather, having destroyed or placed in suspension all his former opinions by rational doubt, to seek to prove the existence of God from scratch. It is only after proving the existence of God that Descartes is able to meditate upon him.[22] Whereas for Anselm it is a fair question to ask what part the ontological argument plays in his life as a believer, it is impossible to ask a similar question of Descartes, because he does not approach the question of demonstrating the existence of God as a believer, but as someone recovering from sceptical doubt, a scepticism so all-encompassing as to include the question of God's existence, by the application of the clear and distinct ideas of his reason.

We have seen that though a concept of God might have its source in authoritative revelation, it nevertheless might be regarded as plausible on general grounds; it might not be unique to special revelation. It might also be that while Anselm thought that he derived the concept from special revelation, he did not in fact do so. A concept of God that has its origin and use in contexts that are other than Christian may be appropriated for

Christian use. This point about appropriation can be illustrated from the procedure of other Christian thinkers.

This appropriation does not necessarily involve conceptual change. To appropriate a concept of God from other contexts seems to be St Paul's procedure in Acts 17, and Augustine's in the *City of God* and elsewhere, and (to look no further) the procedure of John Calvin who says (alluding to Cicero), that there is 'no nation so barbarous, no people so savage, that they have not a deep-seated conviction that there is a God'.[23] By this, of course, Calvin means that the God of which people are deep-seatedly convinced is the true God, the only God.

Augustine's procedure in fact seems to be two-fold; if natural theology seeks an explanation of nature, he then argues that any proposed explanation which terminates within nature cannot be a true explanation, but to be a true explanation it must terminate only in something that is the source of nature:

> This their natural theology refers all these things to the world, which (would they avoid scruple of sacrilege) they should of right refer to the true God, the world's Maker and Creator of all souls and bodies.[24]

In this he seems to be echoing St Paul's thought that before their conversion the Galatians were slaves to those who by nature are no gods (Galatians 4:8), and his teaching, reported by Demetrius of Ephesus, that man-made gods are no gods at all. (Acts 19:26). They are no gods because their nature as gods was such as necessarily to disqualify them from taking the role of Creator and Lord of all, just as, at Lystra, St Paul points out that Zeus and Hermes compare unfavourably to the living God who made heaven and earth and sea and everything in them (Acts 14).

Alternatively, if such explanation terminates in something that is or could be the source of nature (as in the thought of Plato, or at least in Plato as interpreted by Augustine) then like St Paul at Athens (Acts 17), Augustine argues that this God is identical with the Christian God.[25] In disputing with the Epicureans and Stoics, St Paul appears to commit himself to the thought that, if we are created, our Creator must be the sort of being who could not be a human artefact. It is notorious that Augustine endorses the Platonic philosophy in the most positive terms. The Platonists are the 'good god-conceiving men'.[26] They did 'well perceive that God was no bodily thing . . . that no mutable thing was God . . . that all forms of mutable things . . . have their origin from none but Him that is true and unchangeable'.[27] 'From this invariable and simple essence of His they understood Him to be the uncreated Creator of all existence'.[28]

And therefore these learned men did well observe that the first form of things could not have existence in a mutable subject. And therefore beholding degrees of diversity in the forms of souls and bodies, and that the separation of all form from them directly destroyed them, they inferred a necessity of some unchangeable and consequently all-excelling form, which they held the beginning of all things, uncreated, all-creating, exceeding right. Thus what they knew of God he did manifest unto them by teaching them the gradual contemplation of his parts invisible by His works visible: as also His eternity and divinity, who created all things both visible and temporal.[29]

Anselm may be taken to be doing something similar; we may think of him as appropriating Platonic and Neoplatonic materials into a definition of God which he nevertheless considered to be consistent with the divine revelation, and – more to the point – to have been borne in upon him, Anselm, by God himself. Even if we agree that it had its source in the Bible alone, or in some particular philosophical tradition alone, or in some combination of the two, it is not for these reasons alone that Anselm held that it is thought to be acceptable, as a definition, to most reasonable people. The more relevant question is, do or ought reasonable people to accept this as a definition of God? For the purposes of concluding an independent argument the source of a definition is of less importance than its adequacy.

Another reason for questioning the Barthian position is the relationship between the *Proslogion* and the earlier work, the *Monologion*. The *Proslogion* is intended to cover the same ground as the *Monologion*, but by employing 'one argument' instead of many. But the *Monologion* is undoubtedly a work that proceeds by reason alone, and although the *Proslogion* is addressed to believers, we may reasonably presume that it also is intended to be a work of natural reason. It is entirely appropriate, therefore, that Anselm should say:

> I thank You, good Lord, I thank You that what at first I believed through Your giving, now by You enlightening I so understand that even if I did not want to believe that You exist, I could not fail to understand (that You exist).[30]

Thus understanding is attained irrespective of believing.

So Barth's claim that the ontological argument is a piece of revealed theology is unconvincing on two counts. Anselm's definition of God may be regarded as independent of revelation even if it has its source in revelation, or even if Anselm (mistakenly perhaps) believed that it had. And even if it were not independent of revelation, one could accept the biblical definition of God (supposing that Anselm's definition is biblical) as an *assumption*, on the basis of which an argument for God's existence is then mounted. Whether that definition is regarded as a purely human invention, or taken to be the revealed name of God, the validity or invalidity of the argument is unaffected. If someone who takes the definition as an assumption (whatever its source, human invention or divine revelation), is convinced of the validity of the argument which employs it, it is still open to him to reject the assumption, provided that he has good reason to do so. That a conclusion must follow from certain premises does not entail that the premises must be accepted as true.

There is further reason to think that Anselm thought that what he was doing was not simply reflecting intelligently on the characteristic and distinctive claims of Christian theology. As we have already noted, he refers to his project as a search for an 'independent proof', independent in the sense that the credibility of belief in God's existence did not depend on the authority of the special revelation, but had a credibility that was independent of it. Not that that credibility ought, in Anselm's view, to rest on some alternative authority – 'reason' or 'experience', say. Rather, his aim, consistent with his understanding of the *credo ut intelligam* programme, was to provide a proof of God's existence which arose from the inherent character of the concept of God, to show that there is a necessity to God's existence, the God who makes himself known through revelation. So Anselm intended the ontological argument to be an argument which essentially draws out the implications of the concept of God, a concept which was itself implied by Anselm's Christian faith even though elements in that concept were drawn from Platonic sources.

There is a circle in Anselm's thinking here, though not a vicious one. Anselm is in search of an argument to support his belief, and it may seem incongruous, even question-begging, that he should address God in an endeavour to obtain such an argument, and even more incongruous that God should grant his request! It may be asked, how can Anselm be serious in his intellectual endeavours if he is already a believer? Perhaps it is this worry that lies behind Barth's interpretation of Anselm; how can Anselm be doing natural theology when he is behaving as a believer?

But, as Marilyn Adams points out, there is no more incompatibility in seeking such an argument from God than there is in getting help from one's teacher in trying to develop arguments against solipsism.[31]

Let us now look at various aspects of the argument of the first four chapters having in mind not so much its validity and soundness as an argument as its place in fulfilling Anselm's faith seeking understanding programme.

PROSLOGION: THE FIRST FOUR CHAPTERS

The opening chapter has to do with the presence and absence of God; with the fact that though mankind has been made for God's presence, it has been banished by his sins. In this absence, Anselm asks God to renew his presence: 'Teach me to seek You, and reveal Yourself to me as I seek; for unless You instruct me I cannot seek You, and unless You reveal Yourself I cannot find You.'[32] So Anselm begins with his own dissatisfaction with the fact that he does not enjoy the presence of God, a dissatisfaction which has its source in the sins of mankind.[33] He pursues his programme as a Christian, in a clearly Christian context of belief in the fall and in human sin. And he sees his meditative, contemplative thrust as an expression of the desire for a fuller acquaintance with God. To gain a greater under-standing of God through this meditative practice is to come to be more directly acquainted with God, though never fully or comprehensively acquainted with him:

> Lord, I do not attempt to comprehend Your sublimity, because my intellect is not at all equal to such a task. But I yearn to understand some measure of Your truth, which my heart believes and loves. For I do not seek to understand in order to believe but I believe in order to understand. For I believe even this: that I shall not understand unless I believe.[34]

Take an example; if a friend acts in a strange or unexpected way and at a later time, by thinking about what he has done more carefully, you come to understand why he acted as he did, the motives and reasons behind his action, and how these cohere with his wider interests or beliefs, say, then as a result of this reflection it is reasonable to say that you know the person better than you did before. One's acquaintance with a person grows not only extensively, through being acquainted with him longer, but also intensively, by being acquainted with him more deeply; and so it is here with Anselm. The *Proslogion* is a sort of meditative interlude as a result of which Anselm believes that he knows God more deeply. He is not postulating the existence of God, as Kant argued that it was necessary to do, nor is he projecting the existence of God in the manner criticised by Feuerbach and Marx. Rather he is seeing what the idea of God as the one who is most worshipful, an idea that corresponds (he believes) to the revealed character of God, implies about the being of God himself. And in that way, Anselm is coming to know truth about God more deeply, and so to know God, who is the truth, more deeply.

So although Anselm has never, as a believer, had direct acquaintance with God, 'Never have I seen You, O Lord my God; I am not acquainted with your countenance',[35] he hopes and aims through the exercises of the *Proslogion* to go further along the road to direct acquaintance by reflecting upon the character of God, the character that God necessarily has. 'Teach me to seek You, and reveal Yourself to me as I seek; for unless You instruct me I cannot seek You, and unless You reveal Yourself I cannot find You'.[36] In order to be acquainted with someone, it is necessary to know who it is one is to be acquainted with; and Anselm's programme can be seen as an effort at such knowledge. Anselm knows full well that he will never comprehend God, but he sees no objection to the idea that he might know God better by knowing more about God, and that he might know God in a way that reflects God's distinctiveness.

Anselm's believing is both a moral and a conceptual precondition of understanding; it is an aspect of what Kretzmann called the 'way of faith'. Believing reflects the intention and desire to understand; and what is believed, believed on the authority of revelation, sets the parameters of the understanding sought. For though the understanding amplifies what is believed, the conceptual and propositional content of what is believed, this is like the filling in of the details of a picture the outlines of which are already discerned.

Such understanding as he gains as a result of his meditation is not private to Anselm, some Gnostic higher knowledge, a religious private language. It is an understanding which it is possible to publish (as in the *Proslogion*) and to defend (as against Gaunilo); nevertheless it is an understanding, Anselm believes, that could not have been achieved without the special help of God. For the Lord is 'the giver of understanding to faith'.[37] The arguments Anselm employs he thinks of as the gift of God. Part of the renewal of God's image in Anselm involves him in being brought to understand more fully some measure of the divine truth which he already believes.

On most interpretations Chapter 2 presents the ontological argument, or at least one such argument; it is, for Anselm, the result of God's granting understanding of what Anselm believes him to be. There is both a conceptual and an epistemological dimension to Anselm's project. In gaining understanding Anselm will also gain certainty. Understanding provides a greater awareness of God and, in establishing the necessity of his existence through argument, faith approaches knowledge.

There is a sense in which, for Anselm, faith is all right as it stands. It is not deficient for the purposes for which it is intended. But it is intellectually incomplete; it does not amount to knowledge. And because it is accompanied by a love of the one who is trusted, there is about it an impetus for further knowledge. To desire and to gain understanding is to proceed along the path towards such knowledge, knowledge which is ultimately visionary in character, but knowledge which is nevertheless informed by, and so is continuous with, the knowledge of the character and reality the one who is thus known possesses.

To be more precise, understanding involves for Anselm the gaining of insight into the nature of something. God has a nature, yet he is not a member of a kind of thing, and so gaining understanding does not involve coming to know what kind of thing God is, and so what his general nature is. For God is unique, incomparable. And Anselm is striving to gain insight into the character of God's uniqueness, his independence. In common with the main tradition of Christian theology he makes a distinction between the independence of God's existence and the contingency of his creation. Whereas the creation is dependent upon God, God does not, in turn, depend upon anything else. Rather, he is the source of all being; he exists *a se*, from himself. 'Except for You alone, whatever else exists can be conceived not to exist'.[38] What Anselm believes that he has shown in the argument is that the necessity of God's existence is not merely causal, it is not merely that which in fact all creation owes its existence to and which, though it in fact exists, might not, but it is ontological or metaphysical in character. Anselm's stress on modality surfaces again here; there is no possible world in which God fails to exist. 'Assuredly this being exists so truly that it cannot even be thought not to exist.'[39]

So for Anselm understanding, at least understanding the nature of God, is concerned with the unfolding of an aspect of the necessity of the Christian faith, with the explaining away of the elements of contingency and seeming arbitrariness about God and his character as they appear in the faith of the Church; in this case, with explaining away the possible contingency of God's existence. God does not simply exist as a matter of brute fact, the terminus in a process of understanding or explanation. There is an inner necessity to his being that terminus, namely that no one else and nothing else could be it, and that only one who exists necessarily could be. What may seem at first sight, and to faith, as simply a matter of sheer contingency, and as such may give rise to intellectual puzzles and to meet intellectual resistance, will be seen, as understanding grows, to have a necessity to it, and therefore the best of reasons for it. So while initially it may seem that God simply exists, what Anselm aims to convey, as a result of his own increased understanding, is that God does not just happen to exist, as an inexplicable, contingent fact, but that he must exist.

Reason does not therefore seek to establish truths about God additional to revelation, but explores revealed truth more deeply. Reason is, at least in this aspect of its use, not so much creative or normative, as reflective. Reason is instrumental, and the use of this instrument on the divine revelation augments understanding. Nevertheless, reason thus employed might have the effect of detaching truths about God from their revealed source; in the case of God himself, it must have this effect, if Anselm's procedure is sound. (As we shall see later, understanding is not always intended to have this effect.) To understand means that if we presuppose some elements of the faith, we understand the article of the faith in question when we see it to be necessary, its denial to be impossible, given those elements. It is this that Anselm applies to the existence of God, in the following way.

Suppose that we start off with the Christian concept of God, the central article of the Christian faith; *I believe in God the Father Almighty*. If we reflect on the concept of God's almightiness, then according to Anselm we shall see that real existence is implied by that concept, and that to deny the existence of God, having accepted this concept of God, is both metaphysical and spiritual folly. If we really have in our understanding the idea of 'Almighty' then we shall have the idea of something than which no greater can be thought. We shall realise, by logical implication, that such an idea cannot only be in our understandings, but must also be in reality.[40] The God who really exists must necessarily exist. For to suppose the opposite leads to a contradiction, namely that that than which a greater cannot be thought would be that than which a greater *can* be thought, and thus that there might be someone or something more mighty than Almighty God. Here is Anselm's characteristic use of the *reductio ad absurdam* as a test of rationality. If a proposition can be shown to be absurd, then the denial of that proposition must be necessary. If it is absurd to suppose that there might be something greater than Almighty God, then it is necessarily the case that there cannot be anything superior to Almighty God.

In the view of many (for example Barth, and Norman Malcolm), Anselm employs another argument in *Proslogion* Chapter 3 from that deployed earlier. Whereas the first argument, in *Proslogion* Chapter 2, claims that a being which exists in reality is greater than a being which exists merely in the understanding, and the conclusion is therefore that there exists a being than which no greater can be conceived, the second argument contends that a being whose non-existence is logically impossible is superior to a being whose non-existence is logically possible, that there exists a being which cannot even be conceived not to exist. That is, while earlier in the *Proslogion* Anselm argues that God alone can not exist, in *Proslogion* Chapter 3 he claims that God cannot even conceivably not exist. Understood in this way, this is a modal version of the ontological argument.

Alternatively, it has been thought that this is not so much a separate argument as Anselm drawing out a central attribute of God whose existence he has proved in *Proslogion* Chapter 2, that the existence of that God is inconceivable.[41]

The reasoning of the second argument, if that is what it is, depends once more upon the contrast between necessary and contingent existence. God's existence is not merely causally necessary, but according to Anselm it is unique in being logically or metaphysically necessary. Consequently, everything which exists besides God is logically contingent:

> all and only things which have a beginning or an end or are composed of parts – and whatever (as I have already said) at any place or time does not exist as a whole – can be thought not to exist. But only that in which there is no conceivable beginning or end or combination of parts, and only that which exists as a whole everywhere and always, cannot be thought not to exist.[42]

There is a great deal compressed in these statements; if God is a necessary being then he has neither temporal nor spatial parts; he is not in time nor in space, but timeless and spaceless; and he is metaphysically simple.

It is possible to distinguish between different kinds of necessity; call these causal and metaphysical necessity respectively. Something is a causally necessary being when it is the cause of something, perhaps the cause of everything, and when it just happens to exist. Something is metaphysically necessary if its non-existence is inconceivable. Anselm argues that only God's existence is metaphysically necessary, that he exists in all possible worlds; that a 'possible world' in which God does not exist is not in fact a possibility. And that because he is logically necessary in this sense, he is also ontologically necessary as well.

The consequences of such a view of God's existence are puzzling and profound. If God exists necessarily in this sense, then not only is atheism impossible, and the person who is an atheist cannot fail to be in error, but also any state of affairs incompatible with the existence of God is also impossible. Anselm would presumably say that the fact that we can imagine such a possibility, a world without God, or a world of irremediable evil, say, is because such thought experiments are confined to the words, and do not embrace the realities that those words denote.

If God's existence is metaphysically necessary then to suppose God's non-existence implies a contradiction. We can see from this that according to Anselm the fool is such because he fails to remove *prima facie* contradiction in his thinking about God. So the gaining of understanding involves (at least) the removal of apparent contradictions.[43] For, Anselm reasons, it is contradictory (and so reveals a failure of understanding) to suppose that God, the being than which no greater can be thought, could be thought not only not to exist, but also not only possibly not to exist.

In his article 'Anselm's Ontological Arguments' Norman Malcolm argues in connection with what he regards as Anselm's *second* argument that necessary existence is a property of the concept of God and that therefore God's existence is either necessary or impossible. Malcolm claims that there are different senses of 'exist' and that we are not to expect that the necessary existence of God is like the existence of some physical state of affairs:

> Is the Euclidean theorem in number theory, 'There exists an infinite number of prime numbers', an 'existential proposition'? Do we not want to say that in some sense it asserts the existence of something? Cannot we say, with equal justification, that the proposition 'God necessarily exists' asserts the existence of something, in some sense? What we need to understand, in each case, is the particular sense of the assertion. Neither proposition has the same sort of sense as do the propositions, 'A low pressure area exists over the Great Lakes', 'There still exists some possibility that he will survive', 'The pain continues to exist in his abdomen'. One good way of seeing the difference in sense of these various propositions is to see the variously different ways in which they are proved and supported. It is wrong to think that all assertions of existence have the same kind of meaning. There are as many kinds of existential propositions as there are kinds of subjects of discourse.[44]

No doubt Anselm would agree that there is a difference between necessary and contingent existence; this is, in fact, the point behind the ontological argument, at least in the second version identified by Malcolm. The problem with the suggestion that there are as many kinds of existential propositions as there are kinds of subjects of discourse is that it is hard to make sense of without a way of identifying how many kinds of subjects of discourse there are. An alternative approach, one more likely to be favoured by Anselm, would be to argue that the criterion for the real existence of anything is its causal potential, its potential to affect other things. And God, who causes all contingent existence, cannot himself be contingent; for if he were contingent then he might not have existed, and something that exists but which might not have existed could not be God.

Later on Malcolm says:

> In the Ninetieth Psalm it is said: 'Before the mountains were brought forth, or ever thou hadst formed the earth and the world, even from everlasting to everlasting, thou art God'. Here is expressed the idea of

the necessary existence and eternity of God, an idea that is essential to the Jewish and Christian religions. In those complex systems of thought, those 'language-games', God has the status of a necessary being. Who can doubt that? Here we must say with Wittgenstein, 'This language-game is played!'[45]

There is a sense in which Anselm might agree with these remarks, but a sense in which he would demur. As we have already seen he concurs with the idea that the idea of God as a necessary being is essential to Christianity. But this does not imply that Christianity is merely a system of thought, at least a system of thought that does not say things about the universe of necessarily and contingently existing things. For Anselm there is not one language-game in which the idea of God's necessary existence figures, and another language-game in which it does not, each language-game being equally valid. The idea of God's necessary existence is basic to one complex language-game, the language-game in which contingently existing things figure, since for Anselm this necessary being who is God is also the creator of all non-necessary beings; they, as Malcolm says earlier in his article, depend upon God. If what the players in this language-game say about God is true, then it would be true were there to be no such language-game.

But although the proof of God's existence is an 'independent argument', in the sense discussed, it is not wholly independent in the sense that once Anselm has acheived it he loses interest in the roots of the idea of God whose existence he is striving to prove. For Anselm seeks a theological confirmation of the conclusion of his argument when he turns from considering the proof abstractly to face God directly:

> And You are this being, O Lord our God. Therefore, Lord my God, You exist so truly that You cannot even be thought not to exist. And this is rightly the case. For if any mind could conceive of something better than You, the creature would rise above the Creator and would sit in judgement over the Creator – an utterly preposterous consequence.[46]

When Anselm says that his conclusion is rightly the case, he is thinking in terms of a theological confirmation of his conclusion, a confirmation arising from faith. This confirmation lies, it seems, in the fact that if a being that is greater than God could be thought (something which Anselm believes to be impossible) then the distinction between the Creator and the creature would be overturned. But Anselm does not quite mean this, but rather that if *per impossibile* the creature could think of something or someone that was superior to the Creator, even though that thing did not exist, but only existed in the mind, then he would 'sit in judgement on the

Creator', that is, presumably, apply a standard to the Creator by means of which he was judged inferior to some other possible individual. Anselm is working on the assumption that only God can be the Creator; and that since God is a being than which a greater cannot be conceived, only such a being can be the Creator. By these remarks on the Creator and the creature Anselm shows us that he is still working within the parameters of the 'life of faith'.

It is not obvious that this is preposterous in quite the way Anselm intends. What *would* undoubtedly overthrow the Creator–creature distinction would be a situation in which the creature was able to think of something that the Creator could not think of; then the power of the creature would be greater than that of the Creator and the Creator–creature distinction would be overturned.[47] This, for Anselm, is not simply a nice conceptual point about the idea of God. It has wider theological presuppositions and implications. To suppose that God's existence were not metaphysically necessary would involve a reversal of the fundamental theological distinction between the creature and the Creator. For to suppose that God might not exist is to suppose that it is conceivable that there is something that is greater than God, and this in turn supposes that the creature might have in mind something greater than God, and this would mean that, in the sense suggested, the creature could rise above God.[48]

If, as Chapter 3 concludes, God is not only a being than which no greater can be thought, but also one whose non-existence cannot be thought, then, as Anselm states in Chapter 4, 'it is so readily clear to a rational mind that You exist most greatly of all'.[49] How then can the fool have said in his heart that there is no God? The explanation for this, according to Anselm, is to distinguish between two kinds of thought; to think of the word, and to think of the thing signified by the word. The fool is able to say (and to think) that there is no God because in thinking he is thinking only of the word. If he were to think of the reality which the word denotes, then he would think that that reality is such that it cannot fail to exist. 'Anyone who comprehends this, surely understands that God so exists that He cannot even conceivably not exist'.[50] To understand is to grasp with the mind the nature or kind of reality that is understood, even if that reality is not fully comprehensible to the human mind.

Anselm concludes with the recognition that this argument has come as the result of divine illumination:

> I thank You, good Lord, I thank You that what at first I believed through Your giving, now by Your enlightening I so understand that even if I did not want to believe that You exist, I could not fail to understand.[51]

NOTES

1. Anselm, *Proslogion*, p.89.
2. For discussion of this point see Adams, 'Praying the *Proslogion*'.
3. For discussion of the meditative framework of the *Proslogion*, see Adams, 'Praying the *Proslogion*'.
4. Anselm, *Proslogion*, p.103.
5. Anselm, *Proslogion*, p.101.
6. Anselm, *Proslogion*, p.91.
7. Anselm, *Proslogion*, pp.102f.
8. Anselm, *Proslogion*, p.112.
9. Campbell, *From Belief to Understanding*, p.173.
10. Anselm, *Proslogion*, p.104.
11. In the view of some philosophers the ontological argument, far from representing a gain in understanding, is an exercise in misunderstanding. In this vein O. K. Bouwsma in 'Anselm's Argument' claims that the enterprise is a misapplication of the language of praise.
12. Anselm, *Proslogion*, p.89.
13. Anselm, *Proslogion*, p.95.
14. Barth, *Anselm: Fides Quaerens Intellectum*, p.75.
15. Barth, *Anselm: Fides Quaerens Intellectum*, pp.76f.
16. Barth, *Anselm: Fides Quaerens Intellectum*, p.152.
17. Barth, *Anselm: Fides Quaerens Intellectum*, p.131.
18. Anselm, *On the Incarnation of the Word*, p.23.
19. Barth, *Anselm: Fides Quaerens Intellectum*, p.131.
20. Anselm, *Reply to Gaunilo*, p.134.
21. Anselm, *Proslogion*, p.89.
22. Descartes, *Meditations*, p.131.
23. Calvin, *Institutes*, p.44.
24. Augustine, *City of God* I, p.220.
25. Augustine, *City of God* I, pp.231–5.
26. Augustine, *City of God* I, p.229.
27. Augustine, *City of God* I, p.230.
28. Augustine, *City of God* I, p.231.
29. Ibid.
30. Anselm, *Proslogion*, p.95.
31. Adams, 'Praying the *Proslogion*', p.21.
32. Anselm, *Proslogion*, p.93.
33. Ibid.
34. Anselm, *Proslogion*, p.93.
35. Anselm, *Proslogion*, p.91.
36. Anselm, *Proslogion*, p.93.
37. Ibid.
38. Anselm, *Proslogion*, p.95.
39. Anselm, *Proslogion*, p.94.
40. Ibid.
41. For discussion of this point, see Oppy, *Ontological Arguments and Belief in God*, p.12.
42. Anselm, *Reply to Gaunilo*, pp.127f.
43. Anselm, *Proslogion*, p.94.
44. Malcolm, 'Anselm's Ontological Arguments', p.59.
45. Malcolm, 'Anselm's Ontological Arguments', p.62.
46. Anselm, *Proslogion*, pp.94f.
47. Anselm, *Proslogion*, p.95.
48. Anselm, *Proslogion*, p.94.
49. Anselm, *Proslogion*, p.95.
50. Ibid.
51. Ibid.

6

Anselm's Understanding of the Incarnation

As we have already seen, the slogan 'Faith Seeks Understanding' does not describe a monolithic procedure, but a goal. The core idea is of an articulation of the propositions accepted by faith into a more developed form that better displays their inherent structure and hence contributes to the reasonableness of believing them. In the hands of Anselm of Canterbury this articulation becomes a project of a more precise and more ambitious kind, as we noted in Chapter 5. Understanding is conveyed to the extent that we are able to see that one proposition is consistent with another, when previously we had imagined that they were inconsistent, or had no connection with each other. But we gain understanding in a more characteristically Anselmian sense when our reason is able to discern that some Christian doctrine is grounded in the nature of things, particularly in the nature of God, the God than whom no greater can be conceived, and that there is a necessity, or at least an appropriateness, to it.

In this chapter we examine further facets of this Anselmian method by considering aspects of another of Anselm's great works, his *Cur Deus Homo*, on the necessity and nature of Christ's atonement. This book has an important place in the development of the Christian doctrine of the atonement of Christ, but we shall be considering it as an another of Anselm's endeavours to gain understanding through philosophical analysis and reflection. In Chapter 9 of the *Proslogion* Anselm briefly shows that the mercy of God is consistent with his justice. In the *Cur Deus Homo* he develops this with reference to Christ's atonement. In the case of the atonement we are concerned not only with the nature of God, but also with his will, and so one of the things that we shall be concerned about is the sense in which, according to Anselm, the will of God, and the atonement as an expression of the will of God, is necessary, grounded in the nature of things. We may see Anselm's procedure in the *Cur Deus Homo* as an extension of that in the *Proslogion*.

Anselm shows clearly at the outset of the work that he is writing it in furtherance of his programme of faith seeking understanding. The work is in the form of a dialogue between Anselm and Boso.

Boso states:

> Indeed, assisted by the prevenient grace of God I am, it seems to me, holding so steadfastly to faith in our redemption that even if I were not in any respect able to understand what I believe, nothing could wrest me from firmness of faith. Accordingly, I ask you to disclose to me that which, as you know, many are asking about along with me: viz., for what reason and on the basis of what necessity did God – although He is omnipotent – assume the lowliness and the weakness of human nature in order to restore it?[1]

What Boso means is not that he had at that time no reason for his faith, but that there was not aware of any *necessity* about these reasons; because of this his beliefs had the appearance of arbitrariness, and so had a character which was unbecoming to God.

This endeavour after understanding is not only in line with what Anselm states in the *Proslogion* but it is also to be found elsewhere in Anselm's writings. For example:

> But before I examine this question I will say something to curb the presumption of those who, with blasphemous rashness and on the ground that they cannot understand it, dare to argue against something which the Christian faith confesses – those who judged with foolish pride that what they are not able to understand is not at all possible, rather than acknowledging with humble wisdom that many things are possible which they are not able to comprehend. Indeed, no Christian ought to question the truth of what the Catholic Church believes in its heart and confesses with its mouth. Rather, by holding constantly and unhesitatingly to this faith, by loving it and living according to it he ought humbly, and as best he is able, to seek to discover the reason it is true. If he is able to understand, then let him give thanks to God. But if he cannot understand, let him not toss his horns in strife but let him bow his head in reverence. For self-confident human wisdom can, by thrusting, uproot its horns more quickly than it can, by pushing, roll the stone. For when certain men

begin to grow 'horns' of self-confident knowledge, then . . . they are accustomed to mount up presumptuously unto the loftiest questions of faith before they possess spiritual wings through firmness of faith. Consequently, when they try to ascend to those questions which first require the ladder of faith (as it is written, 'Unless you believe you will not understand'), but try to ascend in reverse order by means of first understanding, they are constrained to fall into many kinds of errors on account of their defective understanding.[2]

'To search for the reason why his faith is true', a reason grounded in the necessity of things. The faith supplies the premises of reasoning and the conclusions; it is 'foolish pride', showing a defective understanding, to question either. What Anselm seeks is a satisfactory way of showing how premises and conclusion are linked. So the understanding Anselm seeks is not intended as a condition of faith, but as a consequence of it. There is nothing wrong with holding the propositions of the faith 'on trust', but such an attitude is intellectually unsatisfactory because it is incomplete. Understanding must be guided by what is true, by the propositions of the faith; it cannot depart from them, nor ought our understanding be 'prior', operating in *a priori* fashion, imposing what is to be true from outside the faith.

ANSELM'S PROJECTS

In the Preface to the *Cur Deus Homo* Anselm sets out two distinct projects, to be taken up in the two books of the work.

The first of these contains the answers of believers to the objection of unbelievers who repudiate the Christian faith because they regard it as incompatible with reason. And this book goes on to prove by rational necessity – Christ being removed from sight, as if there had never been anything known about Him – that no man can possibly be saved without Him. However, in the second book – likewise proceeding as if nothing were known of Christ – I show with equally clear reasoning and truth that human nature was created in order that the whole man (i.e. with a body and a soul) would some day enjoy a happy immortality. And I show the necessity of man's attaining this end for which he was created, and [that it can be attained] only by means of a God-man. And I show that all the things which we believe about Christ ought, necessarily, to occur.[3]

In this chapter we shall sample Anselm's method further chiefly by examining Book I of the *Cur Deus Homo*, and particularly the *remoto*

Christo aspects of it. In this Book Anselm is concerned to show that only Christ could save; in Book II, that mankind will be saved, but only through Christ the God-man. Our concern will be to explore the sense in which Anselm came to hold that only Christ could save by using arguments as if nothing were known of Christ.

It is by rational necessity that Anselm attempts to prove that no one can be saved without Christ and that everything we believe about Christ had, in some sense, to happen. In this, Anselm is surely echoing the modal language used in the New Testament about Christ, that it was necessary that he suffered (Acts 17:3) and that it was not possible that death should hold him (Acts 2:24), and drawing out what he took to be its implications. Unlike Augustine, in furthering understanding Anselm gives great emphasis to modality, to the concepts of necessity and possibility. For Anselm, to say that something is in accordance with reason is not merely that it is 'reasonable' in the loose and informal sense in which we often use this term, but that it can be shown that there is some proposition or set of propositions which necessitates it. This endeavour has an apologetic aspect, in rather the way which Anselm's procedure in the *Proslogion* had, the provision of answers to the objection of unbelievers who repudiate the Christian faith because they regard it as incompatible with reason. The apologetic element is more prominent here than in the *Proslogion*, but it is an apologetic conducted among Christians.

To show that something is reasonable in a certain set of circumstances if often to show that a person had reason for doing what he did, and that this reason is not bizarre or otherwise eccentric. But for Anselm, to show that an action is reasonable in given circumstances is to show that features of these circumstances, together with certain aims and ends of the agent, *require* an action of that certain type, and of no other type.

So Anselm outlines a somewhat complex and ambitious programme. Does all of it fall under the programme of faith seeking understanding? There is reason to think that it does. The internal elucidation of the faith, and the rejection of the objections of unbelievers, the apologetic aspects, are here connected by Anselm. Any valid answer to an objection is also part of the elucidation of the faith. Any elucidation of the faith can in principle be employed for apologetic purposes. After all, no one has the copyright to any argument, and so the uses to which any argument may be put are various, not constrained by the original purpose for which the argument was formulated.

In response to Boso, Anselm agrees to take up the task of elucidating the Incarnation along these lines, but with two warnings: the first is that the subject cannot be discussed without 'an analysis of ability, and necessity and will and of certain other notions which are so interrelated that no one of them can be fully examined apart from the others.'[4] These remarks provide us with a clue as to how Anselm wishes to proceed; he needs to use the concepts of power, necessity and will in order to show in what way the atonement of Christ was necessarily grounded in the divine will.

The second warning is that Boso must not expect a *complete* explanation. This is because the subject is 'beautiful in appearance above the sons of men, so it is also adorned with a rationale which exceeds human understanding'.[5] The reason for this caution lies ultimately in divine incomprehensibility, that God has reasons which are not *at present* epistemically accessible to his creatures, and perhaps never will be. Were they to be epistemically accessible, then their rationale would be evident. As we saw when discussing the *Proslogion*, there may in principle be a barrier to full understanding. So Anselm cautions against any attempt to demonstrate exhaustively the truth of any of the tenets of the faith. What he aims to offer is not a full explanation of a divine perfection, on completely *a priori* grounds, but something more modest than this.

Anselm starts from a position where the propositions of the faith, which include beliefs about what God has done, are accepted by faith, and so are not known to be either necessary, or not necessary. It is the aim of the faith seeks understanding project to show that (in the relevant sense) they are necessary. ('Indeed, your saying that God showed in this manner how much he loves you is not at all defensible unless you show that He could not at all have saved man in any other way.')[6] He is concerned with displaying the internal coherence of the faith, understood not simply as consistency, but as something stronger. He aims to show that the seeming arbitrariness and even inappropriateness of human redemption by Christ (involving, as it does, the humiliation of God the Son) is only apparent, and that it is required by the nature of things, in particular by the nature of God and by human sin.

In order to get a clearer grasp of what Anselm means by rational necessity in the case of the atonement, a distinction needs to be made between the deducibility of one proposition from another proposition (or propositions) and the requirement that a person act in a certain way. Just as we say that the conclusion of a valid argument *must* follow from its premises, so we sometimes say, in a somewhat parallel fashion, that a person 'had no alternative' than to act as he did; what the person did he (in some sense) *had* to do. Anselm wishes to show that given the character of an agent, God, and the ends and aims of that agent, and given the circumstances in which he acted, namely human sin, there is a clear sense in which God 'had no alternative' than to act as he did. This may seem to constrain God; that is why Anselm says that in order to gain understanding of this issue we must have some knowledge of the concepts of *ability* and *will* as well as of *necessity*.

So we may be able to get clearer about Anselm's projects if we can see what Anselm means when he says that one of his aims in the first Book of the *Cur Deus Homo* is to prove by logical arguments that it is impossible for any man to be saved without Christ. What he is setting out to prove by logic is something more restricted than these words at first suggest. What they suggest is that Anselm is going to prove *by logic alone* that no man can be saved except by Christ, but of course any proposal of that kind would be preposterous. For any logical argument requires one or more premises, and logic – what in the first chapter we called procedural reason – by itself certainly cannot provide these. What Anselm is in fact attempting to prove is that given that human beings need to be saved from their sin and *given that God wills such salvation*, then salvation is only possible through the atonement of Christ, and hence that the atonement is necessary. These two proposition are, logically speaking, assumptions about the nature and circumstances of an agent, God. They form premises of Anselm's 'logical argument', assumptions which Anselm is entitled to make in view of his faith, and in view of the dialectical situation which he has constructed, since his opponents also hold them. The premises of his argument are propositions which are derived from the teaching of the Church alone. Of course insofar as they appeal to the character of God, Anselm holds that this character can be established independently, by the 'one argument' of the *Proslogion*. But what cannot be independently established is that God wills what he does; for there is no necessity to this. The necessity applies to the means that God chooses to effect a certain freely chosen end. And what Anselm is claiming, somewhat audaciously, it may be thought, is that given that God has as his end human salvation, he does not have a choice as to the means to effect that end.

In fact there is a general reason to be cautious about emphasising the *necessity* of the Incarnation in any sense, for as Brian Leftow has shown,[7] Anselm is wary of imputing necessity of any sort to the divine actions. The reason for this is that according to Anselm something done under necessity is, strictly speaking, compelled to be done. God, being omnipotent and morally perfect (perfect in wisdom), cannot be compelled to do anything. The necessity by which God does what he does is, if the language of necessity is to be used at all, is, so to speak, 'internal necessity', the necessity which arises from God's own character and his own choice, a choice unconstrained by any factors external to him, and wholly in accordance with his character. At one point Anselm says:

And when we say that God does something as if under the necessity of avoiding dishonour (which, surely, He is in no danger of encountering) we must, rather, interpret this to mean that He does it under the necessity of maintaining His honour. Indeed, this necessity is nothing other than the immutability of His honour – an immutability which He has from himself and not from another, and which therefore is improperly called necessity. Nevertheless, let us say that it is necessary that God's goodness – on account of its immutability – accomplish with man what it began, even though the entire good which it does is by grace.[8]

The language of necessity is permissible provided that it is understood as expressing the immutability of God's nature.

Perhaps we can express the point as follows. According to Anselm the creation of the universe is the result of the free creation of God. The force of saying that it is free is that God could, consistently with his nature, have created other universes, universes in which, for example, there are no human beings, and so no possibility of human sin. So there is no necessity about this particular world. No doubt, Anselm thinks, God has a good reason for creating this world, but this reason does not (to use the terminology of Leibniz) *necessitate* so much as *incline* God to create. But given this world, and given that God permits the occurrence of human sin within it, it is up to God whether to pardon that sin, or whether to leave the human race to face the consequences of its own disobedience. However, should God in his wisdom and goodness choose to pardon sin, he can only do so in a way that is consistent with his own perfect nature, with that goodness. So there are ways in which God cannot pardon sin. But (once again) the 'can only' here is not the 'can only' of external constraint, but of God's own moral character. There are, then, as Leftow puts it, reasons for God's decision to create this universe, reasons which are inaccessible to us, according to Anselm; and then there are reasons why, given this creation, and given human sin in it, God 'had to' become incarnate.[9] These have to do both with the divine character and with the divine purposes.

And so, contrary to what Jasper Hopkins says,[10] Anselm is not (in *Cur Deus Homo*) attempting 'to prove that the nature of God is such as to will the very means of incarnation proclaimed in Scripture'. For to suppose this would be to suppose that the Incarnation was *absolutely* necessary, derivable from the nature of God alone. What Anselm attempts to show is that *if God wills the redemption of mankind* then redemption *must* have a certain character; it is not absolutely necessary, but conditionally or hypothetically necessary. Anselm nowhere attempts to show that God must have human redemption as one of his aims. So the conclusion Anselm endeavours to draw is not one which he attempts to derive from the nature of God *simpliciter*, but from the character of God as revealed in his willingness to redeem human beings from sin, a willingness which is not necessitated by God's nature.

So what does Anselm mean when he says that he is undertaking to argue for the necessity of the Incarnation *as if Christ did not exist*? This expression is meant to indicate that Anselm is offering an argument of a particular form. What he is in effect saying is 'Let us put from our minds the fact that Christ has come and redeemed us; I will show that, never-theless, given certain facts about God and ourselves, facts about the divine will, and the nature of human sin, facts having to do with the nature of things, and facts about the divine will, Christ had to come and to do what he did'. *Remoto Christo* is not meant to herald a piece of natural theology on Anselm's part, or of theological rationalism, but an argument of a more restricted type; he is temporarily, or for the sake of the argument, setting aside any appeal to the creed of the Church, to the fact that Christ has come, to support the conclusion that what special revelation testifies to is actually required by the very nature of any divine atonement for human sin, i.e. by the nature of things. So he is spelling out the moral and metaphysical character that, in his view, any atonement *must* have, if there is to be one. And he is doing this in the interests of meeting the charge that there is something *ad hoc* and therefore unbecoming about the atonement.

Harking back to our earlier discussion of Norman Kretzmann's view, let us call any strategy which seeks to replace the authority that grounds the Christian faith, the authority of divine revelation, in a rational proof, the *supplanting strategy*. Anselm, I am arguing, is not a supplanter, not here at least. For this reason, in an otherwise penetrating treatment of Anselm's methodology John Mcintyre is surely mistaken in saying that Anselm nowhere in his writings makes the Church's traditional doctrine author-itative for him.[11] For instance Anselm writes,

> If I say something which a greater authority does not confirm, then even though I seem to prove it rationally, it should be accepted as certain only in the sense that it appears to me for the time being to be thus, until God somehow reveals the matter to me more fully.[12]

This authority is his life-line as he ventures into the metaphysical deeps of rationality and necessity. Anselm has the basic conviction that internal rationality is something which the Christian faith has, and that it is a good thing that it has it. His task is to try to display this rationality insofar as it is possible for a human being to do so. He never countenances the idea that the Incarnation is necessitated by the nature of things apart from the divine will to redeem mankind.

But, it might be objected, does Anselm not refer to 'unbelievers'? And so is he not writing for their benefit, and therefore doing apologetics? In a way, he is. Nevertheless, we must not imagine that in commending his faith to unbelievers Anselm had in mind the mind-set of a modern secularist or humanist.[13] We can see this by noting that at the outset of the *Cur Deus Homo* he has two types of objection in view:

> not in order to approach faith by way of reason but in order to delight in the comprehension and contemplation of the doctrines which they believe, as well as in order to be ready, as best they can, always to give a satisfactory answer to everyone who asks of them a reason for the hope which is in us.[14]

So part at least of Anselm's project is to so display the character of the faith, and particularly, in this case, the character of the atonement, that those who make objection to it may have their objections met. This part of his work is essentially defensive. Put in terminology more recently used, part of the reason for Anselm writing the *Cur Deus Homo* is to provide a defeater-defeater, a counter-argument for those who object to the atonement on the grounds of reason. To do this, Anselm has to show that it is reasonable, in the sense discussed.

OBJECTIONS TO THE ATONEMENT

What rational objections to the atonement does Anselm have in mind?

The first objection we might call the *arbitrariness* objection. It is a commonplace that the Christian faith depends crucially upon contingent historical facts, for example, upon the fact that God was incarnate in Jesus Christ at a particular time and place. There was no logical necessity to these particularities; they could have been otherwise. They are historical facts, and so are contingent, an expression of the will of God. And this is true of the entire narrative of the gospel.

Given this contingency, we may suppose that though Jesus Christ the Son of God came into the world to save sinners, he need not have done so; for his coming was historical, and so contingent. Yet if it could be shown that a proposition such as 'The Son of God came into the world to save sinners' is required by other propositions which are themselves true, then what at first sight appears to be contingent and arbitrary will be shown not to be. The element of arbitrariness, which appears to be present in any free action, will be reduced, if not eliminated altogether. For the central tenet of the Christian faith will have been shown to be grounded in the nature of things, and so (in some sense) necessary, and so not contingent or arbitrary. More on this in due course. And if it can also be shown that this proposition is required by propositions some of which are necessarily true, then this will further strengthen the claim that there is about the Incarnation a kind of necessity.

In answering the arbitrariness objection Anselm attempts to show that more of those propositions that form the rational foundations of a Christian doctrine than we might at first think are necessary truths. In order to understand what Anselm is getting at here let us distinguish between hypothetical and categorical necessary propositions, as follows. Suppose we consider the proposition 'Anything that is green is coloured'. This is true, necessarily true. Its truth is independent of any human wishes or desires. Let us say that it is categorically necessary. But consider, by contrast, 'Anyone who wants to speak must open her mouth'. It does not follow from this that anyone must, of logical necessity, open their mouth, but that *if* a person wishes to speak then a logically necessary condition of speaking is that they open their mouths. Whether or not a person opens their mouth depends entirely upon whether she wishes to speak. If she does not wish to speak, then there is no need for her to open her mouth.

This distinction can be applied to theology. If something is unconditionally or categorically necessary it applies universally, both to God and man. Anselm would hold that it is categorically necessary that God, the most perfect being, exists, as we saw from his *Proslogion*. Further, what we have called categorically necessary truths are categorically necessary for God also. Not even God can make something green which is not coloured. If God wills something, there is no categorical necessity about this. He need not have willed it. But if he does so, then there are certain logical requirements for his attaining that goal. Given the divine nature, the goal chosen must be in accordance with that nature, as must the means for attaining that goal. God cannot attain the goal willy nilly, but only in a certain way. In particular, in attaining his goal God cannot violate the principles of his own nature. This, at any rate, is what Anselm believed. And what he attempted to do in *Cur Deus Homo* was to show that an action or type of action which may at first seem to be arbitrary is in fact necessitated by the nature of God. Given that God freely wills to pardon human sin, he is restricted in the action-types he can undertake in order to achieve this. If God willed to pardon human sin, and such a will is fully consistent with the divine nature, though not necessitated by it, then he could not, consistently with the nature of things, simply choose any way of achieving that end, but one way, or one type of way, of achieving it was necessitated.

But necessitated by what? Anselm would answer, by the necessity of things. Here matters get a little complicated, because 'necessity' and 'necessary' can be used in various senses. One obvious sense in which these words are used is as equivalent to 'forced' or 'compelled', when there is some external agency at work compelling someone to act against their will. As we have seen, Anselm wishes to rule out this sense of 'necessary' in the case of God. It is certainly no part of his aim to show that the atonement was an event that was externally compelled, that God was constrained in so doing. For this would call in question God's freedom in providing for an atonement.

Besides cases of compulsion, such as those cited, there are necessities of nature, the sort of regularities expressed in scientific laws. However such necessities are to be explained, whatever the precise relation of an event to the law of nature which it exemplifies, the necessity in question is nevertheless a contingent necessity, it follows from the natures of the powers in question, or from observed regularities between sets of events. These powers or regularities could have been other than they are; they are contingent. Anselm shows little interest in natural necessities of this kind, either. He certainly does not think that the atonement was scientifically or physically necessary, having the same necessity by which a weight, when it is released, must fall to the ground.

Rather, what is of intense interest to Anselm is what might be called metaphysical necessity, the necessities which follow from the nature of God and the principles of power and justice that, in his view, the divine nature necessarily expresses or embodies.[15] According to Anselm God, in view of his perfection, is such that necessarily he could not fail to be just. Anything that could fail to be just could not be God. God is just in every possible world in which he exists (and, Anselm would add, he exists in *every* possible world).

If God is just, not simply in the sense that justice is part of his essence, nor even if God is just in the sense that he is justice, but rather if justice is present in every possible world, because God exists in very possible world, then for the atonement to be required by justice is for it to be required by the nature of things in a more fundamental sense. But the requirements of justice do not by themselves necessitate the atonement; they only necessitate it if, in addition, God wills the removal of sin. For atonement is a divine action. And the will of God is not part of the fundamental nature of things in precisely the same sense as God's justice is, since though God's will must always fulfil the principles of justice, it need not fulfil them in precisely the way in which it has in fact fulfilled them.

Some human actions are explained by reference to weakness of will, or by the will being overcome through tiredness or inattention. But unlike you or I, God cannot be afflicted with weakness of will. So that even if I have a moral obligation to do something, and so doing that thing is in a certain sense required, or even if it is necessary that I do it, nevertheless I may fail to do it. But according to Anselm God cannot fail; his actions always faithfully transmit his character, and insofar as his character is necessary, they reflect that necessity.

So what is at work in Anselm's reasoning is a sort of principle of simplicity, an attempt to remove the apparent arbitrariness of what has been called the 'scandal of particularity', and therefore the removal of one kind of objection to the faith.

The second objection is linked with the first:

> For what reason, and on the basis of what necessity did God become a man and by His death restore life to the world (as we believe and confess), seeing that He could have accomplished this restoration either by means of some other person (whether angelic or human) or else by merely willing it?[16]

What exactly is this objection? It is an objection to the very idea of the atonement by the incarnate Son, arising from the idea of divine perfection; an apparent incompatibility between perfect being theology and the degradation of God involved in Christ's atonement. As Boso puts it at the outset of the dialogue:

> for what reason and on the basis of what necessity did God – although He is omnipotent – assume the lowliness and the weakness of human nature in order to restore it?[17]

> The unbelievers who scoff at our simplicity raise against us the following objection: that we dishonour and affront God when we maintain that He descended into the womb of a woman, that He was born of a woman, that He grew, being nourished by milk and food for human beings, and – not to mention many other things which seem to be unsuitable for God – that He experienced weariness, hunger, thirst, scourging, and (in the midst of thieves) crucifixion and death.[18]

Let us call this the objection from *unfittingness*. It can be put in the form of a dilemma; either God could not have redeemed sinners by his word alone, in which case he is not omnipotent, but of only limited power, or he could have willed to save by his word alone, but chose not to, but chose to save through the Incarnation. In this case he is foolish, since he willed by becoming incarnate to suffer degradation for no good reason. So either

God is lacking in power, or in wisdom. But God is not lacking in power or wisdom. So the doctrine of atonement by the God-man must be rejected.[19]

In other words, Boso wishes to be shown how it is that the Incarnation is consistent with the idea of divine perfection, and in particular, consistent with the perfection of omnipotence.

From this we can see that Anselm understood himself, in the *Cur Deus Homo*, as carrying further the project of the *Proslogion*. In the latter (as we have seen) he used as a presupposition the idea of God as the most perfect being, and sought to establish the real existence of such a being from this idea alone, and to solve certain paradoxes which his understanding of God's maximal greatness created. Now, in Book I of the *Cur Deus Homo*, he attempts to show that the atonement through Christ is consistent with such divine perfection, in particular with divine justice, wisdom and omnipotence. Nevertheless he holds, as we have already noticed, that the Incarnation is 'a rationale which exceeds human understanding'.[20] So Anselm's basic view is that the Incarnation is an expression of divine perfection, even though the full demonstration and appreciation of this fact is beyond human powers.

ANSELM'S REPLIES

How, then, does Anselm answer the arbitrariness and the unfittingness objections? Because this chapter is not intended as a full-length study of Anselm's thought in the *Cur Deus Homo*, but chiefly of his philosophical procedure in seeking to fulfil the faith seeking understanding programme, we shall illustrate Anselm's faith seeking understanding project by concentrating attention upon Anselm's arguments in Book I of the work, the objection from arbitrariness.

As we have seen, Anselm's entire argument is in answer to objections raised against the very idea of redemption through divine incarnation. And he answers these objections by using premises or presuppositions which his opponents grant; presuppositions such as the nature of satisfaction, and even the nature of necessity itself.[21] This shows both the power and the limitation of Anselm's strategy; it is powerful, if it its cogent, against those who accept certain moral and theological premises, but powerless against those who do not.

Anselm argues against the arbitrariness objection *a posteriori*. He proceeds from the fact of the Incarnation, which he does not seek to interpret in any other way than the way understood in the Church of his day. He does not attempt to offer a 'reductionist' account of the Incarnation and the atonement, to suppose that it is a mere symbolic act, or a metaphor. According to Anselm, God became incarnate in Jesus Christ, and though God himself is unable to suffer (being impassible) he was nevertheless, in the person of the incarnate Son, in union with passible human nature. And – so he wishes to show – such an Incarnation and atonement were (in some sense) necessary, being the outcome of certain states of affairs which themselves are (in a certain sense) necessary.

So what Anselm does is to proceed by assuming the truth an intuitively appealing principle, sometimes referred to as the Transfer Principle. He then attempts to show that Christ's incarnation is a case of this Principle. John Martin Fischer has explained the Principle as follows:

> One starts with a modal property . . . which attaches to something. The principle states that if the thing has the property, and there is an appropriate connection between the first thing and a second thing, then the second thing has the property. That is to say, given an appropriate link, the modal property is projected or transferred from the first thing to the second.[22]

We can apply this to what Anselm is proposing, as follows. The divine character involves a set of modal properties, for whatever character God has he has it necessarily. Consistently with that character, God wills A; so there is an appropriate connection, the connection of consistency, between the divine character and the divine will.[23] (Because of weakness of will and other factors, there is not the same consistency between human character and human will.) Therefore (by the Transfer Principle) whatever God wills must have the moral character that God himself has. In less abstract terms, given the necessity of the divine character, and the divine will to redeem mankind, it was necessary that there be an atonement of the appropriate kind.

So on this interpretation Anselm is not simply arguing that given certain premises a certain conclusion follows, but more precisely, given a certain necessary state of affairs, and the divine will a consistent expression of his nature, then other necessary states of affairs follow.[24]

And what Anselm seeks to show is that the proposition of his faith 'Mankind is redeemed by the God-man' is entailed by a set of necessary propositions about the divine nature, and so (appearances to the contrary) is itself necessary. So *given that God willed a certain end*, he could only carry out that end only in one way.

Karl Barth, consistently with his view of Anselm's procedure in the *Proslogion*, argues that these principles are revealed truths; whether they are or not, the important point is that they are necessary truths, as Anselm sees it. They are drawn from revelation, but are necessary truths about God. So we may say that Anselm's principles are divine perfections which

Anselm is drawing out the consequences of. Anselm's overall procedure is *ad hoc*; sometimes (as in the *Proslogion*), the premises are those of natural theology, at other times, as in the *Cur Deus Homo*, the principles are particular divine perfections; either way, Anselm's preparedness to argue from them in a particular polemical situation are what unifies them as parts of his faith seeking understanding project.

Anselm holds as part of his faith that the redemption of mankind is a free act, an act of God's love and grace:

> For the more miraculously and wondrously he has restored us from such grave and such deserved evils in which we found ourselves – restored us to such great and such undeserved goods which we had lost – the more He has demonstrated the greater degree of His love and graciousness toward us.[25]

God was not constrained, either by logic, or by any external necessities of nature, such as the laws of physics or chemistry, to redeem humankind. One reason why the Incarnation and the atonement could not be actions or events which are absolutely necessitated is that, as we have seen, otherwise they would compromise the divine freedom. So there are necessities and non-necessities in the divine atonement; the non-necessities of the divine will are subsumed under the necessities of the divine nature. (There is a sense in which God was 'constrained' by his own nature but, as Anselm convincingly shows, to suppose that this is a case of real constraint is to be misled by the surface grammar of the expressions in question.)

> For whenever we say 'God is not able', we are not denying His ability but are signifying His insuperable ability and power. For nothing else is meant except that no thing can make Him do what He is said to be unable to do. (This kind of expression is often used; and so, frequently, the reason a thing is said to-be-able is not because there is any ability in it but because there is an ability in some other thing, and [the reason the thing is said] not-to-be-able is not because there is any inability in it but because there is an inability in some other thing. For, in fact, we say 'This man is able to be overcome' in place of 'Someone is able to overcome this man'; and [we say] 'That man is not able to be overcome' in place of 'No one is able to overcome that man'. For to be able to be overcome does not constitute an ability but constitutes an inability; and not to be able to be overcome does not constitute an inability but constitutes an ability.)[26]

Anselm is also concerned, for similar reasons, to show that Christ was not himself externally constrained during the Incarnation. One can only be compelled by God to do something when one does not want to do it; and one does not want to do what God wants only when one has sin:

> Therefore, God did not compel Christ to die, for in Christ there was no sin. Instead, Christ willingly underwent death – not by obeying a command to give up His life, but by obeying the command to keep justice. For He persevered so steadfastly in justice that He incurred death as a result.[27]

That is, Christ behaved in a consistently divine way.

So what Anselm has to do, in pursuit of this part, the central part of his programme, is to provide his readers with a set of propositions each of which will be granted by them to be necessary, and which will, together with a statement about the fact (though not the necessity) of the divine will, necessitate the event of the Incarnation.

Before we enquire as to what these propositions are, and whether they will do the job, it is necessary to clear away one possible misunderstanding. The Christian doctrine of the Incarnation is that God became man, Jesus of Nazareth, born in Bethlehem of Mary a virgin; that Joseph, a carpenter, was his earthly father. And of course there are many more such details. What is said to be true by the Christian Church is not only that God is incarnate, but that he is incarnate in a particular historical matrix, and that all sorts of minor matters were true of that incarnate one.

It would be a mistake to suppose that in setting out to establish the necessity of the atonement Anselm must show that every detail of what took place was necessary;[28] that it was necessary, say, that Jesus' father Joseph was a carpenter; or that Jesus had a particular meal on a particular day; or that he dressed in a particular way. That Jesus ate a particular diet, and dressed in one way rather than another, are truths, and they are truths about the incarnate son of God. But Anselm is not arguing, nor does he need to argue (as Leibniz would argue) that every minute particular that is true of the incarnate Son of God is necessarily true of him, part of his individual essence.

Here we might gain help by distinguishing between action types and action tokens. Two actions may be two tokens of the same type of action; say, two switchings on of the light. To be two such tokens, the actions must have a certain common character. But it is not necessary, in order for two actions to be two switchings, that every particular fact about them must be reduplicated. A switching on of the light with the left hand is equally as much a valid switching as one accomplished with the right hand. Similarly with the Incarnation. It is necessary for any Incarnation that the Son of God become man. An Incarnation is an action type; an atonement is an action type. But it is not necessary for a valid Incarnation that the God-man is employed as a carpenter; it is not necessary for the atonement that the cross on which Christ hung was made of oak, say, and not of cedar.

So it is necessary to distinguish between the Incarnation as a metaphysical or ontological doctrine, and the Incarnation as an event described with full historical particularity. What concerns Anselm is to establish the reasonableness (in the sense already discussed) of the Incarnation as a unique metaphysical event, the event in which God the Son assumed human nature for the redemption of men and women. It is no part of Anselm's project to argue that *whatever* happened to Christ had the same necessity as his becoming God incarnate had, even though he no doubt believed that whatever happened to Christ happened for a good reason.

So what did Anselm take to be those necessary truths which, taken together, necessitated the Incarnation, given a prior divine decree or resolve to redeem men and women from their sin?

Anselm first establishes (in the discussion as far as Bk I Ch.10) that Christ died not of necessity, but of his free will. 'For he was omnipotent; and we read of Him that "He was offered because it was His own will".'[29] He then proceeds in the way which we have already noted, by setting aside the fact of Christ, arguing as if Christ had never been:

> Let us suppose the incarnation of God and the things we say about *that* man never occurred. And let us agree that (1) man was created for happiness, which cannot be possessed in this life, that (2) no one can attain happiness unless his sins have been forgiven, and that (3) no man passes through this present life without sin.[30]

This is an important passage because it sets the parameters of the discussion to follow, and underlines the point made previously, that what Anselm is seeking to do is to establish the *conditional* necessity of the Incarnation. In setting aside the Incarnation he is setting aside from consideration the remedy that Christians believe has in fact been provided for men and women to be freed from their sins and re-established in happiness. But it is important to note that Anselm is not setting aside the convictions that man was made for happiness, and is sinful; the need to have happiness restored, and other matters shortly to be noted, all of which in Anselm's view render an atonement conditionally necessary. Given this need, he now proceeds to show that it can only be met by the Incarnation of God the Son.

So it is from Chapter XI of Book I that the central argument of that Book proceeds. If the atonement was not absolutely necessary, but only conditionally necessary, and if it was partly conditioned by the character of the divine desire or will to redeem, what else conditioned it? Presumably what else conditioned it has to do with human nature, with the fact that man was made for happiness, but is sinful, and that were he to remain in this condition God's purpose for mankind would fail. It is necessary that what God purposes will come to pass, and if his purpose for mankind is happiness then that happiness will be achieved in a way that is consistent with, and is an expression of, God's nature.

Since redemption is redemption from sin, Anselm needs a definition of sin. In his view sin is a failure to repay to God's one debt, i.e. obligation of obedience, and as continuing guilt due to this failure. But this is not a definition in a merely arbitrary or conventional sense, but one which, Anselm holds, arises from the nature of things. Man is created as having obligations; it is part of the nature of mankind to have moral obligations to his Creator. Contrary to what is widely assumed, such moral oughtness is not reducible to a commercial oughtness for Anselm.[31] If and when mankind fails to meet these obligations, and sins, such sin is dishonouring to God, and in order to overcome the insult to God some compensation must be rendered to him. Satisfaction to God for sin against him is therefore necessary, a satisfaction which covers the fulfilment of man's original obligation (which he failed to meet) together with satisfaction for subsequent disobedience. 'This [repayment of stolen honour] constitutes the satisfaction which every sinner is obliged to make to God'.[32] This is a necessary truth about sin, for Anselm. And another necessary truth is that God's justice requires his honour to be satisfied. Atonement for sin, therefore, must have a character that is appropriate for meeting this predicament.

Anselm's argument, therefore, requires particular definitions of human sin and of divine justice. To the extent that his opponent does not accept these definitions Anselm's apologetic strategy will fail, and he will be forced to provide defences of these definitions which he would hope his opponent would accept.

But could not God by his mere mercy freely forgive such sin?[33] This is the objection from divine omnipotence that we noted earlier. If God is free and omnipotent, why may he not simply choose to forgive? Anselm's basic answer to this question is that while God is free he is not free to be lawless, and that sin is committed within a framework of divine law. God's will must be in accordance with his nature. It is not fitting, therefore, for God to condone sin by merely forgiving it. For to forgive is not to punish, and God has no reason not to punish; indeed his rectitude requires that he punish. Sin cannot simply be forgiven, for this would be unjust, 'dis-ordered' in Anselm's terminology.[34] So for Anselm the nature of divine justice is not to be understood primarily in terms of fairness, disinterestedness, or equality (outcome conceptions of justice); the nature of justice involves inputs, inputs of human moral or immoral actions, and justice, the divine justice, requires that the immorality of sin be punished.

Anselm says at one point:

> This kind of divine mercy (viz. the kind that freely forgives sin without satisfaction) is utterly contrary to God's justice, which allows only for punishment to be requited for sin. Therefore, as it is impossible for God to be at odds with Himself, so it is impossible for Him to be merciful in this way.[35]

Note again the prominence of modalities in Anselm's argument. Forgiveness without satisfaction is a form of mercy contrary to God's justice, and to suppose that God might be merciful in this way is to suppose a contradiction. Such a supposition would undo the resolutions of the divine perfections that Anselm proposed in the *Proslogion*. So he appeals to the essential justice of God. For while God is omnipotent, and free, he is not free to do what is inconsistent with his nature, and it would be inconsistent with his nature to forgive sins merely by an act of the will.

Therefore it is a necessary truth, a truth grounded in the nature of things, in the nature of sin and the nature of punishment, which itself is rooted in divine justice, that sin must be punished:

> But as for the statement that what God wills is just and what He does not will is not just: we must not interpret this to mean that if God were to will any kind of unfittingness, it would be *just* simply because He willed it. For the supposition 'God wills to lie' does not warrant the inference 'Lying is just', but, instead, warrants the inference 'This being is not really God'.[36]

Anselm takes an objectivist view of ethics, and regards ethical principles as necessary truths, as being such that not even God is exempt from exemplifying them. So either sin must be punished by the punishment of the offender, or it must be atoned for by another, it cannot be merely forgiven by an act of will. Such an act would be arbitrary and unprincipled. God must uphold his honour. The necessity for God to uphold his own honour is also a conceptual truth for Anselm, another aspect of what Anselm means by the nature of things. Other conceptions of God are possible, of course, but Anselm would reject these as not being in accord with the faith of the Church, and more pertinently as not being in accord with the idea of God as the most perfect being.

Mcintyre alleges a fundamental incompatibility between asserting that

God's honour remains unchanged and that the gravity of human sin lies in the fact that it robs God of his honour.[37] He says that Anselm cannot both assert that God's honour is immutable (as he does in 1.14) and that sin consists in dishonouring God, and that this threatens to cut the nerve of the whole argument of the book.[38] However for Anselm, as we have noted, to rob God of his honour is to fail to give due *recognition* to his character (and perhaps also, to want, if it were possible, to dethrone God), and this for Anselm is the root of all sin. This does not make sin illusory. And as, for Anselm, to rob God of his honour is to fail to give due recognition to it, it is hard to see where the incompatibility that Mcintyre alleges lies. It is axiomatic for Anselm that God's nature cannot change or be changed. But sin consists in the refusal to recognise God's immutable honour, and in the intention (*per impossible*) to dishonour him. According to Anselm, God *upholds* his honour (he does not *recover* his honour) by punishing the sinner or accepting satisfaction in another way.

Further, according to Anselm, God's honour is maintained in that Christ's atonement is a case of good coming out of evil. Mcintyre misunderstands the position.[39] Anselm is stating that God's honour must be upheld, by the punishment of the sinner if necessary. God does not merely take away the prospect of a reward (leaving mankind in a position of neutrality), he punishes him. Such punishment is not a payment which can ever finally be made, and so it cannot be said to be something 'with which to make repayment to God'.[40]

So Anselm presents the honour of God (not the honour that he has essentially, which cannot be lost or compromised in any way[41] but the willing *recognition* of that honour by his intelligent creatures, which can be) as a kind of 'zero-sum' game. Just as, if we are dividing up a cake between us, if you have a larger piece then I must have a smaller, so, if God's honour is not recognised willingly by his creatures, it must be recognised unwillingly by them. If God's honour is not freely recognised then that recognition must be imposed by God. So either God's honour is upheld willingly by his creatures, or unwillingly. But if unwillingly, then the creature is compelled by God to honour him by enduring punishment:

> Similarly, even though men and evil angels do not want to submit to the divine will and ordinance, they are unable to escape from it. For if they want to get out from under God's directive will, they run beneath His punitive will. And – if you ask about the route they traverse – they make their way only under His permissive will. And that which they perversely will or do is redirected by Supreme Wisdom towards the order and beauty of the aforementioned universe.[42]

Nothing falls outside the will of God in one or other of these senses. There is no escape from the requirement of living in a moral order. Not only is the recognition of the honour of God a zero-sum game; but Anselm holds by his remarks on the permissive will that dishonour serves the overall plan of God as does honour.

This redirection of a perverse will by Supreme Wisdom is in fact Anselm's principal way of showing that God cannot be dishonoured in himself.

> If where wickedness tries to disturb right-order Divine Wisdom did not provide for the making of satisfaction and the exacting of punishment, then in the universe (which God ought to order) there would occur a certain marring as a result of the violation of the order's beauty; and God would seem to fail in His governance. Just as these two results are unfitting, so they are impossible; therefore either satisfaction or punishment must follow upon every sin.[43]

In his account of Christ's atonement making satisfaction for others Anselm is unmoved by any thought that one person cannot be punished for the sins of another, and therefore that the substitution of Christ for the sinner is immoral.[44]

This is Anselm's third necessary truth, that it is necessary that God's honour be upheld.

What then follows (Chapters XVI–XVIII) is a statement of God's will or intention couched in the strange idea, apparently widespread in the theological thought of this period, that God wills to replace the number of the fallen angels with the same number of redeemed men and women. The redemption of mankind itself, for Anselm, is not a free act of God if by that is meant an act undertaken without good and sufficient reason; rather it has as its reason the replacement of fallen angels.

But this admittedly obscure proposal, made more obscure by the fact that Anselm holds that there are more elect men and women than fallen angels,[45] does not appear to have the logical character which the structure of Anselm's argument requires. For while there may be an *appropriateness* to the replacement of fallen angels by redeemed men and women, this can hardly be necessary. For why may not the fallen angels themselves be redeemed by the Son of God becoming not incarnate but taking the nature of an angel?[46] While Anselm is elsewhere willing to acknowledge his bafflement at why God should have mercy on *this* person and not *that*,[47] it is hard to see why he ought not to have expressed the same bafflement at why God has mercy on *any*.

The fourth necessary truth, following from this, is thus that a definite number of men and women must be saved, to replace the number of the fallen angels. The importance of this for Anselm's overall project does not lie in its theological rationale or in its detail, but the fact that it enables him to introduce into the argument a proposition about what God wills or desires. Given that God wills or desires the salvation of some men and women (either to replace the fallen angels or for some other sufficient reason), a will that is not itself necessary, then it is necessary that this salvation be effected in a certain way, by means of the atonement provided by the God-man.

So far Anselm has established, consistently with his own theological outlook, a number of necessary truths about God, his honour, and the sin of man. Next comes a crucial step. If man is obliged to honour God his maker throughout his life, but fails through sin to do so, how can the original position of mankind be restored? Even if man began again to honour God after his sin, his sin would remain.

But what is sin? Here follows another crucial move in Anselm's argument. As noted earlier, his basic position is that sin is primarily and essentially an offence against the honour of God, not man; and hence as an offence against God it has an infinite demerit, since God is infinite:

> Now, on the one hand, if God forgives what man ought willingly to pay – forgives it simply because man is unable to pay it – what does this amount to other than that God forgives what He cannot obtain? But it is a mockery to attribute this kind of mercy to God.[48]

> Finally, in the case of obedience, what do you give to God that you do not already owe Him, to whose command you owe all that you are, all that you have, and all that you can do?[49]

> If even had I not sinned I would – in order to keep from sinning – owe to God myself and whatever I can do, I have nothing with which to make payment for my sin.[50]

How is his sin to be removed, if God cannot consistently with his own nature forgive him by an act of free pardon, since such an act would be an act of injustice? Anselm reiterates the point that God cannot merely forgive a sinner:

> But this kind of divine mercy is utterly contrary to God's justice, which allows only for punishment to be requited for sin. Therefore, as it is impossible for God to be at odds with Himself, so it is impossible for Him to be merciful in this way.[51]

There can never be any conflict between the divine attributes, as Anselm has maintained in the *Proslogion*; never be any conflict because they are aspects of the one unified, essential nature of God.

How, then (Boso asks) shall man be saved, if he neither pays what he owes nor ought to be saved unless he pays?[52] (This is the sixth necessary truth, that satisfaction for an offence ought to be commensurate with the seriousness of the offence.)

There must be some other source of divine payment, if there is to be mercy at all. But what can that source be? There are, abstractly considered, three alternatives; either man might not be saved, or be saved by Christ, the God-man, or be saved in some other way. Unbelievers agree in denying the first. Anselm believes himself to have shown that there is no non-divine source of salvation; hence it must follow that the only way of salvation is through the offering of Christ the incarnate Son.

Anselm aims to show that the necessity of salvation through Jesus Christ follows from the impossibility of mankind saving itself, and the imperative need for God's original creative purpose not to be frustrated. But this follows only from his use of other auxiliary premises, as explained.

This is the conclusion of Book I of *Cur Deus Homo* – that only Christ the God-man can provide satisfaction for sin, and that given the divine will to save, it was necessary that he provide it.

NOTES

1. Anselm, *Cur Deus Homo*, p.50.
2. Anselm, *On the Incarnation of the Word*, pp.11f.
3. Anselm, *Cur Deus Homo*, p.43.
4. Anselm, *Cur Deus Homo*, p.50.
5. Anselm, *Cur Deus Homo*, p.51.
6. Anselm, *Cur Deus Homo*, p.55.
7. Leftow, 'Anselm on the Incarnation'.
8. Anselm, *Cur Deus Homo*, p.102.
9. Leftow 'Anselm on the Incarnation', p.169.
10. Hopkins, *A Companion to the Study of St. Anselm*, p.63.
11. Mcintyre, *St Anselm and his Critics*, p.20.
12. Mcintyre, *St Anselm and his Critics*, p.51.
13. Note that in Chapter 25 of Book I Anselm has unbelievers admitting that man by some means may be made blessed. These are unbelievers *respecting the Christian message*, it seems, or sceptics about some particular aspect of Christian teaching, not total unbelievers.
14. Anselm, *Cur Deus Homo*, p.49; this last phrase echoes I Pet. 3:15.
15. See, for example, Anselm's discussion of impossibility and inconsistency in Bk.I, Chs 12 and 15.
16. Anselm, *Cur Deus Homo*, p.49.
17. Anselm, *Cur Deus Homo*, p.50.
18. Anselm, *Cur Deus Homo*, p.52.
19. Anselm, *Cur Deus Homo*, Bk.I Chs 6 and 8.
20. Anselm, *Cur Deus Homo*, p.51.
21. Mcintyre, *St Anselm and his Critics*, p.48.
22. Fischer, *The Metaphysics of Free Will*, p.23. See the whole of Chapter 2, 'The Transfer Principle: Its Plausibility'.
23. This claim to consistency is of course crucial; for this reason the Transfer Principle is not applicable to human actions, which are subject to weakness of will.
24. And so this interpretation of Anselm differs from that of Karl Barth, as reported by Mcintyre, *St Anselm and his Critics*, p.30.
25. Anselm, *Cur Deus Homo*, p.52.

26. Anselm, *Cur Deus Homo*, pp.125f.
27. Anselm, *Cur Deus Homo*, p.61.
28. When Anselm says he aims 'to show that all the things we believe about Christ ought, necessarily, to occur' (p.43) he probably has in mind the central creedal statements about Christ.
29. Anselm, *Cur Deus Homo*, pp.65f.
30. Anselm, *Cur Deus Homo*, p.67.
31. For discussion of this point, see Mcintyre, *St Anselm and his Critics*, Ch.2.
32. Anselm, *Cur Deus Homo*, p.68.
33. Anselm, *Cur Deus Homo*, I.XII.
34. Anselm, *Cur Deus Homo*, p.69.
35. Anselm, *Cur Deus Homo*, p.94.
36. Anselm, *Cur Deus Homo*, p.70.
37. Mcintyre, *St Anselm and his Critics*, p.112.
38. Mcintyre, *St Anselm and his Critics*, p.111.
39. Mcintyre, *St Anselm and his Critics*, pp.108f.
40. Mcintyre, *St Anselm and his Critics*, p.109.
41. Anselm, *Cur Deus Homo*, p.72.
42. Anselm, *Cur Deus Homo*, p.73.
43. Ibid.
44. On the morality of substitution, see Quinn, 'Swinburne on Guilt, Atonement and Christian Redemption'.
45. Anselm, *Cur Deus Homo*, pp.83f.
46. In Book II of *Cur Deus Homo*, (p.136) Anselm claims that since, though fallen angels have the same nature, though they are not of the same race, and since no one abetted their fall, no angel ought to be saved by a God-angel.
47. *Proslogion*, Chapter 11.
48. Anselm, *Cur Deus Homo*, p.94.
49. Anselm, *Cur Deus Homo*, p.87.
50. Anselm, *Cur Deus Homo*, p.88.
51. Anselm, *Cur Deus Homo*, p.94.
52. Anselm, *Cur Deus Homo*, p.95.

7

Jonathan Edwards on Original Sin

So far in this book we have looked at three case-studies of the faith seeks understanding motif drawn from two formative Christian theologians and philosophers, Augustine and Anselm, who worked in conscious fulfilment of that project, though in rather different ways. It is fair to say that much mediaeval philosophy was done in fulfilment of this project. Yet it would be a mistake to think that the faith seeking understanding approach finished at the time of the Reformation; Leibniz, for example, thought of himself as a faith seeking understanding philosopher. In this fourth study we move many centuries and many miles to consider the work of Jonathan Edwards (1703–58), the New England Puritan theologian and philosopher, best known as a philosopher for his masterly work on the freedom of the will.

We have seen that though the motivation for the faith seeking understanding programme was not directly apologetic, its fruits can be used to defend the faith against objections. What is characteristic of the faith seeking understanding approach, however, is that the apologetics that ensue are not exclusively *ad hominem*. That is, the strategy is not simply to show that the objections made to the faith rest upon mistakes made by the objector, but to develop a further understanding of the faith in order to answer the objections, and so, in a sense, to legitimise them as objections. In the example of faith seeking understanding that we are taking from Jonathan Edwards there is a strong apologetic thrust, but one that arises out of what Edwards regarded as a developed understanding of the faith, and particularly the metaphysics which underlies that faith. It was thus Edwards' conviction that the faith, if properly understood, has the intellectual resources to meet the objections that were being made to it.

Edwards lived during the period of the ascendancy of deism, the era of rationalist attacks upon Christian theology characteristic of the Enlightenment. What is noteworthy is that although he was himself theologically conservative, and particularly concerned to uphold the Puritan theology of his New England forbears, he did not hesitate to employ philosophical tools and resources of a type that the deists themselves used to defend the positions that they attacked. This is clear in his work on the freedom of the will, in which he makes use of arguments from John Locke. It is also true in the argument we are about to consider. Although Edwards' philosophical sources (apart from Locke) are not easy to identify we find Edwards keen to use philosophical arguments to elucidate aspects of his theological position, a position which he held chiefly and pre-eminently because it was a matter of revelation. In general, Edwards had the conviction that if a theological proposition is true than it must be both philosophically cogent and (where appropriate) consistent with empirical evidence. In providing philosophical elaborations of positions derived from the faith, Edwards is clearly working in the faith seeking understanding tradition even though he himself did not, as far as one can tell, avow this motif in so many words. He seeks a general philosophical understanding, one rooted in the nature of things as he understood them, and not simply an *ad hominem* argument, in order to show the reasonableness of the faith that he is defending; in the case that we are to examine, to defend the Christian doctrine of original sin.

According to the doctrine of original sin the human race inherits the guilt of Adam which he incurred as a result of the Fall. All mankind is guilty not in the first instance because of the evil of their own actions, but because they are 'in' Adam, and are descended from him. They are 'originally sinful' in Adam; sin is not to be explained chiefly through imitation, but through racial inheritance. The sin of Adam is in some sense (a sense to be clarified later) the sin of the race. This doctrine, variously expressed, and held with varying degrees of strength and precision, is central to Christianity; for without it the atonement of Christ, and the idea of Christ as the 'last Adam' become unintelligible. Accordingly, while the first three of our case studies have been concerned chiefly with aspects of theology, Edwards is chiefly concerned with anthropology, with a proper understanding of creaturely existence through time, in order to rebut objections to original sin.

The Great Christian Doctrine of Original Sin Defended, completed shortly before Edwards' death in 1758, is in four Parts; the first is an examination of the empirical evidence for the truth of the doctrine; the second the Scriptural basis for holding the doctrine; the third 'The Evidence of the Doctrine from the Redemption by Christ', and the last takes up and provides answers to certain objections. Edwards considers three chief objections; that original sin is a contradiction in terms since all sins presuppose individual choice; that the doctrine of original sin makes God the author of sin; and what Edwards calls the 'great objection', 'that such imputation (the imputation of the sin of Adam to his posterity) is unjust and unreasonable, inasmuch as Adam and his posterity are not one and the same'. So the chief philosophical question that Edwards addresses is a moral objection; how can it be equitable to hold a person responsible for the guilt arising from the actions of another? Is it not unfair and arbitrary to do so? And he offers an answer to this moral objection by making a metaphysical claim about identity.

In order to answer the objection Edwards made use not only of John Locke's account of personal identity, but also of some radical ideas about identity and time, and particularly about identity *through* time. The source of these ideas is not clear, though Edwards may have derived them from the Occasionalism of Malebranche.

IDENTITY THROUGH TIME

In order to consider Edwards' defence of the doctrine of original sin from moral objections it is first necessary to think about some of the problems raised by the idea of the endurance of things, especially of people, through time.

In thinking about the persistence of people through time we are confronted by two sets of conflicting intuitions. On the one hand it is natural to say that people change over time. They are born, they mature, grow old and die, a process which involves dramatic physical and psychological change. Let us call these intuitions the *phenomena of difference*. On the other hand there are *phenomena of sameness*, for we are strongly inclined to say that the individual who is born, matures, grows old and dies is the very same individual throughout these changes; that is, numerically the same individual. He is not simply the same *kind* of individual, as Peter and Paul are two of the same kind, two human beings; it is Peter (say) – one individual – to whom all these phenomena of difference occur; it is one and the same person who is born, matures, grows old, and dies.

But how are we to think of this one persisting individual? Again, broadly speaking, there are two ways of answering this question. Let us call these the *exact* and the *inexact* answers. We can best approach these answers by first considering conflicting views about the persistence through time of individual things; not only people, but such things as tables and trees.

Several distinguished twentieth-century philosophers have held the view than an individual, such as a person or a chair, is best understood as a succession of non-overlapping temporal parts or stages. A temporal part may be thought of as an individual thing which exists for only a moment. A thing which we think of as persisting for more than a moment may then be said, on this doctrine, to be made up of a series of momentary temporal parts. According to this view the parts that go to make up, say, a chair at any given moment, are wholly diverse from its parts at other times of its existence. So what we call the chair, the persisting object, is a logical construction out of chair parts or chair stages, temporal parts. So Quine has written:

> A physical thing – whether a river or a human body or a stone – is at any one moment a sum of simultaneous momentary states of spatially scattered atoms or other small physical constituents. Now just as the thing at a moment is a sum of these spatially small parts, so we may think of the thing over a period as a sum of the temporally small parts which are successive momentary states. Combining these conceptions, we see the thing as extended in time and in space alike; the thing becomes a sum of momentary states of particles, or briefly particle-moments, scattered over a stretch of time as well as space.[1]

and,

> The solution of Heraclitus's problem, though familiar, will afford a convenient approach to some less familiar matters. The truth is that you *can* bathe in the same *river* twice, but not in the same river stage. You can bathe in two river stages which are stages of the same river, and this is what constitutes bathing in the same river twice. A river is a process through time, and the river stages are its momentary parts.[2]

This view of the persistence of individual things, including people, as an uninterrupted series of momentary states, the doctrine of temporal parts, is to be distinguished from at least two other views. According to some philosophers it is necessary and sufficient for an individual, including a person, to persist through time that the individual is spatio-temporally continuous as the same sort of thing. As he is commonly interpreted, John Locke held this sort of view about, for example, the persistence of both trees and men and women through time. That is, if we suppose (somewhat crudely) that a tree existing at some time *t1* consists of four parts organised in a characteristically organic fashion, then that tree as it exists at *t2* (a time immediately subsequent to *t1*) might consist of five parts, four of the same numerically identical parts that it possessed at *t1*, and a further part which it has gained. This is familiar to us from the idea of growing things gaining cells; on this view the parts (or cells) that they retain through the period under consideration, are identically the same cells:

> In the state of living creatures, their identity depends not on a mass of the same particles but on something else. For in them the variation of great parcels of matter alters not the identity: an oak growing from a plant to a great tree, and then lopped, is still the same oak; and a colt grown up to a horse, sometimes fat, sometimes lean, is all the while the same horse, though in both these cases there may be a manifest change of the parts, so that truly they are not either of them the same masses of matter, though they be truly one of them the same oak, and the other the same horse.[3]

At any time there are some parts shared by immediately previous and immediately subsequent times, as well as other parts not shared, as parts are lost or gained. Identity does not consist in a persisting core or essence, but in the continuous organisation of an individual of a particular kind.

Locke applies this to personal identity; the principle of identity is consciousness. However else a person may change,

> Since consciousness always accompanies thinking, and it is that that makes everyone to be what he calls *self*, and thereby distinguishes himself from all other thinking things: in this alone consists *personal identity*, i.e. the sameness of a rational being. And as far as this consciousness can be extended backwards to any past action or thought, so far reaches the identity of that *person*: It is the same *self* now it was then, and it is by the same *self* with this present one that now reflects on it, that that action was done.[4]

According to still other philosophers there are at least some things in the universe, notably persons, which are not merely partly numerically identical at each time they exist, with what has gone before, as is true of organic things such as trees and animals, but are wholly numerically identical at each time at which they exist. They can never lose or gain parts, through the processes of growth and decay, because they do not have parts. They are metaphysically simple things which cannot themselves change as individuals, even though these simple things gain or lose characteristics through time. They may have bodies which change, and (in a different sense) they may have thoughts which develop, but they are distinct, as individuals, both from their bodies and their thoughts; they *have* both bodies and thoughts. This is the view of Thomas Reid, who said that the identity of a person is 'perfect identity', and in the twentieth century such a view is held by R. M. Chisholm and Richard

Swinburne,[5] among others. Thus in the course of explaining his views Chisholm defends the following claim:

> If a person may be said to exist at a certain place P at a certain time *t* and also at a certain place Q at a certain time *t1*, then we may infer that something existing at P at *t* is identical with something existing at Q at *t1*.[6]

By asserting such identity Chisholm has in mind what we have called numerical identity. P and Q are numerically the very same thing; it is not merely that they are numerically different but qualitatively identical things. It follows from this view of personal identity that however closely united to his body a person may be, he cannot be identical to his body since his body consists of numerous organically organised parts, which are continuously being lost and gained. Such a view would thus appear to entail a dualistic account of the relation between body and soul.

Edwards is a dualist, but of a rather different kind. He differs from both Locke and Reid, and the philosophical positions that each represents, because he holds that nothing that is created exists for more than a moment. In other words, there is nothing in time which has numerical identity for more than a moment. Locke's view requires that parts of persisting things exist for more than a moment; they may endure for years. Reid held that the soul or self was a simple, numerically identical persisting thing. However, Edwards regarded the beliefs or intuitions to which Locke and Reid appeal as unreliable; the metaphysical reality is otherwise. Let us call Edwards' view a version of the doctrine of temporal parts.

It is this metaphysical doctrine about the identity of all created things, and not just of persons, that Edwards used to help to further understand and defend the Christian doctrine of original sin. However, his understanding of the doctrine of temporal parts is radically different from Quine's, for while Quine held that the doctrine was the best way of thinking about the world, Edwards held that the nature of created reality is such that nothing exists for more than a moment. The doctrine of temporal parts is not just a useful way of thinking about things, it is how things actually are; nothing endures for more than a moment. While Quine's doctrine was essentially *de dicto*, Edwards was essentially *de re*. Edwards expressed this, naturally enough, in terms of the Christian doctrine of creation, and was at pains to stress the idea that the relation between the Creator and any of his creatures is what he called an *immediate* relation of causal dependence. Contrary to the convictions of the deists, the creation is not a law-like state of affairs which persists under its own physical impetus once it is created. Rather, it is a state of affairs which owes its first existence, and each phase of its subsequent existence, to new actions of creation. Its lawlikeness is an expression of the wisdom and faithfulness of the Creator. So the relation between Creator and creation is not mediated via physical laws and powers, but is immediate:

> That God does, by his immediate power, *uphold* every created substance in being, will be manifest, if we consider, that their present existence is a *dependent* existence, and therefore is an *effect* and must have some *cause*: and the cause must be one of these two: either the *antecedent existence* of the same substance, or else the *power of the Creator*. But it can't be the antecedent existence of the same substance. For instance, the existence of the body of the moon, at this present moment, can't be the effect of its existence at the last foregoing moment. For not only was what existed the last moment, no active cause, but wholly a passive thing; but this also is to be considered, that no cause can produce effects in a *time* and *place* in which itself is *not* . . . From these things, I suppose, it will certainly follow, that the present existence, either of this, or any other created substance, cannot be an effect of its past existence. The existences (so to speak) of an effect, or thing dependent, in different parts of space or duration, though ever so *near* one to another, don't at all co-exist one with the other; and therefore are as truly different effects, as if those parts of space and duration were ever so far asunder: and the prior existence can no more be the proper cause of the new existence, in the next moment, or next part of space, than if it had been in an age before, or at a thousand miles distance, without any existence to fill up the intermediate time or space. Therefore the existence of created substances, in each successive moment, must be the effect of the *immediate* agency, will, and power of God.[7]

Thus Edwards did not believe that anything that is created *could* persist for more than a moment of time; so that neither the approach of Locke,[8] nor that of Reid, appealed to him. His commitment to the doctrine of temporal parts requires him to take a different account of the metaphysics of time from that considered earlier when we discussed time and creation in Augustine. For Edwards must hold that a moment is a short period of time, since everything that exists in time exists for only a moment; therefore the present cannot simply be the conceptual boundary between two periods of time, it must have duration.

Shortly we shall look at the reasons why he favoured neither the views of Locke nor Reid. But first we must look at what Edwards had to say about original sin.

ORIGINAL SIN

In common with all orthodox Christianity Edwards accepted the doctrine of original sin upon Scriptural authority, notably St Paul's teaching in Romans 5. When Adam sinned there is a sense in which all the human race sinned 'in' him, and that Adam's posterity, being 'in' him, shared his guilt, and as a consequence is born with 'original sin'. Sin was transmitted through the human race by propagation, not by imitation.

In the history of Christian thought about the relation of Adam to his posterity there have been two main views about how this relation is to be understood. According to the 'realist' view, held by thinkers such as Augustine and Anselm, when Adam sinned, the race of mankind was really 'in' him. Because Adam was the first man, the entire human race was encapsulated in Adam, so that when he sinned, the race really and literally sinned in him. To use the language of later philosophy, Adam was a concrete universal, an individual, but one who nevertheless had a unique and universal relation to all his potential progeny. Adam encapsulated human nature as such, the entire human race. Augustine expressed this in the following way:

> For in him were we all, since we all were that one man . . . we had not our particular forms yet, but there was the seed of our natural propagation which, being corrupted by sin must needs produce man of that same nature, the slave to death, and the object of just condemnation. And therefore this came from the bad using of free will.[9]

> Nor, indeed, are those sins of infancy so said to be *another's*, as if they did not belong to the infants at all, inasmuch as all then sinned in Adam, when in his nature, by virtue of that innate power whereby he was able to produce them, they were all as yet the one Adam; but they are called *another's*, because as yet they were not living their own lives, but the life of the one man contained whatsoever was in his future posterity.[10]

Anselm held essentially the same view. By 'man's defeat the whole of human nature became corrupted'.[11] More precisely:

> In each man are present together a *nature*, by which he is human, as are other men, and a *person*, by which he is distinguished from other men, as when he is called 'this man' or 'that man' or is called by his proper name (e.g., 'Adam' or 'Abel'). The sin of each man is in both his nature and his person; for example, the sin of Adam was in his

humanity (i.e., in his nature) and in the one who was called Adam (i.e. in the person) . . . If Adam and Eve had kept their original justice, those who were to be born of them would originally have been just, even as were Adam and Eve.[12]

What concern us here are the implications of this view for questions of identity. The identity of the race of mankind with the individual, Adam, is a matter of the sort of nature that Adam has. If he was an individual human being only, like you and me, then it would be obviously absurd to suppose that you and I were literally Adam. This would mean that Adam was both you and I, that you and I had Eve as our wife, and so on. Rather, on this view Adam's *nature* was such that he was both an individual and the entire race, and so all the race are corporately identical, though not strictly identical, with Adam, since each is an individual substance of that one nature.

So that on this view there is no problem of how the responsibility of Adam, particularly the guilt that follows sin, is shared by his progeny; it is shared because there is a kind of identity between Adam and the race, an identity of nature deriving from the fact that in Adam all human nature was embodied. So that Adam was not only one individual human being, he was, though an individual, nevertheless also the entire human race as well, because the entire race was 'in' him. So when Adam sinned, you and I sinned, and so the reason why you and I are guilty is that you and I sinned in Adam, and are born, that is, become individual substances, as having sinned in Adam.

The main alternative position, certainly in the covenant theology of Puritan and Reformed tradition in which Edwards stood, was to think of Adam as an individual person, but as someone who stood in a unique *representative* relation to all his potential progeny. On this view Adam, an individual human being, was appointed by God to stand for the entire human race. He was, as the jargon had it, the *federal* head of humanity, just as, in a parallel fashion, Christ is the federal head of the new humanity. As our representative, a representative appointed by God and not by ourselves (for clearly we could not appoint him), we stood to benefit or lose by whatever Adam did. And so when Adam, our representative, sinned, we are justly treated by God as having sinned:

> For the bond between Adam and his posterity is twofold: (1) natural, as he is the father, and we are his children; (2) political and forensic, as he was the prince and representative head of the whole human race. Therefore the foundation of imputation is not only the natural connection which exists between us and Adam (since, in that case, all his sins might be imputed to us), but mainly the moral and federal (in

virtue of which God entered into covenant with him as our head). Hence Adam stood in that sin not as a private person, but as a public and representative – representing all his posterity in that action and whose demerit equally pertains to all.[13]

Because he, as our representative, has failed, we are judged to have failed too, even though we have never ourselves stood, nor could have stood, in the position in which Adam himself stood. The failure is representative, rather than personal. In view of this arrangement, Adam's sin is justly imputed to those whom he represented. We do not simply suffer the consequences of his failure, we are personally implicated in his sin. We bear the consequences, as he did. The only identity there is, is the identity of individual persons; however, one of these individuals can be appointed by God to represent others. On the Augustinian view original sin is a matter of metaphysics, the metaphysics of person and nature, on the federal view, a matter of a divinely instituted arrangement.

As a result of the deep conviction that he had about the immediate dependence of the creation upon the Creator, Edwards did not accept either of these views, the realist or the federal view. Instead he developed an account of the relation between Adam and his progeny in a different direction as part of his overall defence, both philosophical and theological, of the Christian doctrine of original sin. As we have noted, in Part IV of his work, the part dealing with rational objections to the doctrine, he offers answers to objections about the propriety of the close relation between Adam and the race, and in Chapter III of this Part he offers what can best be described as a metaphysical excursus in an attempt to answer 'that great objection against the imputation of Adam's sin to his posterity . . . that such imputation is unjust and unreasonable, inasmuch as Adam and his posterity are not one and the same'.[14] He applies the doctrine of temporal parts to explain and justify the relationship between Adam and his posterity.

Edwards' argument is a reply to the claim that the relation between Adam and his posterity required by the doctrine of original sin is contrary to the nature of things. He replies, in effect, that not only is there an alternative metaphysical explanation of the nature of things than that implied by the realists and the federalists, but that this alternative is the only one open to a theist. Anything which could change is a dependent thing. Whatever is dependent is immediately dependent; and whatever is immediately dependent cannot persist for more than a moment:

A father, according to the course of nature, begets a child; an oak, according to the course of nature, produces an acorn, or a bud; so according to the course of nature, the former existence of the trunk of the tree is followed by its new or present existence. In the one case, and the other, the new effect is consequent on the former, only by the established laws, and settled course of nature; which is allowed to be nothing but the continued immediate efficiency of God, according to a constitution that he has been pleased to establish.[15]

A thing's 'new and present existence' is an existence that is numerically distinct from its immediate past existence. Nothing can exist for more than a moment; the fact that nature, the temporally continuous order of things, is as orderly as it is, is due to the wisdom and power of God, not to the inherent natures of things that he has created.

These words expresses a characteristic Edwardsean concern. It is not sufficient, for Edwards, for a thorough defence of a Christian position, that it is shown to be scriptural and in accordance with the facts. In addition, an attempt must be made to answer objections to the apparent injustice and unreasonableness of a position made by those who do not accept the authority of the revelation on the matter in question. Edwards' argument is *ad hominem* to the extent that he assumes that his objectors believe in a Creator and that the universe is his creation. But what he offers is an 'independent argument,' an argument that does not depend simply upon a careful exposition of the doctrine of original sin from the Bible, but is grounded in the nature of things as Edwards understood them. And the only way to meet such objections is to show, by arguments that the objectors must themselves accept, that their fears are groundless. In this Edwards follows the idea of Christian philosophy characterised by Kretzmann in Chapter 2.

In taking this strategy, it is clear Edwards did not wish to dilute or amend the doctrine being defended; this is another characteristic of the faith seeks understanding project:

> A Christian philosopher may engage in the intellectual exploration and development of fundamental doctrinal propositions in the conviction that the doctrine itself is eminently understandable and acceptable, but in need of clarification of a sort most likely to be accessible through analysis and argument.[16]

It is at this point, then, that the characteristic faith seeking understanding concern emerges, in a situation in which faith seeks understanding by answering objections about the reasonableness of a position, by developing the implications of that position more fully. Such a defence carries interesting theological implications; for example, it implies that what God has done or arranged is reasonable (in some clearly recognisable sense of that term), and furthermore that the reasonableness of any such arrangement can be demonstrated; or, at the very least, that objections that it is *un*reasonable can be satisfactorily rebutted. It is this assumption, that the divine arrangements must be reasonable, that Edwards shares with his deist opponents, though he comes to very different conclusions from them as to what this means in fact.

It is the development of Edwards' answer to this objection that leads him to discuss the nature of identity, particularly the identity of individual things, and to adopt a version of the doctrine of temporal parts that we outlined earlier.

EDWARDS AND IDENTITY THROUGH TIME

Edwards begins his positive account of the metaphysics of Adam's relation to his posterity by first offering a version of John Locke's view of identity through time which he gives in his *Essay Concerning Human Understanding*. Writing of the continued identity of trees and plants Locke argued:

> That being then one plant which has such an organization of parts in one coherent body, partaking of one common life, it continues to be the same plant as long as it partakes of the same life, though that life be communicated to new particles of matter vitally united to the living plant, in a like continued organization, conformable to that sort of plants.[17]

Edwards argued in a similar way:

> God, according to an established law of nature, has in a constant succession communicated to it many of the same qualities, and most important properties, as if it were one.[18]

'As if it were one', that is, numerically one, though in fact (of course) it is not numerically one. A series of momentary parts, qualitatively similar in important respects, is treated both by ourselves and by God as if it were numerically one thing. The law of nature referred to here is a law established by God.

This is also the case with a man, and with the union of body and soul and, more relevantly for our purposes, with personal identity. Edwards once again begins with the Lockean account of personal identity through time, according to which same consciousness is *necessary* for personal identity. Unlike Locke, however (at least on most interpretations of what Locke wrote), Edwards did not regard same consciousness as *sufficient* for persisting personal identity:

> And if we come even to the *personal identity* of created intelligent beings, though this be not allowed to consist wholly in what Mr Locke supposes, i.e. *same consciousness*; yet I think it can't be denied, that this is one thing essential to it.[19]

That is, persisting personal identity requires having the same persisting consciousness. But, as we shall shortly see, Edwards understands this sameness in a rather different way from Locke. For it is here that Edwards' idea of creaturely dependence, mentioned earlier, begins to play a crucial role in the argument.

According to Edwards any individual which is what he called 'dependent', that is, created, depends both for its initial existence and also for its continued existence upon the operation of laws of nature, and the laws of nature in turn depend upon, or are expressions of, the upholding agency of God.

So far it seems that all that Edwards is doing is adding a further, an explicitly theological stage, an account in terms of divine creation, to the familiar Lockean account of identity. However, this second stage of Edwards' account contains a radical twist. He imparts this twist by reaffirming that the divine upholding of all the forces of nature, including the laws of nature, is *immediate*. That is, any individual which exists at a time is caused to exist at that time only by an exertion of the power of God, the effect of which is contemporaneous with the individual at that time. This divine power is causally *necessary and sufficient*, without the instrumentality of any other force or agency, to uphold that individual at that time. In particular, no created thing that existed at any moment prior to the moment in question could cause the existence of anything at that moment or subsequently. For how could what has gone before contribute causally to what is present, Edwards asks, since what has gone before no longer exists? How can that which no longer exists now have any causal influence upon the present?

> That God does, by his immediate power, *uphold* every created substance in being, will be manifest, if we consider that their present existence is a *dependent* existence, and therefore is an *effect* and must have some *cause*; and the cause must be one of these two: either the *antecedent existence* of the same substance, or else the *power of the Creator*. But it can't be the antecedent existence of the same substance. For instance, the existence of the body of the moon at this present moment, can't be the effect of its existence at the last forgoing moment. For not only was what existed the last moment, no active cause, but wholly a passive thing; but this also is to be

considered, that no cause can produce effects in a *time* and *place* in which itself is *not* . . . Therefore the existence of created substances, in each successive moment, must be the effect of the *immediate* agency, will, and power of God.[20]

This requires a little explaining. What Edwards is saying is that nothing that is created exists for more than a moment. Why not? Why could not something created exist for several moments? Because, according to Edwards, in order for this to happen what exists at an earlier moment would have to causally contribute to what exists later by enabling what exists to persist. But how could what no longer exists contribute to anything? What no longer exists has no causal powers. Such a contribution would, in any case, be a kind of *creatio ex nihilo*, and would rival and undermine the powers of the Creator, because one created thing would be causing another created thing to exist, or to endure. In order to see how radical this view is, let us compare it with how Descartes argues in his *Meditations*. In the third *Meditation*, in arguing against the possibility that he has always existed, Descartes puts forward a very similar idea to that expressed by Edwards:

For though I assume that perhaps I have always existed just as I am at present, neither can I escape the force of this reasoning, and imagine that the conclusion to be drawn from this is, that I need not seek for any author of my existence. For all the course of my life may be divided into an infinite number of parts, none of which is in any way dependent on the other; and thus from the fact that I was in existence a short time ago it does not follow that I must be in existence now, unless some cause at this instant, so to speak, produces me anew, that is to say, conserves me. It is as a matter of fact perfectly clear and evident to all those who consider with attention the nature of time, that, in order to be conserved in each moment in which it endures, a substance has need of the same power and action as would be necessary to produce and create it anew, supposing it did not yet exist, so that the light of nature shows us clearly that the distinction between creation and conservation is solely a distinction of the reason.[21]

Like Descartes, Edwards tends to think of divine conservation as a continuous creation, and what we call natural causes are simply the factors which precede but which do not bring about what follows them. And nature is nothing, 'separate from the agency of God'; that is, there are no agents which have their causal power independently of the causal power of God. Indeed, Edwards faces the stark possibility that perhaps there are, strictly speaking, no agents other than God. As he puts it,

> God's *preserving* created things in being is perfectly equivalent to a *continued creation*, or to his creating those things out of nothing at *each moment* of their existence. If the continued existence of created things be wholly dependent on God's preservation, then those things would drop into nothing, upon the ceasing of the present moment, without a new exertion of the divine power to cause them to exist in the following moment.[22]

This goes significantly beyond Descartes, in that Edwards is claiming that no created being can be preserved in being beyond a moment. Nothing created that exists can exist for more than a moment. Not even God can preserve in existence for more than a moment a being that is numerically identical or that has numerically identical parts. By itself Edwards' argument from causation is not sufficient to enable him to conclude to the doctrine of temporal parts, since there would appear to be no inconsistency in the idea that although no past phase of a numerically identical individual (say, at time $t1$) could contribute causally to any present ($t2$) or future phase ($t3$), nevertheless God could causally uphold one numerically individual thing through the period $t1$–$t3$. And there are times when Edwards appears to take this view, a view very similar to Descartes. Thus at one point Edwards concurs with the view that the present existence of created substances is the effect or consequence of past existence, according to the nature of things.[23]

However, there is one further element in Edwards' account which takes him beyond Descartes, to embrace an even more radical position. He claims that God's immediate creative or conserving activity:

> is altogether equivalent to an *immediate production out of nothing*, at each moment, because its existence at this moment is not merely in part from God, but wholly from him; and not in any part, or degree, from its antecedent existence. For, the supposing, that its antecedent existence *concurs* with God in *efficiency*, to produce some part of the effect, is attended with all the very same absurdities, which have been shown to attend the supposition of its producing it wholly.[24]

So there are in what Edwards says two different doctrines about divine creation, identity and time. According to the first of these, if A is a dependent individual existing in time (as, according to Edwards, all individuals except God are), then A will not continue to exist for a moment longer unless God wills its continued existence. This is also the view of Descartes, as we have seen. But according to the second, the stronger doctrine, if A is a dependent individual then A will continue to exist for a moment longer *only if God re-creates A for that moment*, and continues to recreate the individual for all succeeding moments of its existence. the re-created A is thus a numerically distinct individual from the first created A, though qualitatively similar, or even qualitatively identical.

These two accounts, the one that Edwards shares with Descartes, and the stronger account, are different in the following respect. It is compatible with the weaker doctrine that at any moment after the first moment of A's existence A may consist partly, or wholly, of numerically identical parts that A had at the immediately previous time. Or, if A has no parts, A may be wholly numerically identical with the same individual that it was at the immediately previous time. By contrast, the second, stronger doctrine requires that A's existence at a time cannot consist in the persistence of any of the same parts, numerically speaking, that A had at an immediately previous time; or, if A has no parts, of A itself. This is because, according to Edwards, the existence of a created substance 'be wholly the effect of God's immediate power, in that moment, without any dependence on prior existence, as much as the first creation out of nothing'.[25]

Hugh McCann and Jonathan Kvanvig employ a similar argument to that used by Edwards, in arguing for the impossibility of a diachronic causal nexus.[26] That is, they deny that earlier events can be causally responsible for later events, on the grounds that if time is a densely ordered continuum, that is, an ordered continuum with no gaps, then either any earlier event has an interval between it and some later event, or not. If there is an interval, then e occurs before $e1$ but the two events are not temporally contiguous, and so the earlier cannot cause the later; if there is no interval, then they occur at the same time, and the two events are in fact one event, and the question of one event causing the other cannot therefore arise.

So that if there *is* an interval between e and $e1$, then e cannot be the cause of $e1$ since there is a gap between e's going out of existence, and $e1$'s coming into existence:

> Nothing can exercise direct productive efficacy if it does not exist at the time of the exercise. So if e and $e1$ are point events occurring at different times, there is no direct productive relation between them.[27]

And to suppose the relation is indirect raises precisely the same problems again, this time between e and any intervening event or events, and $e1$.[28] Given his remarks about the 'course of nature' Edwards would appear to endorse the position of Kvanvig and McCann that everything immediately depends upon God, but that nevertheless scientific laws have explanatory force.

Kvanvig and McCann conclude that the creative activity of God is responsible for the existence of things, but that He employs no means to see to their continued existence, or to make sure they have any of the character they do.[29]

Like Edwards, Kvanvig and McCann have a concern about the integrity of scientific laws.[30] They say that the divine activity can be explained in a (realist) law-like way, so long as the laws are not supposed to express productive relations. Similarly with explanatory asymmetries, which are largely temporal. However, the authors deny the stronger of the Edwardsean claims, 'We need not think of the universe as appearing anew at each moment of its existence in order to reach this result'[31] because God, in creation, brought about the being of the universe, and it is this being that he immediately conserves in existence.

Edwards himself appears to oscillate between the weaker and the stronger doctrine. On the one hand he thinks that nothing in the past can have any causal influence on anything that exists in the present. The temporally unfolding universe is like a rapidly changing series of stills, each still having an existence independent of all the other stills. There is no temporal overlap between the stills, nor any temporal gap between any of them, and so no still can exert any causal influence upon another. So the continued existence of anything, its persistence through time, requires a series of *creationes ex nihilo*: that is, it requires the power of God to be immediately and continuously exerted:

> The antecedent existence is nothing, as to any proper influence or assistance in the affair: and consequently God produces the effect as much from *nothing*, as if there had been nothing *before*. So that this effect differs not at all from the first creation, but only *circumstantially*; as in the first creation there had been no such act and effect of God's power before: whereas, his giving assistance afterwards, *follows* preceding acts and effects of the same kind, in an established order.[32]

This is the stronger doctrine. On the other hand Edwards, in common with Descartes, allows that 'the established course of nature is sufficient to continue existence, where existence is once given'.[33] And with this weaker doctrine goes the idea of God conserving or preserving his creation, as distinct from God continually creating his creation by a series of *creationes ex nihilo*.

However he may oscillate between the two positions, it is the stronger,

more radical position that Edwards needs in order to rebut the objection
which he is considering at this point in his treatment of original sin, the
objection that the imputation of Adam's sin to his posterity implies
falsehood because it contradicts the true nature of things.

Edwards' reply to this is that Adam is constituted the 'root' of the human
race by virtue of a 'a real union between the root and branches of the world of
mankind'.[34] There are no unions (i.e. identities) through time in any part of
the creation except those established in accordance with the wisdom and
faithfulness of God. Just as the union between various stages of a tree are
constituted by the likeness of those stages, so the propriety of constituting a
union between Adam and his posterity is based on the establishment of God:

> From what has been observed it may appear, there is no sure ground
> to conclude, that it must be an absurd and impossible thing, for the
> race of mankind truly to partake of the sin of the first apostacy, so as
> that this, in reality and propriety, shall become *their* sin; by virtue of a
> real union between the root and branches of the world of mankind
> (truly and properly availing to such a consequence) established by the
> Author of the whole system of the universe; to whose establishment is
> owing all propriety and reality of union, in any part of that system;
> and by virtue of the full consent of the hearts of Adam's posterity to
> that first apostacy. And therefore the sin of the apostacy is not theirs,
> merely because God *imputes* it to them; but it is *truly* and *properly*
> theirs, and on that ground, God imputes it to them.[35]

Imputation is a reckoning of what is true, and what is true is the union of
Adam and the race. Imputation is not therefore a fiction, nor an arbitrary
act, but it is founded on the nature of things. Edwards' argument can be
expressed as follows:

1. The identity of any dependent individual depends wholly upon
   the arbitrary will of the Creator (established as the only rationally tenable position, by the previous argument).
2. Therefore there is no 'natural' identity through time of anything.
3. Therefore it is possible that Adam and his posterity may, for
   certain purposes, be constituted a unity by God.
4. God has in fact constituted a unity between Adam and his
   posterity, as is shown in Scripture, and by the consent we all
   give to the sin of Adam.
5. Therefore the objection that the divinely-constituted unity
   between Adam and his posterity contradicts the true nature of
   things is invalid.

Note that the 'possibility' referred to in (3) is metaphysical possibility. Edwards is arguing that the unity constituted by God does not violate nature, since nature is itself the constitution of God. It does not violate that orderly set of arrangements instituted by God.

The weaker thesis, the one which Edwards shares with Descartes, according to which God preserves or conserves the unity of already created things, would not be sufficiently powerful to establish the desired conclusion, the conclusion expressed in (5) above. For Edwards is arguing that there is no unity through time of anything except that which God constitutes. What he does *not* mean by this, and cannot mean, is that at any time there are antecedent 'natural' unities which God continues in being; rather, according to the stronger doctrine which Edwards needs, God's will is the necessary and sufficient causal condition for the first existence and then for the continued existence of any dependent thing. If Edwards held only the weaker thesis then he would at once lay himself open to the charge that there was an antecedent 'nature of things', which constrained what God could and could not do, and this would embarrass his insistence on the idea of divine immediacy.

However, strong as this doctrine is, and necessary for Edwards' defence of the doctrine of original sin, it must not be confused with an even stronger doctrine which Edwards did not hold but which he has been mistakenly thought to hold.

In *Person and Object* Roderick Chisholm has this to say about Edwards' position:

> But God, according to Jonathan Edwards, can contemplate a collection of objects existing at different times and 'treat them as one'. He can take a collection of various individuals existing at different times and think of them as all constituting a single individual. Edwards thus appeals to a doctrine of truth by divine convention; he says that God '*makes truth* in affairs of this nature'. God could regard temporally scattered individuals – you this year, me last year, and the Vice-President the year before that – as comprising a single individual. And then he could justly punish you this year and me last year for the sins that the Vice-President committed the year before that.[36]

While Edwards stresses that the divine constitution is causally sufficient for the continued existence of any dependent thing, he also maintains that the divine will is 'arbitrary', and this may seem to provide a justification for Chisholm's interpretation of his position. As Edwards himself put the point:

And there is no identity or oneness in the case, but what depends on the *arbitrary* constitution of the Creator; who by his wise sovereign establishment so unites these successive new effects, that he *treats them as one*, by communicating to them like properties, relations and circumstances; and so, leads us to regard and treat them as one. When I call this an arbitrary constitution, I mean, that it is a constitution which depends on nothing but the divine will; which *divine will* depends on nothing but the *divine wisdom*.[37]

As this quotation makes clear Edwards did not hold that just any set of things whatsoever could, by the divine will, be constituted into a unity. For instance he did not hold that my left shoe today, the Taj Mahal ten years ago, and my favourite cherry tree tomorrow, could be constituted into a unity simply by the divine will.

Edwards' phrases 'arbitrary constitution' and 'treats them as one' can be misleading if they are taken in isolation. It is important to bear in mind that by 'arbitrary' Edwards simply means 'dependent upon the will' (*arbitrium*), and that the divine will and the divine wisdom cannot in his view be separated. The divine will is necessarily an expression of the divine wisdom. Similarly, the phrase 'treats them as one' may suggest either whimsy or even mindless tyranny, but Edwards makes clear the sense in which he intends his readers to take this phrase by adding that God can only treat new effects as one 'by communicating to them like properties, relations and circumstances'; in the case of Adam and his posterity, the properties include significant moral properties.

So there are necessary conditions for God, given his wisdom and justice, to treat two successive momentary individuals as the same individual, namely sufficient qualitative similarity between or among them. On this particular point Edwards remained a faithful Lockean in his treatment of identity, including personal identity. Locke had argued that two things, say A in 1993 and B in 1994 are identical if they are of the same kind and there is spatio-temporally continuous history of that kind linking them. The only difference between Locke and Edwards is that whereas Locke thought of the natures of things as being relatively independent of God, Edwards thinks of them as being immediately constituted by the wisdom of God. But both Locke and Edwards agree that not just anything can constitute a nature.

According to Edwards for any number of 'temporal slices' to be constituted one continuous thing they must be spatially and temporally continuous, and have sufficient qualitative identity (though not, of course, numerical identity) to make it possible for a wise God to treat them as one.

What counts as sufficient qualitative identity will vary from case to case. This is what Edwards means when he refers to God treating successive effects of his will as one by communicating to them *similar* properties, relations and circumstances. That is, in the wisdom of God the 'stills' which make up temporally continuous individuals are qualitatively similar in character, besides being spatially and temporally contiguous, having a degree of similarity appropriate to the kind of thing in question.

For there to be the continuous identity of an individual that individual has to be of a certain kind; a horse, a house, a mouse, a man or whatever. So that while continuity of numerically identical parts is not necessary for the continued existence of an individual of a certain kind, not necessary because (Edwards held) such a condition is impossible to satisfy, yet sufficient continuity of qualitative parts is necessary for the continued existence of something. John Locke expressed the continued identity of a plant in the following terms:

> That being then one plant which has such an organization of parts in one coherent body, partaking of one common life, it continues to be the same plant as long as it partakes of the same life, though that life be communicated to new particles of matter vitally united to the living plant, in a like continued organization, conformable to that sort of plants.[38]

It is vital for Edwards that his account of the relation between Adam and his posterity conforms to this Lockean principle. However, in using this principle Edwards is not claiming that it is reasonable to suppose that Adam and his posterity are *the same person* because of the communication of life. This would obviously not work. For Adam had millions of progeny, and if Adam is identical say with Jones, one of his progeny, and also identical with Smith, another, then it would follow that Smith and Jones are themselves identical with each other; hardly a satisfactory result. What Edwards' use of the Lockean principle is intended to show is not that Adam and Smith are the very same person, but that it is reasonable *to regard them* as the same person for certain purposes because of the similarity between them, and the impossibility of there ever being strict numerical identity through time. In other words, he uses the Lockean principle to set up an argument from analogy.

Since according to the doctrine of temporal parts nothing that exists at a time can be numerically identical with anything that exists at any other time, the only remaining question, as regards identity, is whether or not there is sufficient similarity or analogy between Adam and each of his descendants on the one hand, and different sets of objects which are commonly and justifiably regarded as a unity for certain purposes on the other hand. As we have seen Edwards, using Locke's principle, judges that there is. If we are justified in treating these as a unity, then God is justified in treating Adam and his posterity as a unity, a forensic unity.

Another analogy which Edwards uses is between Adam and his posterity on the one hand, and the past actions and present responsibilities of a person on the other. A person, let us call him Jones, is responsible for many of his actions in the past but, according to the doctrine of temporal parts, he cannot be strictly identical with the individual who performed those actions, but he must be a later temporal part or slice of that individual, no later slice of anything having a closer relation to the earlier Jones than the later Jones does. The later Jones is responsible for the actions of the earlier Jones even though he is not strictly identical with the earlier Jones. These relations between the earlier and later Jones are established by the will of God, according to Edwards:

> It appears, particularly, from what has been said, that all oneness, by virtue whereof pollution and guilt from past wickedness are derived, depends entirely on a divine establishment. 'Tis this, and this only, that must account for guilt and an evil taint on any individual soul, in consequence of a crime committed twenty or forty years ago, remaining still, and even to the end of the world and for ever. 'Tis this, that must account for the continuance of any such thing, anywhere, as *consciousness* of acts that are past; and for the continuance of all *habits*, either good or bad: and on this depends everything that can belong to *personal identity*.[39]

Edwards is not claiming that Cain is as much a unity with Adam as a previous temporal slice of Jones is a unity with the present temporal slice of Jones. Rather, he claims that there is enough of a similarity between the cases to make the analogy a plausible one. Just as the question, Why should the present Jones be praised or blamed for something done in the past by an individual related to him but not strictly identical to him? can be satisfactorily answered, according to Edwards, only by drawing attention to the relations between the two phases of Jones, so the question, Why should Cain be held responsible, and so guilty for something done by Adam, not strictly identical to him? can only be answered in a similar way, by reference to the relations that God has constituted between Adam and Cain, relations which are not dissimilar to those that obtain between the earlier and the later Jones.

But why does not Edwards simply rest content with using the Lockean account of identity coupled with the weaker version of the doctrine of temporal parts? The obvious reason is that he believed the strong doctrine of temporal parts to be true. Moreover, as we have already noted, if Adam's relation to his posterity were regarded as a straightforward instance of Lockean identity through time it would have the absurd consequence of making Adam to be the same individual as Cain and as each of his descendants.

So Edwards needs both the stronger doctrine of temporal parts, in order to rebut the objection about the true nature of things, and he needs the positive analogies which he derives from Locke in order to show that things existing at different times may still be regarded as unities for certain purposes, even though they are not strictly identical, and could never have been.

COMMENT

The primary aim of this chapter, and of all the case studies we are considering, is to illustrate the faith seeking understanding project at work in various contexts. But the Edwardsean doctrine of immediate divine upholding, and the doctrine of temporal parts which is its corollary, is so extraordinary that it is worth spending a little time assessing it further. In asking whether it is plausible, there seem to me to be a couple of things that we need to consider.

Firstly, the view is counterintuitive. That is, we all naturally assume that we exist as numerically the same persons from day to day, despite many changes to our personalities and circumstances. It is hard to accept the Edwardsean view, therefore, that nothing is numerically identical with anything that existed a moment ago, but that everything, each moment, is created anew. Another way of making the point is to stress that the view that Edwards implies is part of the true understanding of personal identity seems to form no part of the view of Christian believers, so that the development of understanding would seem to require the overturning of some of the first ideas of faith. To say that this view is counterintuitive does not mean to say that it is false; nor is it unusual for a philosophical view to be counterintuitive. But given that it is counterintuitive Edwards needs to have a particularly strong reason for affirming that it is true.

Secondly, the view of personal identity we find expressed in *The Great Christian Doctrine of Original Sin Defended* appears to be at odds with other things Edwards claims elsewhere in his writings. For example in his most famous work, *The Freedom of the Will* (1754), Edwards maintains in no uncertain terms a version of causal determinism as applied to human actions. There he says that our actions are caused by our volitions, our desires. If the idea of causation being used here is a temporal notion, that is, if part of what it means to say that X causes Y is that X is an event that precedes Y in time, and brings Y to pass, then what Edwards is saying is that Smith's volition at *t1* brings about Smith's action at *t2*. But then this would appear to presuppose both the existence of Smith at these two times, and the real causal efficacy of Smith's desire; Smith's desire brings about his action at a later time. But as we have seen, in his work on original sin Edwards appears to be denying that either of these are possible.

If this is a failure in consistency, then it has serious repercussions for Edwards' work as a theologian and philosopher if we think of him in the faith seeking understanding tradition. For, as we have stressed, one of the intended fruits of understanding is to display the coherence, that is, the internal consistency, of the Christian faith, and so to rebut the charge that the faith is unreasonable or arbitrary.

Of course there may be some way of showing that this inconsistency between two of Edwards' great works is apparent, and not a real inconsistency. And it would clearly be vital to do this if Edwards overall philosophy is to be taken as reflecting a gain in understanding.

NOTES

1. Quine, *Methods of Logic*, pp.222f.
2. Quine, *From a Logical Point of View*, p.65. See also Quine, *Word and Object* pp.114ff. It would, however, be inaccurate to suppose that Quine thought that such a view of time and change was required by the nature of anything; rather it is in his view that description of reality which is attended with the fewest logical difficulties.
3. Locke, *An Essay Concerning Human Understanding*, Vol.i, p.276.
4. Locke, *An Essay Concerning Human Understanding*, Vol.i, p.281.
5. Chisholm, *Person and Object*, Ch.iii; Swinburne, *The Evolution of the Soul*.
6. Chisholm, *Person and Object*, p.97.
7. Edwards, *Original Sin*, pp.400f.
8. Edwards comments on Locke's views as follows: 'and if we come even to the *personal identity* of created intelligent beings, though this be not allowed to consist wholly in that which Mr Locke places it in, i.e. *same consciousness*; yet I think it can't be denied, that this is one thing essential to it. But 'tis evident, that the communication or continuance of the same consciousness and memory to any subject, through successive parts of duration, depends wholly on a divine establishment' (*Original Sin*, p.398).
9. Augustine, *City of God*, Vol.2, p.10.
10. Augustine, *On the Merits and Remission of Sins, and on the Baptism of Infants*, p.74.
11. Anselm, *Cur Deus Homo*, p.92.
12. Anselm, *The Virgin Conception and Original Sin*, pp.144f.
13. Turretin, *Institutes of Elenctic Theology*, Vol.ii, p. 616.
14. Edwards, *Original Sin*, p.389.
15. Edwards, *Original Sin*, p.401.
16. Kretzmann, 'Faith Seeks, Understanding Finds', p.2.
17. Locke, *Essay Concerning Human Understanding* Vol.i, p.277.
18. Edwards, *Original Sin*, pp.397f.
19. Edwards, *Original Sin*, p.398.
20. Edwards, *Original Sin*, pp.400f.
21. Descartes, *Philosophical Works*, Vol.i, p.168.
22. Edwards, *Original Sin*, pp.401f.
23. Edwards, *Original Sin*, p.401.

24. Edwards, *Original Sin*, p.402.
25. Ibid.
26. 'The Occasionalist Proselytizer', p.598. See also Kvanvig and McCann, 'Divine Conservation and the Persistence of the World'.
27. McCann and Kvanvig, 'The Occasionalist Proselytizer', p.599.
28. And even if events are regarded not as points, but as having duration, the problems recur. (For details, see Kvanvig and McCann p.601.)
29. Kvanvig and McCann, 'The Occasionalist Proselytizer', p.610.
30. Kvanvig and McCann, 'The Occasionalist Proselytizer', pp.610f.
31. Kvanvig and McCann, 'The Occasionalist Proselytizer', p.590.
32. Edwards, *Original Sin*, p.402.
33. Edwards,*Original Sin*, p.401. Edwards continues, 'But then it should be remembered, what nature is, in created things: and what the established course of nature is; that, as has been observed already, it is nothing, separate from the agency of God'.
34. Edwards, *Original Sin*, p.407.
35. Edwards, *Original Sin*, pp.407f. See also pp.386f.
36. Chisholm, *Person and Object*, p.139.
37. Edwards, *Original Sin*, pp.402f.
38. Locke, *An Essay Concerning Human Understanding*, Vol.I, p.277.
39. Edwards, *Original Sin*, p.405.

8

John Calvin's Sensus Divinitatis

The final case-study we shall consider brings us into the twentieth century. Although we have touched on central epistemological issues, we have so far been largely concerned with 'faith seeking understanding' as it is applied to the metaphysical or ontological structure of the Christian faith; such matters as the relationship between creation and time, or between the divine will and the atonement, or the character of God's upholding of all things. In this final chapter a central issue in epistemology will take centre stage. We shall be concerned with the question of what is necessary for the chief articles of the Christian faith to be reasonably believed, and with some of the implications of one answer to this question.

As we saw in the first two chapters positive answers to the question of what warrants Christian belief form themselves into two broad traditions. According to one tradition, perhaps the more dominant, belief in the central articles of the Christian faith, and certainly belief in the first article, the existence of God, is justified or warranted when the reasons for that belief are reasons that any rational person would accept. We may call this the *full evidentialist* position, for the reasons sought and given are those that are derived from evidence available to anyone. This position has given rise to the great debates of natural theology.

According to the other tradition, while full evidentialism is a permissible position, it is not required for belief in the existence of God to be rational. We have seen how Aquinas has been claimed by each of these traditions. Some think of the Five Ways as instances of establishing the existence of God according to the requirements of full evidentialism.[1] Others have seen the Five Ways as cases of faith seeking understanding,[2] with the achieving of *scientia* being sufficient for understanding, though not necessary.

Opposition to full evidentialism may take various forms, from the anti-rationalism of a Tertullian to the view that one requires reasons for belief, but that one does not need reasons which are acceptable to any rational person.

Let us call the view that reasons are necessary for belief, but that the reasons in question need not be so strong as to be acceptable to every rational person, *partial evidentialism*. One might support this position by arguing that evidentialism is in general too strong a requirement. Few of our beliefs, if any, meet it. Instead one may argue that some weaker form of appeal to evidence is all that is warranted. One might also draw a distinction between what is required to make a view *reasonable*, and what is required to *justify* that belief, arguing that it might be reasonable for a person to believe in God without, strictly speaking, that belief being justified.[3] Or again, one might argue that the very idea of justification is a person-relative notion; that one cannot speak of the justification or the reasonableness of a belief *simpliciter*, but only in relation to what a person already believes. All these would be among the ways in which one might develop partial evidentialist versions of theistic belief.

An alternative approach to the denial of full evidentialism, and one that we shall explore in this chapter, is to claim, more radically, that the Christian faith itself contains the resources necessary to make belief in God rational. The idea of seeking reasons for faith, whether in furtherance of the full evidentialist or partial evidentialist strategies, is something that is not required at all for Christian faith to be rational. Reasons may be given for Christian belief, but they are not required. Let us call this position *non-evidentialism*. While, like Tertullian and the fideist tradition, this position rejects the need for natural theology, it does this by providing arguments for this position. It provides general reasons why natural theology is unnecessary; it sees no clash between faith and reason; the argument is about what reason requires. Further, it insists on the importance of reason, and allows that though natural theology is not necessary in order to defend the rationality of belief in God, it is nevertheless an allowable and useful activity.

While some cases of full evidentialism can be seen as expressions of faith seeking understanding, and perhaps (as we have noted) Aquinas' Five Ways are examples of this, partial evidentialism and non-evidentialism obviously lend themselves wholesale to the faith seeking understanding treatment. This is particularly true in the case of non-evidentialism. For what it claims is that the Christian faith itself contains the reasons to make belief in God rational. Thus the satisfactory articulation of the faith will not only make its internal rational structure clear and available, it will also display the grounds that make the faith credible or rationally acceptable.

In this chapter we shall largely be concerned with two contemporary defences of non-evidentialist approaches to theistic belief, each of which takes its inspiration from some claims about the knowledge of God made by the Reformer, John Calvin. So far we have studied examples of faith seeking understanding operating on some of the basic concepts of the Christian faith; and also on the text of Scripture. Here it operates by considering ideas from the writings of a Christian theologian.

Early on in his *Institutes of the Christian Religion*, John Calvin asserted that:

> There is within the human mind, and indeed by natural instinct, an awareness of divinity. This we take to be beyond controversy. To prevent anyone from taking refuge in the pretense of ignorance, God himself has implanted in all men a certain understanding of his divine majesty. Ever renewing its memory, he repeatedly sheds fresh drops. Since, therefore, men one and all perceive that there is a God and that he is their Maker, they are condemned by their own testimony because they have failed to honor him and to consecrate their lives to his will. If ignorance of God is to be looked for anywhere, surely one is most likely to find an example of it among the more backward folk and those more remote from civilization. Yet there is, as the eminent pagan says, no nation so barbarous, no people so savage, that they have not a deep-seated conviction that there is a God.[4]

We shall refer to this as the claim that each of us has a *sensus divinitatis*, or *sensus* for short. According to Calvin here, this *sensus* gives to all people the conviction that there is a God, knowledge that does not depend upon argument, nor even on the testimony of other people, but which is immediate. It is this idea of a basic awareness of God that has recently been articulated and defended in a way that is characteristic of the faith seeks understanding tradition.

Alvin Plantinga, Nicholas Wolterstorff and others[5] have developed what has come to be called 'Reformed Epistemology', the basic thrust of which is that, following what they take Calvin to be saying here and elsewhere, argument is unnecessary in order to establish the reasonableness of belief in God, but the belief that God exists may be a basic belief. And even, as we shall see, that one may know that God exists without possessing arguments for that conclusion.

So though John Calvin's appeal to the *sensus* is not perhaps itself a case of faith seeking understanding, his views have been developed by others in the characteristic faith seeks understanding manner.

THE *SENSUS DIVINITATIS*

In order to appreciate what is being proposed, we need to be clearer on what precisely Calvin means by the *sensus*. Some have argued that Calvin means that we have a direct awareness of God, a sort of basic intuition of his existence. Dewey Hoitenga, for example, holds that Calvin is in the Augustinian tradition which we identified earlier on, and holds that the *sensus* is a case of knowledge by acquaintance:

> The term *awareness* (Latin: *sensus*) is drawn from the language of our sensation of physical objects, and suggests therefore that Calvin thinks of our knowledge of God by analogy with our acquaintance with these objects. The important parallel is the *directness* or the *immediacy* of our knowledge of God. The directness and immediacy of such knowledge is to be contrasted with the indirectness and remoteness that characterize both the conclusions derived from reasoning and proof (the hallmark of natural theology) and the beliefs acquired on the testimony of other human beings. If Calvin is clear on anything, it is that knowledge of God is first of all a knowledge by direct acquaintance with him. God is, for Calvin, directly *present* to human minds, analogous to the way in which sense objects (and Augustine's incorporeal objects) are present.[6]

But this is not obvious; it is not obvious that Calvin is saying that each human being is directly aware of God in this manner, the possessor of an unmediated experience of God. Rather, he appears to hold that there is a universal, immediate, intuitive conviction that God exists.

Calvin characterises the *sensus* briefly as 'that by which we . . . conceive that there is a God'. It is 'an awareness of divinity'; by it men 'perceive that there is a God and that he is their Maker'.[7] These expressions confirm Calvin's lack of interest in discursive proofs of God's existence as the basis for religious epistemology. There is a directness, an immediacy about the knowledge of God which make the use of discursive argument unnecessary. But it is necessary to note what Calvin does not say in these expressions. He is not claiming that by virtue of the *sensus* all men *conceive* of God; that is, he is not claiming that there is direct comprehension (or even apprehension) of God's essence. Indeed we know from what Calvin writes elsewhere about the incomprehensibility of God that he would be vehemently opposed to such an idea. For example, Calvin says that God's 'essence is incomprehensible; hence his divineness far escapes all human perception'.[8] Much less is Calvin saying that all men have a direct experience of God. The sentences we are discussing do not amount to an appeal to religious experience, either as a mystical 'encounter' or as some other kind of direct awareness of God. The idea of an experience of God does not enter into any of the terminology that Calvin uses to characterise the *sensus*. Rather Calvin alleges that by the *sensus* all men conceive (or perceive) *that there is a God*; that is, there is recognition by all men of the fact that there is a God. This basic knowledge of God is propositional in content rather than a person to person awareness of God. And Calvin uses the terms 'conceive' and 'perceive' seemingly interchangeably in order to highlight that this knowledge is direct, not inferred from other propositions.

Either way, whether Calvin refers to a direct acquaintance with God, or to an immediate belief that God exists, such a view is in sharp contrast to the tradition of natural theology. Because we are all endowed with the *sensus*, it would seem that for Calvin proofs of God's existence by inferential reasoning are unnecessary, and *a fortiori* the proofs of natural theology are unnecessary.[9]

Further, according to Calvin this internal *sensus* has an external correlate. The *sensus* is triggered by the awareness of the world around us, not by using such evidence as premises for an argument for God's existence, but by activating an otherwise dormant disposition to believe that God exists. Since it is an awareness, it must be an awareness of something, a belief that such and such is the case. So Calvin says:

> Lest anyone, then, be excluded from access to happiness, he (viz. God) not only sowed in men's minds that seed of religion of which we have spoken but revealed himself and daily discloses himself in the whole workmanship of the universe. As a consequence, men cannot open their eyes without being compelled to see him. Indeed, his essence is incomprehensible; hence, his divineness far escapes all human perception. But upon his individual works he has engraven unmistakeable marks of his glory, so clear and prominent that even unlettered and stupid folk cannot plead the excuse of ignorance.[10]

To say that God discloses himself in the workmanship of the universe does not entail that he discloses *himself*. A person may give clues to his whereabouts while remaining hidden from view. The *sensus* does not enable men and women to see God; but as what Jones does may be evidence of what Jones is, so with God. So this 'divine workmanship' to which Calvin refers is the external correlate of the *sensus*. For although the *sensus divinitatis* exists as a natural human endowment, the works of God in creation feed and renew it.[11] The *sensus* is not sufficient to form the conviction that there is a God apart from the evidence which feeds it. At first glance Calvin seems to be full-evidentialist, making a claim about people in general and the sufficiency of the evidence available to all. But clearly Calvin eschews the use of inference in establishing the knowledge of God; and we shall see later that he carefully qualifies these initial statements.

These statements of Calvin are representative of those to which non-evidentialists appeal. In the developments arising from the appeal to Calvin's *sensus divinitatis* Alvin Plantinga has played a pivotal role. It is not stretching things too far to say that Plantinga sees himself as attempting to draw out the epistemic import of Calvin's idea of the *sensus* in a way that is characteristic of faith seeking understanding.[12]

So in the rest of this chapter we shall be concerned not so much with Calvin's own development of the idea of the *sensus*, for in fact there is little by way of philosophical development of it in Calvin, but with contemporary developments which use the *sensus* as the inspiration for making general epistemological claims.

These readings of Calvin may be considered in two phases. There is, in the first phase, Plantinga's use of Calvin's idea of the *sensus* as part of a critique of strong foundationalism (or full evidentialism) and thus of a critique of that natural theology which is an expression of full evidentialism. As we have noted, in Calvin's appeal to the *sensus* there is the idea that the knowledge of God does not need any external support by way of an argument because God testifies to himself immediately in the mind of any human being by using features of the environment in which we live to do so. Such belief is typically of a highly dispositional kind; on this view it is natural or usual to believe in the existence of God in rather the way in which it is natural to believe that there are minds other than my own mind when, for example, I am in the presence of another human being. We have grounds for such a belief, but these are very rarely articulated. It is this idea which has been developed by Plantinga as part of his rejection of strong foundationalism. Let us call this the *first application* of the *sensus divinitatis*.

We have also seen that Calvin sees the *sensus* operating within an environmental framework, a framework which feeds and renews what the *sensus* tells us about the existence and character of God. The *sensus* is thus not purely subjective, a matter of individual feeling, but is correlated and sustained by features of the external world. Nor is the functioning of the *sensus* automatic; in fact Calvin stresses that because of sin the *sensus* malfunctions in us all. Thus there is knowledge of God only where the *sensus* functions properly in the appropriate environment.

So it is that more recently Calvin's remarks about the *sensus* have inspired what I shall call the externalist turn in Plantinga's epistemology, where knowledge (including the knowledge of God) is understood not in terms of the grounds or evidence that a person may have to justify their belief, but in terms of mechanisms operating in such a way as to produce reliable belief. Let us call this the *second application* of the *sensus divinitatis*. We shall look at each of these applications in turn.

FIRST APPLICATION OF THE *SENSUS DIVINITATIS*

Plantinga appeals to and applies Calvin's *sensus divinitatis* as part of a response to the problems that beset strong foundationalism (or full evidentialism), and in particular as one chief source of insight for the defence of the idea that a person is within his or her epistemic rights to have 'God exists' in the foundations of their noetic structure, the structure of their beliefs. In order for a person's belief in God to be rational, that person does not have to be convinced by a rational proof that God exists.

As noted earlier, in Plantinga's view strong foundationalism lies at the heart of classical natural theology. It asserts that a proposition can only be rationally believed if either it is (in Plantinga's terminology) 'properly basic', i.e. self-evident or evident to the senses, or is suitably related to a proposition (or propositions) which are properly basic. Plantinga believes that we find such a view in Aquinas' natural theology, and although as we have seen, there is reason to doubt the accuracy of such an interpretation of the Five Ways, we shall here follow Plantinga's interpretation.

Aquinas writes, 'From effects evident to us, therefore, we can demonstrate what in itself is not evident to us, namely, that God exists'.[13]

He proceeds to attempt such demonstrations in his Five Ways, moving in typical foundationalist fashion from what is evident to us to what is not. Thus, it is evident to us that some things move, and from this (he believes) it can be soundly argued that there must be an unmoved mover, God. The crucial question as to whether or not Aquinas is a strong foundationalist in respect of the existence of God concerns whether Aquinas holds that it is *necessary and sufficient* for faith to be rational that the existence of God can be demonstrated in this way, or merely *sufficient*. If he holds that demonstration is necessary, then Aquinas can fairly be regarded as a strong foundationalist; if only sufficient, then not.[14] Let us then assume that Plantinga is correct is claiming that Aquinas is committed to the *necessity and sufficiency* of the proofs for the rationality of belief in the central article of the Christian faith.

So Thomas, along with many others, argues that it is rational to believe that God exists only if there is evidence available to all from which the existence of God can be derived. One is not rational in believing that God exists without having such evidence, or without such evidence being available to someone who is competent to evaluate it. According to Plantinga, this means that Thomas must have a certain view about what constitutes a rational noetic structure, the structure possessed by the set of propositions that a person believes insofar as he is rational, together with all their logical connections. This view is that a rational person's noetic structure is constituted by a basis, his basic beliefs, together with what is built on this basis, the beliefs which are justified by the basic beliefs. It is only by forming beliefs in accordance with such foundations that rationally justifiable beliefs can be formed:

> According to the foundationalist a rational noetic structure will *have a foundation* – a set of beliefs not accepted on the basis of others; in a rational noetic structure some beliefs will be basic. Nonbasic beliefs, of course, will be accepted on the basis of other beliefs, which may be accepted on the basis of still other beliefs, and so on until the foundations are reached. In a rational noetic structure, therefore, every nonbasic belief is ultimately accepted on the basis of basic beliefs.[15]

So far we have thought of foundationalism as simply a type of structure of beliefs, some beliefs being basic, other beliefs being built upon and supported by these basic beliefs. *Strong* foundationalism (what we earlier called full evidentialism) is the view that a proposition is properly basic, properly among the foundations of a person's noetic structure, if and only if that proposition is either self-evident to that person or evident to that person's senses. A properly basic belief is such that it would be irrational for any person to deny it. So that according to the strong foundationalist the superstructure of belief must be built upon a basis of self-evident propositions.[16] This is the dominant tradition in modern western philosophy, the tradition of Descartes and Locke.

Plantinga's position has two elements: a critique of strong foundationalism, and an alternative proposal. Plantinga's critique of strong foundationalism, in essence, claims that no one is under any obligation to meet its requirements. His alternative proposal appeals to the *sensus* for the idea that theistic belief is permissible, and sees what Calvin refers to as the external correlate, the character of the external world, as providing grounds, though not evidence, for God's existence. The distinction between grounds and evidence is important for Plantinga, as we shall shortly see. First, let us first briefly look at foundationalism and what Plantinga sees are its problems.

Plantinga claims that such foundationalism is self-referentially incoherent.

That is, it does not satisfy, in itself, the conditions it lays down for the rationality of any belief. It states that *a proposition is properly basic for a person only if that proposition is self-evident or incorrigible or evident to that person's senses*. But this proposition, the one that is italicised here, is none of these things. Strong foundationalism is an interesting philosophical proposal. It is one that many philosophers have accepted. But it is not self-evidently true and therefore we are not required, even if we happen to be strong foundationalists, to accept it. The paradox is, no strong foundationalist need accept strong foundationalism. It is neither self-evident nor incorrigible nor evident to the senses, though it may be rationally acceptable to some.

So *strong* foundationalism is not mandatory, though there is nothing to prevent a person accepting the standards of strong foundationalism. But Plantinga does not for this reason reject foundationalism in all its shapes and sizes. He reckons that our noetic structure does have a foundationalist character. But if strong foundationalism is not required, if it cannot be required for the reasons given, then another version or versions of foundationalism, if not required, are most certainly permitted.

The second criticism of strong foundationalism that Plantinga offers is that it is too restrictive. For if strong foundationalism is true, then it rules out as irrational myriads of our beliefs; for example, beliefs about other people than myself, and about other times than the present:

> If I see someone displaying typical pain behaviour, I take it that he or she is in pain. Again, I do not take the displayed behaviour as evidence for that belief; I do not infer that belief from others I hold; I do not accept it on the basis of other beliefs. Still, my perceiving the pain behaviour plays a unique role in the formation and justification of that belief; as in the previous case it forms the ground of my justification for the belief in question.[17]

> I believe, for example, that I had lunch this noon. I do not believe this proposition on the basis of other propositions; I take it as basic; it is in the foundations of my noetic structure. Furthermore, I am entirely rational in so taking it, even though this proposition is neither self-evident nor evident to the senses nor incorrigible for me.[18]

There are two points being made here. One is that according to Plantinga as a matter of fact there are many propositions which we believe, and are entitled to believe, which do not rest upon other, more basic propositions, to make them rationally believable. Plantinga is making a move here that is typical of that type of epistemologist which Roderick Chisholm calls a 'particularist'. He is appealing to particular examples of rational belief, noting their character, and in effect saying, 'If anything is a case of rational belief, this is. And so no theory or criterion of what rational belief must be like which excludes such beliefs can be warranted'.[19]

The second point is that one is fully entitled to believe such propositions even though they are not self-evident to any rational person. In other words, strong foundationalism is unnecessary. As far as one can see, Plantinga does not give an argument for this view, but makes an appeal to our normal procedures. He does not say that we cannot provide a justification for our everyday beliefs, but that we need not do so. We do not first have a theory, and then accept those beliefs which accord with the theory; we have certain beliefs which we take to be paradigmatically rational. These beliefs are not arbitrary, they have grounds: but the grounds are not evidence available to any rational person.

A foundationalist might respond at this point: Plantinga is picking examples of practical, not theoretical belief. No one denies that there are beliefs which we are practically convinced of the truth of; the question is, are such beliefs theoretically justified, and if so, how? The strong foundationalist might go on to claim that although we cannot in practice justify our everyday beliefs, yet many of them are capable of justification, and the carrying out of such a justifying procedure would be a part of any theoretical epistemology.[20]

So strong foundationalism is not required for the justification of a belief; of course strong foundationalism is permitted, but then so are other versions of foundationalism. And among these other versions, according to Plantinga, is what might be termed *theistic* foundationalism. A person is rational, entirely within his epistemic rights, in believing that (say) God has created the world, even if he has no argument for this. Such a belief can form part of the foundations of his noetic structure.

And this brings us back to Calvin, and to the *sensus divinitatis*. For Plantinga explicitly ties the rational permissibility of theistic foundationalism to what Calvin says about the *sensus*. He does not use Calvin as an authority in order to stifle argument, but argues that this is what Calvin meant, or part of what he meant, by appealing to the *sensus*, and claims moreover that this view is entirely acceptable as an account of the rational basis of our claim to know God. Calvin was correct in his claim that we are entitled to believe in God without argument. For if, as Calvin says, we all have such a sense, the innate tendency to believe in God, a tendency brought to fulfilment by the awareness, say, of the grandeur and beauty of our environment, then we do not need to attempt to establish the existence of God by argument, for we already have the belief that God exists, at least if the *sensus* is working properly and is not malfunctioning in some way. So natural theology, insofar as it requires strong foundationalism, may be *possible*, but it is *unnecessary* for the rational justification of belief in God.[21] For because we all are endowed with the *sensus*, any of us may appeal to it in his own case, and so there is no need for proofs of God's existence, arguments for his existence, in order to be rational in believing in his existence:

> Calvin's claim is that one who accedes to this tendency and in these circumstances accepts the belief that God has created the world – perhaps upon beholding the starry heavens, or the splendid majesty of the mountains, or the intricate, articulate beauty of a tiny flower – is entirely within his epistemic rights in so doing. It is not that such a person is justified or rational in so believing by virtue of having an implicit argument – some version of the teleological argument, say. No; he does not need any argument for justification or rationality . . . Indeed, a person in these conditions, says Calvin, *knows* that God exists.[22]

One might understand the debate between Plantinga and classical natural theology as being over the question, Which is the natural human condition? Does the natural human condition include belief in God, and is any failure to believe, or any rejection of such a belief, unnatural? Or is the natural human condition one of unbelief, or perhaps of the suspension of belief, with belief in God, if is to be rational, having to satisfy general norms for rational belief, whatever exactly they are?

So Plantinga argues, *contra* the requirement of strong foundationalism, that it is rational to believe in God on the basis of having the proposition *God exists* in the foundations of one's noetic structure. And as we have seen, he also argues that a person knows that God exists on this basis.

Such a position seems to be open to two strong objections. The first is that if the theist is within his rights to have a proposition such as 'God exists' in the foundation of his noetic structure, then others, with radically different beliefs from the theist, presumably have the same right. So an atheist might have the proposition 'There is no God' in the foundations of his noetic structure. Could not any belief be properly basic? Who is to say which is rational, belief or unbelief? And is this not a recipe for irrationalism and superstition?

Plantinga's answer to this first objection is that it is important to distinguish between *evidence* for a belief, and *grounds* for that belief. Although a person need not have reasons for his belief in God in order for that belief to be rational, nevertheless he would be irrational in his belief that God exists if that belief were not appropriately grounded. The groundedness of his belief that God exists shows that this belief is not arbitrary or whimsical. His belief in God arises from appropriate circumstances and occasions. There is nothing extraordinary about this; a person is entitled in certain circumstances to declare that he sees a tree. These circumstances ground his belief. But these circumstances do not constitute evidence for his belief.[23] Why not?

To answer this, we need to distinguish between person-variant and person-invariant beliefs. A person variant belief is one that is formed by some person in the situation occupied by that person. A person-invariant belief is one which any person in any situation may have. Plantinga is arguing that there are many person-variant beliefs which are justified or rational. In the case of such beliefs a person does not need to have strong foundations for that belief; nevertheless, this does not entitle him to go around declaring that he believes he sees trees when he has no grounds for such a belief; when he is not appeared to appropriately, by trees, then it would be absurd for him to claim to see them:

> We must assemble examples of belief and conditions such that the former are obviously properly basic in the latter, and examples of beliefs and conditions such that the former are obviously *not* properly basic in the latter. We must then frame hypotheses as to the necessary and sufficient conditions of proper basicality and test these hypotheses by reference to those examples. Under the right conditions, for example it is clearly rational to believe that you see a human person before you: a being who has thoughts and feelings, who knows and believes things, who makes decisions and acts.[24]

Plantinga's particularism is once again evident. But there seems to be nothing to stop atheists also appealing to grounds; to the fact of evil, or to the plausibility of naturalism.

So while proper basicality as far as God's existence is concerned does not require evidence for Plantinga, it does require grounds. The grounds are the conditions or circumstances relative to a person, which ground the belief for that person; they are experiences rather than beliefs, though it is hard to see how beliefs would not be formed on the basis of such experiences.

There seem to be two problems with this suggestion. The first problem has to do with the distinction between grounds and evidence itself. Grounds are not, according to Plantinga, formulated as beliefs. The reason given for this is that having a belief grounded may occur when one is unaware. Because one is unaware, the grounds are not formulated as beliefs. But this seems to be taking belief in a very narrow sense, ignoring that it often has a highly dispositional character.

The difficulty of clearly distinguishing between grounds and evidence is compounded by the fact that Plantinga allows that the arguments of natural theology can be used to strengthen belief, even though they are not necessary for the rationality of belief in the first place.[25] And the matter of the relation between grounds and evidence is made even more complex by the fact that Plantinga also recognises that appropriately grounded theistic belief may face at least *prima facie* defeat by counter-evidence, for example, by the evidence of moral evil in the world.[26]

But if it is granted that the groundedness of a belief is sufficient to answer the charges of irrationality or whimsicality, is the fact that certain beliefs are properly basic because grounded in certain experiences sufficient to constitute *knowledge*? In commenting on Plantinga's views Hoitenga appears to argue that such groundedness alone, while sufficient to meet the charge of irrationality, is not sufficient for knowledge.[27] But there are points at which Plantinga seems to think that they are sufficient:

> Calvin claims that one who takes belief in God as basic can nonetheless know that God exists. Calvin holds that one can *rationally accept* belief in God as basic; he also claims that one can *know* that God exists even if he has no argument, even if he does not believe on the basis of other propositions. A weak foundationalist is likely to hold that some properly basic beliefs are such that anyone who accepts them, knows them. More exactly, he is likely to hold that among the beliefs properly basic for a person s, some are such that s accepts them, s knows them. A weak foundationalist could go on to say that other properly basic beliefs can't be known, if taken as basic, but only rationally believed; and he might think of the existence of God as a case in point. Calvin will have none of this; as he sees it, one needs no arguments to know that God exists . . . Now I enthusiastically concur in these contentions of Reformed epistemology.[28]

So there is in Plantinga's account of the fact that belief in God may be grounded and so rational, a parallel to Calvin's idea of our natural awareness of the divine workmanship. The Reformed epistemologist will concur with Calvin in holding that God has implanted in us a natural tendency to see his hand in the world around us, something which is not true of belief in, say, the Great Pumpkin. For rational belief there is required not only a believer, but an appropriate environment in which the noetic faculties may be exercised, appropriate in the sense that they are appropriate for the faculties concerned.

So the grounding condition[29] as we might call it, has both external and internal features. The external conditions are the appropriate circumstances in which a person is placed, and the internal conditions are the awareness of those circumstances and their aptness for forming the belief that God exists. These are, as we have noted, the two sides of Calvin's *sensus*.

The *second* objection to Plantinga's theistic foundationalism is that, in appealing to the *sensus* as they do, both Calvin and Plantinga appear to be appealing to a matter of fact. It is an empirical claim. And in order to be convincing the claim must be in accordance with the facts. And so we need to ask whether it is a fact that all men and women have the *sensus,* and what the implications are if they do not. What is to be said in the case of these men and women who deny that they have a natural awareness of God, to atheists and agnostics, and to those who rely upon classical natural theology? And why, if everyone possess a *sensus divinitatis*, have many thought it necessary to articulate arguments to establish the rationality of believing in God?

To answer this question we need to stress one important feature of Calvin's thought that we only glanced at earlier, the fact that according to him the *sensus* is affected by sin, and so does not function properly. Sin, which affects both each individual person and the environment in which we are placed, has noetic effects upon the *sensus*. Because of this we do not universally recognise God as we recognise, say, the existence of other people:

> Experience teaches that the seed of religion has been divinely planted in all men. But barely one man in a hundred can be found who nourishes in his own heart what he has conceived; and not even one in whom it matures, much less bears fruit in its season (cf. Ps. 1:3). Now some lose themselves in their own superstition, while others of their own evil intention revolt from God, yet all fall away from true knowledge of him.[30]

According to Calvin the presence of sin does not result in the elimination of the *sensus* altogether, but in the reduction of its strength and powers of discrimination; the philosopher has a 'slight taste of his divinity'.[31] But the *sensus* is deficient in the amount and kind of the knowledge of God that it now provides; it is speculative;[32] and it results, at the practical level, in idolatry and superstition. No doubt this is because sin affects not only the *sensus*, but also the environment in which the *sensus* operates.

Can Plantinga's epistemology take account of this aspect of Calvin's thought as well? Plantinga understands this in terms of the suppression of the created tendency to believe in God:

This is the natural human condition; it is because of our presently unnatural sinful condition that many of us find belief in God difficult or absurd. The fact is, Calvin thinks, one who does not believe in God is in an epistemically substandard position – rather like a man who does not believe that his wife exists, or thinks that she is like a cleverly constructed robot and has no thoughts, feelings, or consciousness.[33]

Plantinga takes Calvin to be saying that:

Were it not for the existence of sin in the world, human beings would believe in God to the same degree and with the same natural spontaneity that we believe in the existence of other persons, an external world, or the past.[34]

What is Plantinga saying here? His argument appears to be an appeal to coherence, or perhaps to the explanatory power of a hypothesis. For he is arguing that there is a reason why not all people have the immediate awareness that there is a God, namely that they are affected by sin, which has noetic effects. Sin smothers or distorts the grounds on which a theist bases his belief in God and causes the senses to malfunction. Were it not for sin we would all be theists, with our belief in God grounded by way of an appreciation of our environment, just as we are all in fact believers in other minds. Such an explanation is not one that those allegedly affected by sin are likely to accept, but it is nevertheless a possible explanation, and one which is in accordance with the tenets of Christian theism; it coheres overall with the Christian position.

Of course, as Westphal points out, this raises the question of how Plantinga and others are exempt from or emancipated from this particular consequence of sin. How is it that sin is at work in the beliefs of unbelievers but not in those of believers? Is it faithful to Calvin to suppose that oneself, or one's community, might be exempt from the effects of sin?[35] Presumably the answer must be that divine grace has noetic effects which nullify the noetic effects of sin.

So far what we have seen is that in an appeal to Calvin's *sensus*. Plantinga argues for the rationality of belief in God, and also – perhaps – for the knowledge that God exists, though this latter claim seems open to objection. He does so on the basis of a critique of strong foundationalism, and by an appeal to the groundedness of belief. But more recently Plantinga has used Calvin's idea of the *sensus* as the inspiration for a more radical departure.

SECOND APPLICATION OF THE *SENSUS DIVINITATIS*

It has been widely believed, in twentieth-century discussions of knowledge and belief, that knowledge is justified, true belief. In order for A to know that p, it is necessary that p is true, that A believes p, and that A has evidence of sufficient strength to justify the belief that p. This emphasis upon the ability to justify on the basis of evidence is characteristic of internalism. Since the work of Edmund Gettier, who in a famous paper[36] showed that it is possible for these three conditions to be satisfied and yet for a person to lack knowledge, the search has been on for the elusive fourth condition.

This debate has assumed that knowledge is to be analysed in terms of the evidence for the belief in question that a person himself is able to recognise and appropriate. That is, knowledge is to be analysed in terms of justification. 'Evidence' in the sense relevant to internalist accounts of knowledge is evidence *which the person in question* is aware of and which he could specify and must specify if his true belief is to be justified. Such justification is a personal achievement. It is this internalist feature that makes the language of obligation and permission appropriate to use in epistemology, and as we have seen such language is prominent in Plantinga's critique of strong foundationalism.

Plantinga has gone along with this internalist assumption not only in his critique of strong foundationalism but also in his retention of the foundationalist shape for any rational noetic structure. This is clear not only in his use of the language of epistemic obligation and permission, but also in his discussion of grounds; the justification of any belief for a person is a matter of having grounds or evidence for that person which are sufficient to enable him to fulfil his epistemic obligations.

Given internalism there is a strong analogy between epistemology and ethics. In ethics a person may perform an action because he believes himself to be justified in doing so; because, say, his conscience tells him to do it or because he believes that in doing so he will fulfil some duty, or whatever. But a person may follow his conscience, or do what he believes to be his duty, and what he does may nevertheless be wrong when judged from an objective ethical point of view. He may be subjectively justified, but nevertheless do what is (objectively speaking) morally wrong. May not something similar happen in epistemology? May not a person have what he believes to be grounds for his belief, and yet his belief be mistaken? And *vice versa*?

Further, a person, say a small child, may do the right thing, morally speaking, but be unable to give the grounds for doing what he does. His inability does not detract from the fact that what he did was the right thing to have done.[37]

So according to internalism epistemic justification is something that a person must himself provide; the rational belief that there is a tree in front of me is grounded in the fact that there appears to be a tree there and that I have no reason to think that I am being deceived. Having a justified belief is having a belief that the person who has it is able to justify. Justification is thus a skill or ability which a person has, or has to acquire; it is something that the one justified is able to provide. But is such internalism ever sufficient for knowledge?

Plantinga offers a sustained critique of epistemological internalism, in outline as follows:

If epistemic justification is understood in this way, the internalist way, the way which Plantinga regards as the dominant epistemological assumption of Descartes and subsequently, the fact is that a person may (as in ethics) perform all his subjective duties impeccably but nevertheless not be objectively warranted in his belief or knowledge claim that p. Subjective justification is no guarantee of objective justification, and this is because a person may do all within his control to justify his belief that p but there may be a myriad things outside his control which affect the proper operation of his epistemic equipment. The problem is not simply that the elusive fourth condition for the analysis of knowledge as justified true belief has not so far been located, but that this entire way of thinking about knowledge is radically misconceived.

According to Plantinga, all the variants of epistemic internalism fail in the same way; there is in all of them a failure of proper function. Even though A's internal evidence for p may appear to be sufficient, unbeknownst to A the Alpha Centaurians may have got at him, or he has suddenly received a secret brain lesion, and what has all the appearance to him of a banana may in fact be a bun loaf:

> So suppose I am captured by a group of unscrupulous but extremely knowledgeable Alpha Centaurian superscientists intent upon a cognitive experiment . . . In the course of conducting their experiment, the scientists . . . modify my cognitive faculties . . . when I consider 67 *is prime*, it has for me precisely the phenomenology that goes with simply seeing that a simple arithmetical proposition is true. But of course my faculties have been modified so that they no longer function properly; in particular, most of the propositions of the form *n is prime* that I think I can simply see to be true are false, and most of the ones I think I can simply see to be false are true. It is, so to speak, only by accident that I have the right phenomenology with respect to 67 *is prime*; my captors could just as well have given me the phenomenology that goes with seeing that a proposition of the form *n is prime is false.*

It is clear, I think, that under these conditions 67 *is prime* has very little by way of warrant or positive epistemic status for me. Although it is true and necessarily true, I surely do not know that it is.[38]

Note that the Alpha Centaurians are deployed not in the interests of defending scepticism but to show that more is required for knowledge than truth, belief, and justification. According to Plantinga what is needed to meet the Gettier paradoxes is not the sought-after fourth condition, but an externalist perspective, an account not in terms of an individual's access to his own mental states, but of truths about his cognitive functioning and the environment in which that functioning occurs. Externalism focuses not on grounds to which the knower has access, but sees the knower as a mechanism who functions (or malfunctions); functions when true beliefs are appropriately and reliably produced, malfunctions when false beliefs are produced. So the knower is seen from the outside, hence externalism. The focus is not on reasons which a person may (or may not) be able to produce for his belief, but on what causes him to have (or to fail to have) reliable beliefs.

Plantinga's use of Calvin that we have been examining so far has been based on the assumption that knowledge or justified belief is a matter of having reasons for belief, not reasons that will necessarily convince every rational person, but reasons that provide grounds or evidence for the belief. But more recently, in keeping with this move away from internalism, Plantinga has come to regard Calvin's idea of the *sensus* not so much as providing grounds – in internalist fashion – but as a mechanism for the production of true belief when it functions properly in an appropriate environment. The *sensus* is not a faculty which discerns grounds which support belief or knowledge claims, but a device for producing reliable beliefs. According to Plantinga, Calvin's *sensus* is that mechanism which, when it functions properly in an appropriate environment, produces true beliefs about God. So on this view the question of whether a person is justified in their belief by having reasons or grounds does not arise. What is needed for justification (or for what Plantinga now calls 'warrant') is a set-up which produces reliable beliefs.[39]

Plantinga summarises this position as follows:

Warrant is a matter of a belief's being produced by faculties that are (a) working properly in an appropriate environment, and (b) aimed at truth; and if a belief has warrant for you, then the greater your inclination to believe it the more warrant it has.[40]

Inclination is a matter of being convinced, not of having grounds or reasons which one must be able to produce on demand. This externalist perspective, the idea of proper function in an appropriate environment, has two elements. The first is the idea of a design plan:

> Human beings are constructed according to a certain design plan. This terminology does not commit us to supposing that human beings have been literally designed – by God, for example. Here I use 'design' the way, e.g. Daniel Dennett (not ordinarily thought unsound on supernaturalism) does in speaking of a given organism as possessing a certain design.[41]

We are familiar with the idea of an artefact or a bodily organ having a certain function or purpose, and the associated idea that the organs can either fulfil this purpose – operate normally – or malfunction in some way.

Similarly, Plantinga says, there is something like a set of specifications for a well-formed, properly-functioning human being – an extraordinarily complicated and highly articulated set of specifications. Among these specifications are those for our epistemic faculties, designed for producing beliefs. Sometimes the design is for beliefs which are founded on evidence; at other times the design is for beliefs which have other foundations; for instance, preserving the person in question against disabling psychological shocks.[42] Calvin's *sensus* is a module of our design plan.[43] Naturally in studying human epistemology we are concerned with those beliefs which aim at truth.

The second element is the idea of an appropriate environment. That is, in order to provide us with reliable information our senses not only need to be working properly, in accordance with the design plan, but they need to be doing so in an environment that is appropriate. As we noted earlier, Calvin sees belief in God being triggered by features of this world, daily reminders of God's goodness.

The further, crucial question, the question that brings us back to Calvin's *sensus*, is, can one be functioning properly in this sense (i.e. be operating in accordance with the design plan, and in an appropriate environment) and accept belief in God?[44] Or is belief in God necessarily the result of malfunction?

> When people accept belief in God in the basic way, is it the case that sometimes their faculties are functioning properly and the modules of the design plan governing the formation of this belief are aimed at truth?[45]

Or is it that the theist is cognitively defective in some way, simply in virtue of being a theist as, say, Marx and Freud each thought? It is at this point in his argument that Plantinga again appeals to Calvin's *sensus*:

It is *unbelief, failure* to believe in God that is the diseased, unnatural, unhealthy condition. Unbelief results from an intellectual and spiritual disease, a cognitive dysfunction . . . it is only because of the results of sin, only because of this unnatural fallen condition, Calvin thinks, that some of us find belief in God difficult or absurd. If it weren't for sin and its effects, we human beings would believe in God with the same sort of natural spontaneity and to the same degree that we believe in the existence of ourselves, other persons, and the past.[46]

Plantinga cites the following passage from Calvin

Indeed the perversity of the impious, who though they struggle furiously are unable to extricate themselves from the fear of God, is abundant testimony that this conviction, namely, that there is some God, is naturally inborn in all, and is fixed deep within, as it were in the very marrow . . . From this we conclude that it is not a doctrine that must first be learned in school, but one of which each of us is master from his mother's womb and which nature itself permits no man to forget.[47]

Any failure to believe in God is a failure of proper function. But why a *failure* of proper function? Why is belief in God not a failure of proper function? Consideration of this question leads Plantinga to argue that epistemology is founded in different views of human nature, in ontology:

Our question was: is natural theology needed for belief in God to have warrant? Alternatively: can belief in God taken in the basic way have warrant? And the important point is that this epistemological question is not ontologically neutral: it has ontological or religious roots. The answer you properly give to it will depend upon what sorts of beliefs will be produced by the faculties of a parson whose epistemic faculties are functioning properly: more exactly, by properly functioning faculties or mechanisms whose purpose is the production of true beliefs. This is a question about the nature of human beings, a question the answer to which belongs in philosophical anthropology and hence in ontology.[48]

Ultimately, epistemology is founded on ontology. So, adopting an externalist perspective in epistemology, Plantinga wishes to argue not that it is permissible for a person to have the proposition *God exists* in the foundations of his noetic structure, but rather that no satisfactory account of knowledge can be provided that is not externalist in character. And he appeals once more to Calvin's *sensus* as corroboration of this. The *sensus divinitatis* is capable of a wider application, as propounding a version of externalism in epistemology. The insight of Calvin's which provides inspiration has to do, Plantinga now thinks, with the correlation between the *sensus* and the environment.

TWO QUESTIONS

We have highlighted the internalist and externalist phases of Plantinga's epistemology. What they have in common is the conviction that a person may believe in God without having reasons for doing so; and that such a view finds precedent in Calvin's idea of the *sensus divinitatis*.

There are clearly two sorts of questions that are raised by this use of Calvin's *sensus divinitatis* in the style of faith seeking understanding for the purposes of developing a distinctive view of faith and reason; what are the merits of this view, and is it true to its alleged sources in Calvin? We have already noted certain problems with Plantinga's epistemology, but to follow these up here would take us from our main theme.[49] For the remainder of this section we shall concentrate on the question of whether Plantinga has been faithful to Calvin, and therefore whether his use of Calvin is a plausible case of faith seeking understanding.

The Reformed epistemologists understand Calvin's lack of interest in natural theology as a repudiation of the strong foundationalism of the Enlightenment. Calvin does not scruple to place the proposition that God exists (and many similar theistic propositions) in the foundations of his noetic structure, and to affirm that all men, despite their fallenness, ought to place them there as well.

But is Calvin in fact a foundationalist in any sense? In 'Reason and Belief in God'[50] Alvin Plantinga cites passages from the *Institutes* regarding the *sensus*, including this one:

> Lest anyone, then be excluded from access to happiness, he not only sowed in men's minds that seed of religion of which we have spoken, but revealed himself and daily discloses himself in the whole workmanship of the universe as a consequence, men cannot open their eyes without being compelled to see him.[51]

And then draws the following conclusion:

> Calvin's claim is that one who accedes to this tendency and in these circumstances accepts the belief that God has created the world – perhaps upon beholding the starry heavens, or the splendid majesty of the mounts, or the intricate, highly articulate beauty of a tiny flower – is entirely within his epistemic rights in doing so. It is not that such a

person is justified or rational in so believing by virtue of having an implicit argument – some version of the teleological argument, say. No; he does not need any argument for justification or rationality. His belief need not be based on any other propositions at all; under these conditions he is perfectly rational in accepting belief in God in the utter absence of any argument, deductive or inductive. Indeed, a person in these conditions, says Calvin, *knows* that God exists.[52]

Perhaps Plantinga's comments amount to this, that Calvin offers what is an implicit argument from the premise that there are people who without argument have the belief that God exists, to the conclusion that they are entitled to such a belief. The suppressed premise is something like 'It is rational to believe in God's existence without argument'. But is this a reasonable conclusion to draw from Calvin? There is reason to think that it is not. For one thing, there is no evidence from the passages cited (or from any similar passages) that Calvin has in mind the rationality of religious belief.

Later on Plantinga quotes remarks of Calvin about the fact that the authority of Scripture is based not on 'rational proofs' but the conviction that the Bible is the word of God ought to rest 'in a higher place than human reasons, judgments, or conjectures, that is, in the secret testimony of the Spirit.'[53]

There is a kind of parallel here between Calvin's remarks and the denial of strong foundationalism; according to Calvin in the case of the knowledge of God men do not have reasons, while in the case of the authority of Scripture men do not *need* reasons; at least, no reasons that are to be found only outside the Bible. But there is a significant lack of parallel also, for in discussing the authority of the Bible Calvin is making a normative claim, a claim about where we ought to ground our conviction that the Bible is the word of God. It is not at all clear that these remarks about the self-authenticating character of the Bible also apply, in Calvin's mind, to belief in God's existence.

For what we find in Calvin, I suggest, is little or no interest in the rationality of religious belief.[54] (Rationality in this sense is perhaps as much a child of the Enlightenment as is strong foundationalism; certainly one struggles to find any interest in such an issue in Calvin.) Rather, what Calvin emphasises is not rationality but responsibility. His interest in the *sensus* is not due to an interest in the rational grounds for theistic belief, but to a concern to establish that since all men and women in fact have some knowledge of God, they are culpable when they do not form their lives in a way that is appropriate to such knowledge:

For how can the thought of God penetrate your mind without your realizing immediately that, since you are his handiwork, you have been made over and bound to his command by right of creation, that you owe your life to him? – that whatever you undertake, whatever you do, ought to be ascribed to him?[55]

Since, therefore, men one and all perceive that there is a God and that he is their Maker, they are condemned by their own testimony because they have failed to honor him and to consecrate their lives to his will.[56]

But can one rationally reconstruct Calvin to yield the distinctive tenets of 'Reformed epistemology'?

Perhaps one can. Perhaps what Plantinga has in mind in appealing to Calvin is an argument that is something like the following:

1. The original epistemic condition of mankind was such that every human belief held then was fully rationally justified.
2. Originally, mankind believed in God without needing any reasons for doing so.
3. Whatever presently remains of the original epistemic condition is rational.
4. For any present belief, if that belief is identical with a belief that was part of the original human condition, then that belief was rational.
5. Some people presently believe in God without having any reasons for doing so.
6. Therefore, those who presently believe in God without reasons for doing so are rational.

This seems to be much more plausible an account of the argument implicit in passages from Calvin like those cited. However, there is still an emphasis upon issues of rationality here that is not present in Calvin. For in asserting the universality of the *sensus* Calvin is making a broad factual claim, that as a matter of fact everyone has in them the seed of religion. And, following St Paul in Romans 1, he is more concerned with using this fact about knowledge to establish the responsibility of all people in the sight of God for the use to which they put this knowledge than he is about saying anything about rationality. The point about foundationalism, whether weak or strong, is as Plantinga says, a point about epistemic entitlement; but Calvin says nothing about this, and he may imply nothing about it either.

Calvin may perhaps be more plausibly seen as an externalist, or at least the *sensus* might be taken to operate in externalist fashion. But it is not at all clear that Calvin thinks that his appeal to the *sensus* is a contribution to the proper understanding of human knowledge as such.

Another attempt at harnessing Calvin might be made by using the approach of another 'Reformed epistemologist', Nicholas Wolterstorff. He distinguishes between ineluctable beliefs, propositions we could not have refrained from believing, and eluctable beliefs, which we could have refrained from believing.[57] In the case of propositions ineluctably believed we are rational in continuing to hold such a belief in the absence of an adequate reason to cease from believing it. Ineluctable believing is innocent until it is proved guilty. And so, Wolterstorff claims, someone who comes to belief in God immediately, without reasons, might nonetheless be justified in having and holding such a belief.[58] Wolterstorff does not offer this as a gloss on Calvin, but could it be taken to be such? It is hard to see how. For one thing, Calvin seems to think of the belief in God or the gods that all people have as, if anything, an eluctable belief. Though even this is straining things, for Calvin does not seem to pay much attention to the question of whether someone who, as the result of the working of the *sensus*, believes in God or the gods, could have refrained from so believing.

If all men and women believed in God, then there would (in one sense) be no need to establish the existence of God rationally, but (in another sense) this universality would not settle anything. But in any case Calvin does not say that all men believe in God; he says that all men have the seed of religion, the disposition to believe in God.

Perhaps another attempt could be made in the following way:

1. All men and women ought to believe in the true God.
2. I find myself believing in the true God without having any reasons to do so.
3. Whatever a person finds himself believing he should continue to believe unless there is good reason to desist.
4. Therefore, I ought to continue to believe in God.

This is a rather stronger conclusion than Reformed epistemology needs; but from it we can infer

5. Therefore, I may continue to believe in him.

This conclusion, that a person may believe in God without having any reasons for doing so, is characteristic of Reformed epistemology, and follows on the assumption that if A ought to do X then A is permitted to do X. The problem with this argument, if it is to be used to establish Reformed epistemology, is (1). It is certainly a proposition about the ethics of belief that Calvin appears to hold. And perhaps Calvin believes that he does not need reasons for believing in the truth of (1); perhaps (1) expresses a kind of weak moral foundationalism. But perhaps not; for as we have seen Calvin certainly offers reasons why men and women do believe in God, reasons deriving from the *sensus* and the environment in which it functions.

I suggest that those who look to Calvin as the *fons et origo* of Reformed epistemology are in something of a dilemma at this point. If they appeal to him to provide a premise of a factual kind about the seed of religion working in all people, then they will certainly find evidence for this in Calvin, as we have seen. But it does not follow from Calvin's remarks about the seed of religion that a person is entitled to believe in God reasonlessly, nor does Calvin say that it does. He does not say that it does, nor does he deny that it does. If on the other hand they appeal to a normative proposition as a premise, a proposition about what men and women ought to believe, which they might find warrant for in Calvin's remarks about the responsibility of all men and women before God, it is surely implausible to suppose that such a proposition is acceptable without reason.

The basic problem with appealing to Calvin is that his remarks about the *sensus* are first-order observations. He does not theorise about what he takes to be matters of fact; and where he does theorise, as in his brief remarks about the grounds for accepting the authority of Scripture, these remarks do not seem to be directly applicable to questions about the rationality of belief in God.

MORE RADICAL STILL?

In an earlier chapter we noted that the strongest form of faith seeking understanding is when it is claimed that it is only on the assumption of faith that there can be a true understanding, a matter for which secular solutions are sought. In *Warrant and Proper Function* Plantinga approaches this position, for he argues not simply that externalism is the best approach to knowledge, and that one can give a satisfactory account of theistic belief from an externalist perspective, but that it is irrational to be an externalist without being a theist. 'Naturalism in epistemology can flourish only in the context of supernaturalism in metaphysics'. If Calvin's remarks on the *sensus* have proved to be the inspiration of Plantinga's externalism, then perhaps they may be said to be the impetus for this more radical appeal, though the evidence for this is not clear.[59]

All naturalistic accounts of proper function fail for one reason or another. For example, the function of an organism cannot be equivalent to empirical generalisations about it,[60] nor is it satisfactory to elucidate proper function in terms of what accounts for the survival and proliferation of an organism.[61] If these objections to a naturalistic account of proper function can be sustained, then one has a powerful argument against naturalism. However, the argument Plantinga goes on to develop, in the closing chapter of *Warrant and Proper Function*, is not that naturalism is false, but that it is irrational to accept that it is true.

Naturalism most naturally appears these days as some version of evolutionary epistemology. But there is no obvious connection between the survival of an organism and the production in that organism of true beliefs (as opposed, say, to the production of appropriate behaviour). Furthermore, it may be that the probability of our cognitive faculties being reliable is low, given that we are the products of naturalistic evolution. For perhaps beliefs do not cause behaviour, or are caused by behaviour, or cause behaviour but are maladaptive. Plantinga argues that given these possibilities, and more, the probability of the reliability of our beliefs being accounted for on wholly naturalistic assumptions is low, or at least we should be agnostic about that probability.

Again, perhaps we need to separate out some kinds of beliefs from others. Perhaps it is more plausible to suppose that some sorts of beliefs are reliable, those most obviously and directly having to do with our survival, such as perception and memory.[62] And perhaps therefore we ought to remain agnostic about our theoretically-informed beliefs, including the theoretical beliefs of science, including belief in evolution. And any appeal we may make from the reliability of some beliefs to the reliability of these beliefs is going to beg the question.[63] But then, though naturalism may nevertheless be true, we would have no reason for believing it to be so. But the theist is not in such a predicament, since he has the belief that God has created us in his own image, and equipped with powers to acquire reliable beliefs. But a theist cannot argue for such a position, since arguing would beg the very question at issue; but then the theist is not troubled by scepticism to begin with:

> Once again, therefore, we see that naturalistic epistemology flourishes best in the garden of supernaturalistic metaphysics. Naturalistic epistemology conjoined with naturalistic metaphysics leads *via* evolution to scepticism or to violation of canons of rationality; conjoined with theism it does not. The naturalistic epistemologist should therefore prefer theism to metaphysical naturalism.[64]

So though epistemological externalism might appear naturalistic, and indeed up to a point it is, the most persuasive grounding of such externalism is to be found in a supernaturalist metaphysics. Or rather, it is irrational to be an externalist and not a supernaturalist. From a position where theism is epistemically permissible we are invited to move to an account of warrant which can only be provided in a supernaturalistic framework. So, I must believe in order that I may know.

So while Plantinga is furthering a faith seeking understanding project, he is interpreting that project more radically and more ambitiously than Augustine, and perhaps more ambitiously than Anselm. For Plantinga is attempting not merely to argue for this or that Christian doctrine, not even the doctrine that there is a God, but to place epistemology, the account of all human knowledge, on supernaturalist foundations.

NOTES

1. E.g. Plantinga, 'Reason and Belief in God', p.39f.
2. E.g. Stump, 'Aquinas on the Foundations of Knowledge'; Wolterstorff, 'The Migration of Theistic Arguments: From Natural Theology to Evidentialist Apologetics'.
3. See Audi, 'Faith, Belief and Rationality'.
4. *Institutes*, pp.43f. Calvin refers at this point to Cicero's *The Nature of the Gods*. He goes on, in the following chapter, to assert that this knowledge is smothered or corrupted by sin, but not totally extinguished. As can be seen from the reference to Cicero, the idea of the *sensus divinitatis* did not originate with him, nor does he claim that it did.
5. Representative statements of this position are to be found in Plantinga and Wolterstorff, *Rationality and Religious Belief*; Plantinga, *Warrant and Proper Function*; and Wolterstorff, *Reason within the Bounds of Religion*. A similar outlook is to be found in William Alston, *Perceiving God*.
6. Hoitenga, *Faith and Reason from Plato to Plantinga*, p.150.
7. These expressions are to be found in *Institutes*, pp.43f.
8. *Institutes*, pp.51–3 (see also I.III.I and I.XIII.I).
9. This does not rule out the idea that Calvin may also have thought that proofs of God's existence were possible. Scholars differ on whether or not he did.
10. *Institutes*, pp.52f.
11. It is interesting to compare what Calvin says about the *sensus divinitatis* with Thomas Aquinas' remark that 'the awareness that God exists is not implanted in us by nature in any clear or specific way. Admittedly, man is by nature aware of what by nature he desires, and he desires by nature a happiness which is to be found only in God. But this is not, simply speaking, awareness that there is a God, any more than to be aware of someone approaching is to be aware of Peter, even should it be Peter approaching'. (*Summa Theologiae* 1a 2.1, p.64).
12. Plantinga, 'Augustinian Christian Philosophy'.
13. *Summa Theologiae*, 1a 2.2., p.66.
14. Evidence that Aquinas thought the proofs sufficient, but not necessary, for rational belief in God can be found in passages such as the following: 'The credenda include things that admit of strict philosophical proof, not because these are absolutely speaking objects of faith for everyone, but because they are a prerequisite to the truth of faith; and those who do not have proof of them must at least presuppose them in faith' (*Summa Theologiae* 2a 2ae 1,5 ad. 3m). See also *Disputed Questions on Truth* 14,9. These passages and others are discussed in Vos, *Aquinas, Calvin and Contemporary Protestant Thought*, Ch.4.
15. Plantinga, 'Reason and Belief in God', p.52.
16. Plantinga, 'Reason and Belief in God', p.59. Strong foundationalism is not by any means the only possible form of foundationalism. For a partial taxonomy of foundationalism, see Audi, *The Structure of Justification*.
17. Plantinga, 'Reason and Belief in God', p.79.
18. Plantinga, 'Reason and Belief in God', p.60.
19. Here, besides the influence of Calvin, that of Thomas Reid may be noted.

20. See, for example, Kretzmann, 'Evidence against Anti-evidentialism'.
21. Plantinga. 'Reason and Belief in God', For Plantinga's views on the uses of natural theology see 'The Prospects for Natural Theology'.
22. P.67. Note that Plantinga here uses 'justification' and 'rationality' interchangeably. For some of their differences, see Audi, 'Faith, Belief and Rationality'.
23. Kretzmann, in 'Evidence against Anti-Evidentialism', argues that they do.
24. Plantinga, 'Reason and Belief in God', p.76.
25. Plantinga, 'The Prospects for Natural Theology'.
26. Plantinga, 'The Foundations of Theism: A Reply'.
27. Hoitenga, *Faith and Reason from Plato to Plantinga*, p.187.
28. Plantinga, 'The Reformed Objection to Natural Theology', p.58. Italics in the original.
29. Hoitenga, *Faith and Reason from Plato to Plantinga*, p.190 interprets the grounds in externalist fashion, as conditions for the production of reliable belief. But this does not seem plausible.
30. Calvin, *Institutes*, p.47.
31. Calvin, *Institutes*, p.277.
32. Calvin, *Institutes*, p.41. Cf. the case of Plato, p.46.
33. Plantinga, 'Reason and Belief in God', p.66. For another interpretation of the philosophical implications of this aspect of Calvin's thought, see Westphal, 'On Taking St Paul Seriously'.
34. Plantinga, 'Reason and Belief in God', p.66.
35. Westphal, 'On Taking St Paul Seriously', p.213.
36. Gettier, 'Is Justified True Belief Knowledge?'
37. These points are developed at length by Plantinga in his critique of internalism in *Warrant: The Current Debate*.
38. Plantinga, *Warrant: The Current Debate*, pp.59f.
39. Plantinga is not saying that one ought never to give reasons for one's belief, only that it is unnecessary to do so for such beliefs to be warranted.
40. Plantinga, 'Prospects for Natural Theology', p.300.
41. Plantinga, *Warrant and Proper Function*, p.13 (see this page for more detail).
42. Plantinga, *Warrant and Proper Function*, p.16.
43. Plantinga, *Warrant and Proper Function*, p.48.
44. Plantinga, 'Prospects for Natural Theology', p.303.
45. Plantinga, 'Prospects for Natural Theology', p.303.
46. Plantinga, 'Prospects for Natural Theology', p.308.
47. Calvin, *Institutes*, I.3.3.
48. Plantinga, 'The Prospects for Natural Theology', p.309.
49. The critique of natural theology mounted by 'Reformed epistemology' is discussed by Stephen Davis in another volume in this series.
50. In *Faith and Rationality* ed. Plantinga and Wolterstorff pp.16–93.
51. Plantinga, 'Reason and Belief in God', p.66.
52. Plantinga, 'Reason and Belief in God', p.67.
53. Ibid.
54. For other reasons for the inappropriateness of the Reformed epistemologists' appeal to Calvin see John Beversluis, 'Reforming the "Reformed" Objection to Natural Theology'.
55. *Institutes*, p.42.
56. *Institutes*, p.44.
57. Wolterstorff, 'Can Belief in God Be Rational If It Has No Foundations?', p.162.
58. Wolterstorff, 'Can Belief in God Be Rational If It Has No Foundations?', p.176.
59. Plantinga, *Warrant and Proper Function*, p.194.
60. Plantinga, *Warrant and Proper Function*, pp.198f.
61. Plantinga, *Warrant and Proper Function*, pp.202f.
62. Plantinga, *Warrant and Proper Function*, pp.232f.
63. Plantinga, *Warrant and Proper Function*, p.234.
64. Plantinga, *Warrant and Proper Function*, p.237.

Bibliography

Adams, Marilyn McCord, 'Praying the *Proslogion*: Anselm's Theological Method', in *The Rationality of Belief and the Plurality of Faith*, ed. Thomas D. Senor (Ithaca, Cornell University Press, 1995)

Alston, William, *Perceiving God* (Ithaca, Cornell University Press, 1991)

Alston, William, 'Taking the Curse off Language-Games: A Realist Account of Doxastic Practices', in *Philosophy and the Grammar of Religious Belief*, ed. Tessin and Von Der Ruhr (London, Macmillan, 1995)

Anscombe, G. E. M., 'What is it to Believe Someone?', in *Rationality and Religious Belief*, ed. C. F. Delaney (Notre Dame, University of Notre Dame Press, 1979)

Anselm of Canterbury, *Cur Deus Homo?* trans. J. Hopkins and H. Richardson, in *Anselm of Canterbury III* (Toronto, The Edwin Mellen Press, 1976)

Anselm of Canterbury, *Proslogion*, trans. J. Hopkins and H. Richardson, in *Anselm of Canterbury I* (London, SCM Press, 1974)

Anselm of Canterbury, *Reply to Gaunilo*, trans. J. Hopkins and H. Richardson, in *Anselm of Canterbury I* (London, SCM Press, 1974)

Anselm of Canterbury, *On the Incarnation of the Word*, trans. J. Hopkins and H. Richardson, in *Anselm of Canterbury III* (Toronto, The Edwin Mellen Press, 1976)

Anselm of Canterbury, *The Virginal Conception and Original Sin*, trans. J. Hopkins and H. Richardson, in *Anselm of Canterbury III* (Toronto, The Edwin Mellen Press, 1976)

Aquinas, *Summa Theologiae*, ed. Thomas Gilby, Part One, Questions 1–13 (Garden City, Image, 1969)

Audi, Robert, 'Faith, Belief and Rationality', *Philosophical Perspectives 5, Philosophy of Religion 1991*, ed. James E. Tomberlin (Atascadero, Ridgeview, 1991)

Audi, Robert, *The Structure of Justification*, (Cambridge, Cambridge University Press, 1993)

Augustine, *The City of God* (London, Dent, 1945)

Augustine, *Confessions*, trans. Henry Chadwick (Oxford, Oxford University Press, World's Classics, 1992)

Augustine, *On Christian Doctrine*, trans. D. W. Robertson Jr (Indianpolis, Bobbs-Merrill, 1958)

Augustine, *On the Merits and Remission of Sins*, in *Augustine: The Anti-Pelagian Writings*, ed. Philip Schaff (Grand Rapids, Eerdmans, 1971)

Augustine, *Soliloquies*, trans. Thomas F. Gilligan (New York, CIMA Publishing Co., 1948)

Augustine, *Two Books on Genesis Against the Manichees*, trans. Roland J. Teske SJ (Washington, Catholic University of America Press, 1991)

Augustine, *The Advantage of Believing*, trans. Luanne Meagher (New York, CUA Press, 1947)

Barth, Karl, *Fides Quaerens Intellectum*, trans. Ian W. Robertson (Cleveland and New York, Meridian Books, 1962)

Beversluis, John, 'Reforming the "Reformed" Objection to Natural Theology', *Faith and Philosophy*, 1995

Boethius, *The Consolation of Philosophy*, trans. V. E. Watts (Harmondsworth, Penguin, 1969)

Bonaventure, *The Journey of the Mind to God*, trans. P. Boehner, edited by Stephen F. Brown (Indianpolis, Hackett, 1993)

Bouwsma O. K., 'Anselm's Argument', in *Philosophical Analysis*, ed. J. Bobik (Notre Dame, University of Notre Dame Press, 1970)

Brown, Stuart, 'Christian Averroism, Fideism and the "Two-fold Truth"', in *The Philosophy in Christianity*, ed. Godfrey Vesey (Cambridge, Cambridge University Press, 1989)

Burnyeat, Myles, 'The Sceptic in his Place and Time', in *Philosophy in History*, ed. Richard Rorty, J. B. Schneewind and Quentin Skinner (Cambridge, Cambridge University Press, 1984)

Calvin, John, *Institutes of the Christian Religion*, trans. F. L. Battles (London, SCM Press, 1960)

Campbell, Richard, *From Belief to Understanding* (Canberra, ANU Press, 1976)

Chisholm, R., *Person and Object* (London, Allen and Unwin, 1976)

Descartes, R., *Meditations*, in *Philosophical Works*, trans. Haldane and Ross (Cambridge, Cambridge University Press, 1931)

Edwards, J., *The Great Christian Doctrine of Original Sin Defended*, ed. Clyde A. Holbrook (New Haven, Yale University Press, 1970)

Fischer, John Martin, *The Metaphysics of Free Will* (Oxford, Blackwell, 1994)

Gale, Richard, *On the Nature and Existence of God* (Cambridge, Cambridge University Press, 1991)

Gettier, Edmund L., 'Is Justified True Belief Knowledge?', *Analysis*, 23 (1963), pp.121–30

Hawking, Stephen, *A Brief History of Time* (London, Bantam, 1988)

Helm, Paul, *Belief Policies* (Cambridge, Cambridge University Press, 1994)

Helm, Paul, *Eternal God* (Oxford, Clarendon Press 1988)

Hoitenga, Dewey, *Faith and Reason from Plato to Plantinga* (Albany, SUNY Press, 1991)

Hopkins, Jasper, *A Companion to the Study of St Anselm* (Minneapolis, University of Minnesota Press, 1970)

Hughes, Gerard J., *The Nature of God* (London, Routledge, 1995)

Hume, David, *An Inquiry Concerning Human Understanding* (1748)

Kant, Immanuel, *The Critique of Pure Reason*, trans. Norman Kemp-Smith (London, Macmillan, 1933)

Kant, Immanuel, *The Critique of Practical Reason and other Writings in Moral Philosophy*, trans. L. W. Beck (Chicago, University of Chicago Press, 1949)

Kenny, Anthony, 'Necessary Being', in *British Analytical Philosophy*, ed. Williams and Montefiore (London, Routledge, 1966)

Kenny, Anthony, *What is Faith?* (Oxford, Oxford University Press, 1992)

Kenny, Anthony, *Wyclif* (Oxford, Oxford University Press, 1985)

Kierkegaard, Soren, *Concluding Unscientific Postscript*, trans. David F. Swenson and Walter Lowrie (Princeton, Princeton University Press, 1941)

Kirwan, Christopher, *Augustine* (London, Routledge, 1989)

Kretzmann, Norman, 'Faith Seeks, Understanding Finds', in *Christian Philosophy*, ed. Thomas Flint (Notre Dame, University of Notre Dame Press, 1990)

Kretzmann, Norman, 'Reason in Mystery', in *The Philosophy in Christianity*, ed. G. N. A. Vesey (Cambridge, Cambridge University Press, 1989)

Kretzmann, Norman, 'Evidence against Anti-Evidentialism', in *Our Knowledge of God*, ed. K. J. Clark (Dordrecht, Kluwer, 1992)

Kvanvig, J. and McCann, H., 'Divine Conservation and the Persistence of the World', in *Divine and Human Action*, ed. Thomas V. Morris (Ithaca, Cornell University Press, 1988)

Leftow, Brian, 'Anselm on the Incarnation', *Religious Studies*, 31.2 (1995)

Leftow, Brian, *Time and Eternity* (Ithaca, Cornell University Press, 1991)

Locke, John, *An Essay Concerning Human Understanding*, ed. John W. Yolton (London, Dent, 1965)

Locke, John, *The Reasonableness of Christianity*, ed. I. T. Ramsey (London, A. and C. Black, 1958)

McCann, H. and Kvanvig, J., 'The Occasionalist Proselytizer', in *Philosophical Perspectives 5, Philosophy of Religion*, ed. James E. Tomberlin (Atascadero, Ridgeview, 1991)

MacInerny, Ralph, 'Analogy and Foundationalism in Thomas Aquinas', in *Rationality, Religious Belief and Moral Commitment*, ed. Robert Audi and William J. Wainwright (Ithaca, Cornell University Press, 1986)

McIntyre, John, *St Anselm and his Critics* (Edinburgh, Oliver and Boyd, 1954)

Malcolm, Norman, 'Anselm's Ontological Arguments', reprinted in *The Existence of God*, ed. John Hick (London, Macmillan, 1964)

Malcolm, Norman, 'Is it a Religious Belief that "God Exists"?', in *Faith and the Philosophers*, ed. John Hick (Macmillan, London, 1964)

Oppy, Graham, *Ontological Arguments and Belief in God* (Cambridge, Cambridge University Press, 1995)

Penelhum, Terence, 'Skepticism and Fideism', in *The Skeptical Tradition*, ed. Myles Burnyeat (Berkeley, University of California Press, 1983)

Penelhum, Terence, *God and Skepticism* (Dordrecht, Reidel, 1983)

Phillips, D. Z., *The Concept of Prayer* (London, Routledge, 1965)

Phillips, D. Z., *Death and Immortality* (London, Macmillan, 1970)

Phillips, D. Z., *Faith After Foundationalism* (London, Routledge, 1988)

Phillips, D. Z., *Faith and Philosophical Inquiry* (London, Routledge, 1970)

Plantinga, Alvin, 'Justification and Theism', *Faith and Philosophy* 4 (1987)

Plantinga, Alvin, 'Augustinian Christian Philosophy', *The Monist* (1992)

Plantinga, Alvin, 'The Foundations of Theism: A Reply', *Faith and Philosophy* (1986)

Plantinga, Alvin, 'The Prospects for Natural Theology', in *Philosophical Perspectives 5, Philosophy of Religion*, ed. James E. Tomberlin (Atascadero, Ridgeview, 1991)

Plantinga, Alvin, 'Reason and Belief in God', in *Rationality and Religious Belief*, ed. Plantinga and Wolterstorff (Notre Dame, University of Notre Dame Press, 1983)

Plantinga, Alvin, 'The Reformed Objection to Natural Theology', *Proceedings of the American Catholic Philosophical Association* 54 (1980)

Plantinga, Alvin, *Warrant: The Current Debate* (New York, Oxford University Press, 1993)

Plantinga, Alvin, *Warrant and Proper Function* (New York, Oxford University Press, 1993)

Quine, W. V. O., *Methods of Logic*, 3rd edn (London, Routledge, 1974)

Quine W. V. O., *From a Logical Point of View*, 2nd edn (Cambridge, Mass., Harvard University Press, 1961)

Quine, W. V. O., *Word and Object* (Cambridge, Mass., MIT Press, 1960)

Quinn, Philip, 'Swinburne on Guilt, Atonement and Christian Redemption', in *Reason and the Christian Religion*, ed. Alan G. Padgett (Oxford, Clarendon Press, 1994)

Shoemaker, Sydney, 'Time Without Change', in *The Philosophy of Time,* ed. R. Le Poidevin and M. Macbeath (Oxford, Oxford University Press, 1993)

Stump, Eleonore, 'Aquinas on the Foundations of Knowledge', *The Canadian Journal of Philosophy*, Supplementary Volume 17 (1991)

Stump, Eleonore, 'Revelation and Biblical Exegesis: Augustine, Aquinas and Swinburne', in *Reason and the Christian Religion*, ed. Alan G. Padgett (Oxford, Clarendon Press, 1994)

Stump, Eleonore and Kretzmann, Norman, 'Eternity' (reprinted in *The Concept of God*, ed. T. V. Morris (Oxford, Oxford University Press 1987))

Swinburne, Richard, *The Christian God* (Oxford, The Clarendon Press, 1994)

Swinburne, Richard, *The Coherence of Theism* (Oxford, The Clarendon Press, 1977)

Swinburne, Richard, *The Existence of God* (Oxford, The Clarendon Press, 1979)

Swinburne, Richard, *The Evolution of the Soul* (Oxford, The Clarendon Press, 1986)

Turretin, Francis, *The Institutes of Elenctic Theology*, Volume 1 trans. G. M. Giger, ed. J. T. Dennison (Philadelphia, P & R Publishing, 1992)

Vos, Arvin, *Aquinas, Calvin and Contemporary Protestant Thought* (Grand Rapids, Christian University Press, 1985)

Westphal, Merold, 'Taking St Paul Seriously: Sin as an Epistemological Category', in *Christian Philosophy*, ed. Thomas P. Flint (Notre Dame, University of Notre Dame Press, 1990)

Wolterstorff, Nicholas, 'The Migration of Theistic Arguments: From Natural Theology to Evidentialist Apologetics', in *Rationality, Religious Belief and Moral Commitment*, ed. R. Audi and W. J. Wainwright (Ithaca, New York: Cornell University Press, 1986)

Wolterstorff, Nicholas, 'Can Belief in God Be Rational If It Has No Foundations?', in *Rationality and Religious Belief*, ed. Plantinga and Wolterstorff (Notre Dame, University of Notre Dame Press, 1983)

Wolterstorff, Nicholas, *Reason Within the Bounds of Religion*, 2nd edn (Grand Rapids, Eerdmans, 1984)

Index